INDIA'S BISMARCK

Sardar Vallabhbhai Patel

INDIA'S BISMARCK

Sardar Vallabhbhai Patel

B. Krishna

Indus Source Books

Viceroy Lord Wavell to Under Secretary of State Arthur Henderson:

"Vallabhbhai Patel, India's Bismarck, the man of iron from Gujarat . . ."

*

Viceroy Lord Mountbatten to Sardar Patel:

"You have for years been the 'strong man' of India . . . I do not believe there is one man in the country who would stand up to you when you make up your mind."

*

J. R. D. Tata on the Gandhi-Nehru-Patel Troika:

"While I usually came back from meeting Gandhiji elated and inspired but always a bit sceptical, and from talks with Jawaharlal fired with emotional zeal but often confused and unconvinced, meetings with Vallabhbhai were a joy from which I returned with renewed confidence in the future of our country. I have often thought that if fate had decreed that he, instead of Jawaharlal, would be the younger of the two, India would have followed a very different path and would be in better economic shape than it is today."

Indus Source Books
PO Box 6194
Malabar Hill PO
Mumbai 400 006
INDIA
Email: info@indussource.com
www.indussource.com

ISBN 10:   81-88569-14-3

ISBN 13:   978-81-88569-14-4

Front cover photograph of Patel and Nehru courtesy Homai
Vyarawalla

First edition December 2007
Second edition August 2008
First reprint August 2009

Printed at Decora Printers, Mumbai.

To my brother
Yuvraj Krishan
*(ever supportive & inspiring -
his great admiration for Sardar)*

ACKNOWLEDGEMENTS

My acknowledgements are to those with whom I corresponded; also to those with whom I conversed. I am expressing my gratitude to the former by reproducing their letters in order to let readers know what they actually wrote and how they expressed themselves. This will give them a better understanding of their views. There is, however, a difference between correspondence and conversation. Being face-to-face, the latter is more intimate, lively, giving the listener greater clarity in understanding—even a feeling of living with events.

Half a century later, in 2007, I still cherish sweet memories of my meeting with V. P. Menon at his bungalow in Bangalore one late evening—without prior appointment and without a questionnaire. I just dropped in and wanted to listen to what was uppermost in his mind. I had not met him before, but knew him well through correspondence. Our bond seemed to be Sardar Patel. Because of that, perhaps, he always addressed me as "My dear Balraj". He welcomed me instantly as a friend. During the hour I spent with him I raised no questions, but let the narration flow out uninterrupted. The subject was not integration of princely states, about which Mountbatten had paid him rich tributes in a letter to Patel, terming it "the miracle which you and your faithful VP have produced".

Earlier, Menon had rendered Mountbatten similar "faithful" service with regard to the transfer of power. Strictly adhering to Attlee's mandate, Mountbatten made undue haste in despatching his plan to London by early May, and thereafter showed it to Nehru, who happened to be staying with him at Shimla, in the expectation of support as a family friend. Nehru's reaction was rather violent. He was alarmed by the plan leading to India's balkanisation. His total rejection threw Mountbatten into a crisis. What would London think of him? Would he justify their trust? That worried him most. Menon was in Shimla as Patel's watch-dog. Mountbatten called him for "rescue" operations. It was late evening when Menon started his dictation. Page by page, Eric Mieville (ICS), principal secretary to the viceroy, would take the draft to Mountbatten, anxiously waiting in an adjoining room. Mountbatten breathed a sigh of relief when Nehru gave his approval to the "Menon plan". Added to that, as a soother, was Patel's acceptance from New Delhi. He was "delighted by the turn of events". He saw in it a larger role for himself to play, as Mountbatten realised that the man to negotiate with was Patel. He drew up a six-point deal with him.

The second person who comes to mind is Col. Himatsinhji, brother of the Jamsaheb of Nawanagar. I met him in Mumbai accidentally at someone's residence. Unexpectedly, he gave me information about how India was saved from a great crisis—one that would have pleased Jinnah, being of great gain to Pakistan. The Jamsaheb had finalised plans to form an independent confederation of the Kathiawar States, with allegiance to Pakistan.

Patel moved in to stop this, even when he did not yet exercise authority, transfer of power being two months away. He acted boldly and decisively. The Jamsaheb was to pass through Delhi prior to flying to central India to confer with the princes there. Patel lost no time. He sent Himatsinhji to the airport in his car to bring the Jamsaheb to his residence. The Jamsaheb and Her Highness lunched with Patel. In that short time, Patel's influence worked. The Jamsaheb gave up his confederation plan; on the other hand, he lent his support to Patel in the achievement of Gandhi's dream of a united Kathiawar, to which the Mahatma belonged. But for Himatsinhji, I would not have known this incident about how a crisis was nipped in the bud by Patel, and how an explosive issue was settled so quickly.

Equally revealing was what Mahavir Tyagi, MP and a senior Congress leader, told me about Sheikh Abdullah. Article 370 of the Indian Constitution was being debated in the Constituent Assembly—relating to Kashmir's relationship with India. Suddenly, an emotionally upset Abdullah stunned the House by announcing: "I am going back to Kashmir." His behaviour amounted to an insult to the House; it also questioned India's right to discuss Kashmir, which, he thought, was limited only to Nehru. Nehru wasn't in India to come to his "rescue". Acting as prime minister in Nehru's absence, Patel had to deal with him. As the debate was on, he could not intervene there and then. That evening, Patel sent Tyagi to the railway station to deliver his stern message to Abdullah. The Sheikh had just settled down in his compartment when Tyagi stepped in, and announced: "Sheikh Sahib, the Sardar says you could leave the House; but you cannot leave Delhi." Afraid of what Patel was capable of doing in Nehru's absence, Abdullah quietly got down from the train and cancelled his departure. With Kashmir having been taken away from his charge by Nehru, under pressure from Abdullah, the strict disciplinarian in Patel would never go beyond his jurisdiction.

Two other people whom I remember with gratitude are Kalyanji Mehta of Surat, and Maniben, Sardar's daughter, who not only managed his house all by herself, but served her father as a keeper of records, appointments, meetings, and correspondence. I spent two days with Kalyanji Mehta at his ashram near Surat. He gave me a moving description of how, as *senapati* (commander-in-chief), Patel led his army of 87,000 non-violent peasants to a glorious victory in the Bardoli satyagraha. He inspired them with discipline, obedience, sacrifice, looking upon him as their liberator from the injustice and oppression they suffered from. The British-owned and edited *Times of India* admitted that Patel had "instituted there a Bolshevik regime in which he plays the role of Lenin." Kalyanji Mehta's briefing drew a convincing picture of Patel as Lenin. But one absolutely Gandhian.

I have always felt grateful to Maniben for letting me have direct access to Patel's correspondence and other papers in their original. I could feel the pulse of the man in his changing moods as an administrator or a unifier of over 560 princely states. The correspondence took me closer to him than the printed material could. He could be gentle as well as daunting, depending on what the occasion demanded. Correspondence in original proved lively and animated in regard to his wisdom and diplomacy; above all his boldness. That was why Patel, as Vinoba Bhave confirmed, "knew no retreat" as Gandhi's GOC.

C. P. Ramaswami Aiyar, the highly egoistic non-Travancorean diwan, was the first to have declared Travancore's decision to be completely independent on the transfer of power on 15 August. Prior to Gandhi's capture of the Congress in 1919-20, he was a leading Home Ruler and secretary to Annie Besant. In May 1947, he had come to New

Delhi to see Mountbatten prior to the announcement of the 3 June plan. Patel was most diplomatic in writing to him: "It is in my nature to be a friend of the friendless. You have become one by choice, and I shall be glad if you will come and lunch with me tomorrow at 1 pm."

Correspondence made me realise how impartially, but determinedly, Patel could maintain party discipline, sparing none who crossed the *Lakshman rekha*. His tone and temper would change with the issue, and with each individual. He wrote to Dr. B. C. Roy, chief minister of West Bengal: "I was disturbed to find you writing to the Prime Minister like this. Had it been a personal letter, or had you been talking to him, perhaps as an elder, you could afford this liberty. But in an official communication to him as Prime Minister, I had expected that you could be deferential as is appropriate to the dignity of the high office that he holds, as well as the office which you yourself occupy as serving your own interest."

As party boss, Patel did not spare another chief minister—Gobind Ballabh Pant of Uttar Pradesh. Pant had inaugurated an exhibition of photographs at Varanasi, showing police atrocities during the Quit India agitation of 1942. Patel wrote to him: "In caricaturing official activities in the manner reported in the Press at a time when we are in office is open to serious objection. This is likely to affect the morale of the police force, which, in the present emergency, can hardly be considered proper. It is also likely to agitate the public mind against the Services. For obvious reasons, this must be avoided if administrative efficiency is to be maintained in these difficult times."

Patel was much harsher to Jainarain Vyas, president of the Rajasthan Provincial Congress Committee. He had got a resolution passed by the PCC, calling upon chief minister Hiralal Shastri to resign. Patel told him bluntly: "You should

understand that Hiralal Shastri as Premier is not responsible
to the Provincial Congress Committee, which cannot
appropriate to itself functions of the legislature . . . Your
persistence in the undesirable and harmful course which you
have adopted will merely recoil on you . . . the tactics you
have adopted are a disservice to the organisation we all
belong to."

I am also grateful to General Roy Bucher, the British
commander-in-chief of the Indian Army, for placing in my
hands a copy of the letter he wrote to his daughter Elizabeth:
"I personally never saw him other than absolutely composed,
and determined to uphold law and order throughout India.
Later I was to see him in a rage, and realised how his
colleagues were dominated." Patel was, according to Narhari
Parikh, his biographer, "harder than steel in national matters,
but softer than a flower in personal and private relations".
He was kind and forgiving to friend or foe alike. Patel's hold
over the party was absolute. His strength lay in restraint; his
greatness in forgiveness.

It was so with the princes; even with the Nawab of Bhopal
and the Nizam of Hyderabad. The former had conspired with
Jinnah against India; the latter had waged a war. Bhopal
requested Patel to ensure the safety of his son-in-law, the
Nawab of Pataudi, who was trapped in communal rioting in
his state near Delhi in Haryana. Patel sent an emissary in his
car with instructions: either bring the family back or provide
adequate protection if he wished to stay on. He was
magnanimous to the princes on their "surrender" and offer
of abiding friendship to India. He never allowed the past to
influence the present—the virtue of the truly great.

I express my gratitude to Ramesh Prajapati, administrator
of Sardar Patel Trust, Karamsad, Gujarat, for his valuable
support.

CONTENTS

INTRODUCTION

Patel, along with Gandhi and Nehru, was a leading member of the triumvirate which conducted the last phase of India's freedom struggle. He was the "saviour" and the "builder". Non-violently, he demolished the princely order Lord Wellesley had created; and in January 1946, he had nearly buried Pakistan in Karachi. Post-independence, Patel was the creator of New India just as Surendranath Banerjea was the father of political consciousness to the newly educated class of Indians in the 19ᵗʰ century; and Gandhi, the father of mass awakening pre-independence.

(a) Saviour: Patel saved India from the machinations of the ruling British, and thereby did not allow large Hindu majority areas to fall into the hands of Jinnah. In 1946, in an undivided India, the Cabinet Mission was giving away to Jinnah a Pakistan comprising the whole of Punjab and Bengal, besides Hindu Assam, as fully autonomous parts of Groups B and C. Gandhi favoured the plan since it preserved India's unity. In his "paternal pride" as Congress president, Azad seemed totally committed, confident of securing Congress acceptance. He thought that it would not only keep India united, but also safeguard Muslim interests. Nehru, however, voiced his opposition to grouping, as it related to the NWFP and Assam. He even suggested that there was "a big probability" that "there will be no grouping". Patel was more blunt than others in telling Wavell that the mission's "proposed solution was 'worse than Pakistan', and he could not recommend it to Congress".[1]

India's partition, as conceived by Churchill in 1945 as Britain's prime minister, was implied in Attlee's policy statement of 20 February 1947. It clearly meant the creation of Pakistan in one form or other, but in a divided India. Under it, too, Jinnah was to get the whole of Punjab, Bengal, and Assam. Patel immediately countered it with a policy statement on behalf of the Congress, demanding a division of Punjab—and of Bengal by implication—thereby saving Assam for India. Assam was predominantly Hindu, whereas in Bengal the Hindus were 49% as against 51% Muslims.

(b) Builder: Attlee's statement of 20 February categorically stated transference of power to the princely states, simultaneously with India and Pakistan, thus making the princes completely independent on 15 August. This would have led to the creation of a "Third Dominion", comprising confederations of princely states, and thereby throwing open possibilities of some of the states going over to Pakistan, in "association", if not "accession". This book discusses some of the conspiracies hatched in that direction, which Patel scotched with rare boldness, backed by his towering personality that exuded unquestioning friendliness towards the princes. The states involved were major ones like Travancore, Hyderabad, Junagadh, Jamnagar, and Jodhpur, and some Central Indian states. Through his diplomatic manoeuvres, Patel secured "accession" of all states prior to 15 August, before they could be made independent on par with India and Pakistan, thereby gaining equal status. The exceptions were those of Junagadh and Hyderabad—Kashmir too, but it was under Nehru's charge.

On the ashes of a defunct empire, Patel created a New India—strong, united, put in a steel-frame. That frame was the Indian Administrative Service, which kept a subcontinent bound together as a single unit despite disparities of politics and economy. As saviour and builder, Patel played decisive roles that took India to new pinnacles of success and glory after centuries.

Yet, the saviour and builder of New India was accused of responsibility for the partition of India; and the assassination of Gandhi. Patel never asked for India's partition. He and other Congress leaders were opposed to it. It was thrust upon them by the British through Attlee's policy statement of 20 February. He merely served India's interests by making partition conditional upon division of Punjab and Bengal. He could not have left the Punjabi and Bengali Hindus, as well as the Sikhs, to the cruel mercies of the Muslim League after the genocide of August 1946 in Kolkata. He also looked beyond, in gaining a free hand in the integration of over 560 States.

About Gandhi's assassination, General Roy Bucher, the British commander-in-chief of the Indian Army, wrote to the author in his letter of 24 July 1969: "From my knowledge, I am quite sure that Maulana Azad's charge that Sardar Patel was responsible for the murder of the Mahatma was absolutely unfounded. At our meeting in Dehra Dun, the Sardar told me that those who persuaded the Mahatma to suggest that monies (Rs. 55 crore) held in India should be despatched to Pakistan were responsible for the tragedy, and that after the monies had been sent off, the Mahatma was moved up to be the first to be assassinated on the books of a very well-known Hindu

revolutionary society. I distinctly remember the Sardar saying:
'You know quite well that for Gandhiji to express a wish was
almost an order'." It was on Gandhi's insistence that security
had been withdrawn.

Gandhi commanded every Hindu's veneration, Godse
being no exception. He had bowed to him in reverence thrice
before firing the shots. Gandhi had exhausted the patience
of even Nehru and Patel over two of his impossible demands.
First, asking Mountbatten, at his meeting on 1 April 1947,
"to dismiss the present Cabinet [interim government] and call
on Jinnah to appoint an all-Muslim administration."[2] This
would have killed Patel's dream of creating a unified India.
He had publicly stated in 1939: "The red and yellow colours
on India's map [representing provinces and states] have to be
made one. Unless that is done, we cannot have *swaraj*."[3] In
Nehru's case, Jinnah would have denied him the chance of
becoming independent India's first prime minister—a historic
opportunity Nehru could not have missed under any
circumstance.

Gandhi's second demand was even more difficult.
Addressing the All-India Congress Committee on 15
November 1947, he demanded that all Muslims who had fled
India were "to be called back and restored to peaceful
possession and enjoyment of all that they had had, but been
forced to abandon while running away".[4] It would have
amounted to making Hindu and Sikh refugees from Punjab
and the NWFP vacate the Muslim houses they had occupied
by restoring the same to the Muslims who were living in
refugee camps the government had set up. It would have been
a cruel double tragedy for the Punjabi refugees to suffer so
soon after the Punjab genocide.

A year before Patel's demise, M. N. Roy, once a comrade
of Lenin in Soviet Russia and a Communist of international

fame, wrote: "What will happen to India when the master-builder will go, sooner or later, the way of all mortals? . . . Nationalist India was fortunate to have Sardar Patel to guide her destiny for a generation. But her misfortune is that there will be none to take his place when he is no more . . . when the future is bleak, one naturally turns to the past, and Sardar Patel can be proud of his past."[5] He was India's "Iron Man", who proved to be his country's "saviour and builder". Today's India is what he created and left behind.

Some of Sardar Patel's major achievements:

1. Patel was the backbone of Gandhi's satyagrahas. During the Dandi March in 1930, he played the role of John the Baptist to Gandhi as a forerunner who "baptised" people en route. In a speech as Wasna, on his way to Dandi, Gandhi admitted: "I could succeed in Kheda [in 1918] on account of Vallabhbhai, and it is on account of him that I am here today."

2. In the Bardoli satyagraha in 1928, Patel played the role of a Lenin. The British-owned and edited *Times of India* wrote that Patel had "instituted there a Bolshevik regime in which he plays the role of Lenin".

3. As chairman of the Congress Parliamentary Board, Patel played the role of a strict boss in the conduct of the provincial elections in 1937. In that capacity he declared: "When the Congress roller is in action, all pebbles and stones will be levelled." He did not spare senior leaders like K. F. Nariman and N. B. Khare; not even the indomitable Subhash Chandra Bose. He was an uncompromising disciplinarian. That was a major contribution to the party's unity and strength.

4. Without Patel's support Lord Wavell could not have formed the interim government in August 1946, nor could Lord Mountbatten, in 1947, have implemented transfer of power smoothly and within the time-frame. In return, Patel got for India half of Punjab and half of Bengal and the whole

of Assam. Patel also got termination of paramountcy, which enabled him to achieve integration of over 560 princely states. That was his master-stroke, which demolished Churchill's imperial strategy. What was that strategy? An account is given in the chapter *A Churchillian Plan: Partition of India.*

5.   Briefly discussed is what would have been India's position in Kashmir, Tibet and Nepal had Patel's proposals been implemented. Kashmir had been taken away from Patel's charge by Nehru under Sheikh Abdullah's pressure, while Tibet and Nepal were foreign territories directly under Nehru's charge.

6.   Philip Mason (ICS) has written in the *Dictionary of National Biography*: "Patel has been compared to Bismarck but the parallel cannot be carried far. Patel was courageous, honest and realistic, but far from cynical."

7.   On his demise on 15 December 1950, the *Manchester Guardian* (now *Guardian*) wrote: "Without Patel, Gandhi's ideas would have had less practical influence and Nehru's idealism less scope."

181, Mehr Naz   Balraj Krishna
Cuffe Parade
Mumbai-400 005

1

WHAT WAS VALLABHBHAI?

Early Years

What was Vallabhbhai?" asked Rajagopalachari, and he himself answered: "What inspiration, courage, confidence and force incarnate Vallabhbhai was . . . We will not see the likes of him again."[1] Nehru called him "the Builder and Consolidator of New India . . . a Great Captain of our forces in the struggle for freedom . . . a tower of strength which revived wavering hearts."[2] Gandhi found in him a colleague "most trustworthy, staunch and brave".[3] Vinoba Bhave called him "the accurate bowman of Gandhi's struggle, his disciple and his GOC. He knew no retreat".[4]

Patel's international acclaim was equally eloquent. The London *Times* wrote of him on his demise: "Little known outside his own country, 'Sardarji' neither sought nor won the international reputation achieved by Mr. Gandhi and Mr. Nehru. Yet, he made up with them the triumvirate that gave shape to the India of today."[5] The *Manchester Guardian*'s tribute was more specific: "Without Patel, Gandhi's ideas would have had less practical influence, and Nehru's idealism less scope. Patel was not only the organiser of the fight for freedom, but

also the architect of the new State when the fight was over.
The same man is seldom successful both as rebel and
statesman. Patel was the exception."[6]

Vallabhbhai Zaverbhai Patel was born on 31 October 1875
at Nadiad in the Kheda district of Gujarat. He was the
fourth son of Zaverbhai Galabhai Patel, a petty landowner
from Karamsad, a small village about five miles from Anand.

Patel's origins were humble. His parents were of average
means and had no formal education. However, both his
parents influenced him greatly and moulded his character.
Patel's mother, Ladbai, was a gentle person and an expert
housekeeper. It is from her that he imbibed a spirit of service,
and a taste for cleanliness and orderliness that he observed
throughout his life. She often narrated stories from the epics,
Ramayana and Mahabharata, to her children. These stories
instilled in Patel's mind an irresistible desire to fight injustice.

His father, Zaverbhai Patel, belonged to a class of
cultivators known for their simple character, industrious
habits, and straightforward dealings. He was a firm and
determined man, also deeply religious, a believer in the
Swaminarayan cult. Vallabhbhai had inherited much of his
father's fierce pride and commanding personality. Zaverbhai
was himself a rebel, who travelled all the way from Gujarat
to Central India in 1857 to join the Rani of Jhansi in India's
first war of independence. After the war, Zaverbhai was taken
prisoner by Malharrao Holkar. One day Holkar was playing
chess within sight of his prisoner. Whenever he made a wrong
move, Zaverbhai corrected him. Malharrao was so pleased
that he not only returned to Zaverbhai his freedom but the
two struck up a friendship. In almost similar manner, in 1947,
when India had gained independence, the princes, small and
big, became his son's close and admiring friends. He was the

sole arbiter of their destiny. He magnanimously gave them handsome privy purses, historic palaces, extensive properties, and large personal wealth, besides honourable status as citizens of the new India.

And, like his father, Patel had abiding friendships with many princes—Hindu and Muslim alike, including the Nizam of Hyderabad and the Nawab of Bhopal. Of such relationships, the Maharaja of Gwalior (Scindia) expressed the feelings of many of his brother princes when he stated: "Here is the man whom I once hated. Here is the man of whom I was later afraid. Here is the man whom I admire and love."[7] The Maharaja had confessed to General S. P. P. Thorat: "If we Princes have to have our throats cut again, we will undoubtedly choose the Sardar and V. P. [Menon] to do it."[8]

Both were gentle and persuasive, but firm and determined. Patel could be equally reprimanding. It so happened with the Maharaja of Indore, a camp-follower of the Nawab of Bhopal, the pro-Pakistani chancellor of the Chamber of Princes. With the latter's resignation, Indore was left forlorn. He visited Patel for a patch-up by explaining his position. Sternly Patel told him, "You are a liar."[9] A crestfallen Maharaja returned to Indore and sent by post, duly signed, the Instrument of Accession.

Patel inherited his spirit of a rebel from his father. As a schoolboy, his tender age and his rustic village upbringing could not stem the upsurge of his rebellious spirit to fight injustice. He successfully fought many a battle through boycott and strike on behalf of his victimised schoolmates. He was unusually bold, courageous, outspoken, and daring—more concerned with the cause than with the punishment. He humbled the pride of many, proving himself a born fighter and superb organiser. Such exceptional qualities of leadership were recognised not only by his schoolmates, but also by his teachers. His eventful school life pointed to the man Patel was ultimately going to be—a relentless, unyielding freedom fighter.

Patel's student leadership had many episodes of heroism. He never knew retreat, always emerging victorious. He was just 18, and a sixth standard student at Nadiad, when he led his school on strike. A haughty teacher turned a fellow-student out of class for his failure to bring fine-money imposed on him the previous day. Patel considered it sheer injustice to hurt the pride of a small boy. And it equally hurt Patel's independent, robust mind. The teacher could have waited for another day or two. But, in his high-handedness, he didn't. Patel, on his part, could not tolerate such injustice. At his call, the class staged a walk-out. And his ultimate victory was when he led the entire school on strike—and even organised picketing! On the third day, the headmaster lost his nerve and reached an honourable settlement, with an assurance that no excessive and unjust punishment would be meted out in future.

Patel grew still bolder. He moved out of the school confines into the public life of Nadiad. It was to help a teacher, with poor means and far less influence, who stood for the municipal election. His opponent was an influential, wealthy person—proud of both. In his arrogance he declared that if he were defeated, he would have his moustache— then a symbol of masculine pride and status—shaved off. The student in Patel worked with "such resolute will and steadfastness" that his teacher scored a resounding victory. Along with some fifty boys, and accompanied by a barber, Patel went to the opponent's house, calling upon him to step out to honour his pledge and shave off his moustache!

Patel had "no patience with an indifferent teacher"; nor could he "spare a lazy one." His class teacher was a habitual late-comer. This irked Patel's sense of discipline. If he and his classmates were expected to come on time, why couldn't the teacher as well? He and his fellow-students created a rowdy atmosphere in the class-room just to heap ridicule on him. Out of spite, the teacher punished Patel with the task of writing numbers from 1 to 10. So simple! Yet, Patel refused to comply with an unjust order. But the teacher, in his vengeance, doubled the figure for each day's failure till the figure reached 200. Writing out numbers 1 to 10, 200 times! It was an arduous task, repugnant to Patel's sense of fair play. His ingenuity worked. He simply wrote "200" on the slate, and with an innocent air showed the slate to his teacher.

In Patel's words: "The teacher asked me where were the *padas*? [meaning in Gujarati both "sums" and "buffaloes"]. I told him I could write only 200 when the *padas* [buffaloes] ran away! The teacher was all sound and fury. I was presented before the headmaster, who, instead of punishing me, took the teacher to task for not knowing the correct method of prescribing task."[10]

From Nadiad, Patel moved to a school in Vadodara. His stay did not last even a month. An incident showed how much more rebellious he had grown. One day, he found his math teacher failing to solve an algebraic sum. Patel had the audacity to stand up and boldly tell him, "Sir, you don't know how to work it out." In annoyance the teacher threw a challenge: "If I do not know how to do it, you come here and be a teacher yourself!" An unabashed Patel went to the board and solved the sum. Not stopping at that, he impudently sat on the teacher's chair! Howsoever improper, he was impishly complying with what the teacher had told him to do. The headmaster sent for Patel and warned him to behave himself in future. But Patel's pride was hurt. He retorted: "I do not wish to study in a school where there are teachers of such type."[11]

In 1913, Patel achieved his ambition of becoming a barrister. With his determined spirit and sharp intellect, he

obtained a first class first and was called to the Bar on 27
January. The young barrister immediately returned to India
and set up practice in Ahmedabad. His fearlessness, clear
thinking, and ability to quickly judge people served him well,
and in a short time Barrister Patel was successfully practising
at Ahmedabad. In 1914, an ominous development threw the
Ahmedabad municipality into a deep crisis, which threatened
to smother freedom at the civic level—a freedom which
liberal-minded British rulers had themselves granted. The
threat came from the amended District Municipal Act in
allowing appointment of British ICS bureaucrats, mostly
diehards, as heads of self-governing institutions. The
amendment was anti-national in two ways: one, it curbed
national aspirations influencing civic life; and, two, it
controlled and directed school education and thereby did not
allow national feelings to take root in the minds of
schoolchildren at an impressionable age.

In November 1915, a hardliner, J. A. Shillidy (ICS), took
over as municipal commissioner. It was considered a bad
omen. Municipal councillors became apprehensive of losing
whatever limited autonomy they enjoyed. From the very start,
there developed friction between the two over Shillidy's
unconstitutional interference in the working of the municipal
administration. Not only did he spend money as he wished
without reference to the appropriate municipal body, he even
chose to usurp the president's right to correspond with the
government, make appointments on his own and disburse
largesse as he chose. Further, he even absented himself from
work without intimation to the president. He was arrogant,
assertive, and self-opinionated. His was a sort of dictatorship,
not self-governance that the government had given people
under the Municipal Act.

Municipal affairs had been rendered chaotic. There was
"little organisation, duties were carelessly defined and

procedure negligible". According to the president, R. B. Ramanbhai, "The efficiency of the municipal staff is at a low ebb . . . delays and corruption . . . have been rife."[12] The Bombay Provincial Conference, at its session at Ahmedabad in October 1916 was highly critical of the municipal affairs. Presided over by Jinnah, the creator of Pakistan in 1947, the conference recommended abolition of the office of the municipal commissioner.

Who could take the bull in Shillidy by the horns? And even secure the abolition of the post of municipal commissioner? In the considered view of some, "only someone with Vallabhbhai's skill, shrewdness and fearlessness".[13] Shillidy could be outwitted by one who possessed "[a] tough temperament, rough manners and indomitable spirit to match the arrogance, obstinacy and irritability of Shillidy". And so, "a search for such a person was going on till the eyes of some of the members of the Gujarat Club fell upon Vallabhbhai, who was well-known among his colleagues for qualities of sustained labour, blunt repartee and a tendency of delivering telling blows on his adversaries".[14] Patel alone could meet their expectations. On becoming a councillor in May 1917, he sought to curb the self-acquired autocratic powers of the municipal commissioner through forthright, determined, and bold constitutional moves.

Patel took two steps—both constitutional: First, he put monetary limits on purchase transactions, allowing only those authorised by the board to be entertained by the municipal commissioner. Second, the municipal commissioner was required to accept any of the tenders recommended by the board. Further, Patel got the board to ask the municipal commissioner to furnish a statement of purchases made by him since 1914-15. Still further, the managing committee was to scrutinise it before its submission to the board. It was a battle of wits between Patel and Shillidy. The latter had to eat humble pie on quite a few occasions. Even Shillidy's boss, the commissioner, F. G. Pratt, was, on one occasion, stunned by Patel's "impertinent" behaviour. Patel's boldness had left Pratt speechless.

Patel's battle was a major one to rescue municipal education from British control and influence, and "to remove their strangulating hold from the municipal schools".[15] Under his instructions, the municipality refused to accept government grant and even debarred government inspectors from visiting schools. In the boycott, out of over 300 teachers, 297 stood by Patel. The municipalities of Ahmedabad, Surat, and Nadiad supported him. The presidency government at Bombay got alarmed. The education minister, Raghunath Paranjpe, stepped onto the scene. But no settlement could be reached. The government got tougher. So did Patel.

Patel organised a People's Education Board. He had instant success. It ran 43 schools, including 13 for girls; and it had 270 teachers and nearly 8,400 pupils, of whom over 900 were Muslims and nearly 2000 were girls. These schools incurred a monthly expenditure of Rs. 10,000. Patel had raised Rs. 1.25 lakh through public subscription. In comparison, the government had 57 schools, 250 teachers and around 2000 pupils. Admitting defeat, the government sought a compromise, which Patel generously accepted.

Addressing the Municipal Employees' Association in Ahmedabad in 1940, Patel stated: "It is a matter of pride with me that I have devoted the best part of my life here. I recall those years with great satisfaction."[16] Much later in 1948, he admitted: "To serve our own city must give unmitigated pleasure and satisfaction, which I cannot get in any other sphere. To cleanse the city of the dirt is quite different from cleansing the dirt of politics."[17]

Part I
DIRECT ROLE

2

FREEDOM FIGHTER

Backbone of Gandhi's Satyagrahas

Kheda Satyagraha

The Kheda satyagraha of 1918 ushered in a new era in India's freedom struggle—an era of mass agitation on the basis of non-violent non-cooperation. It was equally significant, according to Congress historian Pattabhi Sitaramayya, that "it brought two great men together".[1] They were highly complementary to each other: if Gandhi provided the soul force, Patel contributed his "muscle power" as a superb organiser. He was to Gandhi what Ashoka was to Buddha, or Vivekananda to Ramakrishna Paramahansa. Socialist leader Yusuf Meherally stated: "Vallabhbhai at long last found a leader the likes of whom the country had not seen for centuries—not since the days of Ashoka and Akbar. The Mahatma had found a lieutenant that those Emperors would have given a kingdom to get."[2]

Gandhi had already attained worldwide fame before returning home from South Africa in January 1915 after conducting a brave, non-violent fight against apartheid. For such heroism, he had earned the admiration of world leaders like Tolstoy and Romain Rolland. He came to be reverentially called "The Mahatma" and his countrymen saw in him an apostle. Early in the century, he was considered to be one of the ten great people in the world. It was but natural that Pherozeshah Mehta should have looked upon him as "a hero in the cause of Indian independence".[3] Yet, Gandhi did not take an immediate plunge into Indian politics. He followed Gokhale's advice to wait for a year or two, in order not only to acclimatise himself to the political climate, but also to test Indian political waters.

In fact, the shrewd Gandhi waited for the right opportunity: one that would concern a cause worthy enough to unite an agitated public. Equally important for him was to find a deputy commander and a band of trusted, self-sacrificing workers who could organise and lead the people in the fight. But he had first to win their confidence in his capability to lead them to victory. He did that in 1917, a year prior to his launching the Kheda satyagraha. He proved his credentials with his victory in three cases in quick succession: first, the viceroy's compliance with his request to abolish indentured labour by a fixed date; second, the removal of the customs barrier at Viramgam in Kathiawar; and third, the British indigo planters' surrender to his challenge in Champaran, Bihar, in agreeing to do justice to the exploited indigo cultivators. These three victories established Gandhi as the new leader of India's non-violent freedom struggle.

"Who should be my deputy commander?" Gandhi asked himself. Patel first appeared to him "a stiff-looking person". Not without reason. Patel enjoyed the reputation of being "a bridge-player, [a] chain-smoking barrister", who had earlier despised Gandhi for being a queer-looking figure from whom

he had "kept himself cynically and sarcastically aloof"; and
was openly "very sceptical and critical about Gandhi's ideas
and plans".[4] In personal appearance, Patel looked "a smart
young man, dressed in a well-cut suit with a felt hat worn
slightly at an angle, stern and reserved, his eyes piercing and
bright, not given to many words, receiving visitors with just a
simple greeting but not entering into any conversation, and
of a firm and pensive expression, almost as if one looking
down upon the world with a sort of superiority complex,
talking with an air of confidence and superiority whenever
he opened his lips".[5]

Such a proud, sophisticated, highly anglicised Patel
underwent a dramatic change under the irresistible spell of
Gandhi's magnetism. It was a complete transformation of
the man Patel was: from an unsparing scoffer to a most ardent
admirer, co-worker, and freedom fighter. Patel not only gave
up his lucrative legal practice, but discarded for good his
western dress and lifestyle. He adopted, instead, the Gandhian
style of austere, frugal living. He started wearing a villager's
dress—coarse, hand-spun *kurta* and *dhoti* and a pair of crude
chappals—even while walking on dusty rural roads. It was a
complete change, good for Gandhi, good for Patel, no less
for the freedom struggle.

Gandhi discovered Patel's uniqueness as a freedom fighter
on the "battlefield" of Kheda. His challenge to the British
was over land revenue—the very foundation of their Indian
empire. Commissioner F. G. Pratt said, "In India, to defy the
law of land revenue is to take a step which would destroy all
administration. To break this law, therefore, is different from
breaking all other laws."[6]

Gandhi appeared to the British to be preaching rebellion
in asking the peasants to withhold payment of land tax. Pratt
expressed his grave apprehensions by telling the peasants:
"If you fight about land revenue today, the whole country

will fight about it tomorrow."[7] The issue involved was very simple and just. The *kharif* crop had been completely ruined by excessive monsoon, while an epidemic of rats and other pests had heavily damaged the *rabi* crop. Revenue rules permitted postponement of assessment if the yield was estimated to be less than 25% and a complete remission if there were a failure of the crop in the following year. Gandhi demanded only postponement, not total remission. That too, until a full inquiry had been conducted by the government. Over 18,000 peasants signed an application submitted to the government on 15 November. The Bombay government refused to interfere with the commissioner's authority.

This encouraged the local officials to conclude that "the peasants were complaining only because they had been instigated and their emotions worked up by agitators. So, if the government accepted the demands of the peasants, it would be the agitators who would gain in reputation, while the reputation of the officers would decline. Thus, to government officers, the fight on this occasion was one chiefly of prestige".[8] It was not so with Gandhi and Patel. They were fighting for a just cause: noble for its purity of motive in urging the government to postpone recovery of land revenue.

Despite that, Commissioner Pratt rode roughshod over the people's hopes and aspirations by being dictatorial. He told the secretaries of the Gujarat Sabha, on whose behalf the satyagraha was being conducted, not the Congress, that "the responsibility for proper administration in Kheda district is that of the collector," and held out the threat: "If I do not hear from you by tomorrow, I shall write to the government recommending that your Sabha should be declared illegal."[9] It was a serious threat, which Gandhi and Patel could not ignore.

Since Gandhi was launching his first satyagraha in India, he and Patel had to prepare the masses for it; and also to educate their lieutenants about how to conduct themselves. Gandhi's advice to them was: "You may be arrested for doing so, but you must regard that as the fulfilment of your work. That is satyagraha."[10] This assumed importance in view of the collector's threat: "If anyone, influenced by the wrong advice which is being given to them, refuses to pay up his land revenue dues, I shall be compelled to take stringent legal measures against him." To this Gandhi replied, "The Government may do what it likes. If the hardship is genuine and the workers skilful, they cannot but achieve success."[11]

Gandhi and Patel moved nearer to the "battlefield": from Ahmedabad to Nadiad. They opened a camp office in the local orphanage, and conducted an on-the-spot inquiry into the conditions of peasants. They jointly visited about 60 villages, while a team of workers surveyed 425 villages out of a total of 600. Their joint operations were at Gandhi's bidding. He had laid down the condition that a sabha worker should accompany him and devote all his time to the campaign until it lasted. "As no one else was prepared to give up his other activities wholly, Vallabhbhai offered his services, much to Gandhi's delight."[12]

Patel enjoyed two advantages: First, he belonged to Karamsad in Kheda. He was born and brought up on its soil and amid its environment, and had practised as a lawyer at Borsad earlier in the century. Second, being the son of a peasant, he knew and understood the people better than Gandhi. Both worked together, moving in the dusty countryside on foot over long distances.

The satyagraha was launched on 22 March 1918 at a public meeting of peasants at Nadiad. Gandhi's inspiring words were: "It is intolerable that the Government should forcibly recover assessment. But that has become the practice in our country. However truthful the people, and however just their case, the Government refuses to believe them and insists on having its own way. There must be justice, and injustice must be ended . . . That people would tell lies for the sake of saving at the most a year's interest—for they are asking only for postponement of assessment—is inconceivable. It is an insult to all of us that the Government dares to make this accusation."

Gandhi exhorted the peasants: "I would, therefore, tell you, that if the Government does not accept our request, we should declare plainly that we shall not pay land revenue, and will be prepared to face the consequences . . . the Government may recover the assessment by selling our cattle and our movable property, confiscate *jagirs* and even put people in jail on the ground that they are not law-abiding. I do not like this charge of lawlessness . . . The people are fighting for a principle, while the officials are fighting for their prestige. The peasants of Kheda have ventured to take up cudgels in the interests of justice and truth."[13]

The satyagraha had run for a few days when Gandhi had to leave for Indore to preside over the Hindi Sahitya Sammelan. He handed over charge to his deputy commander. Patel displayed great qualities of leadership. He had the bluntness of a soldier and the astuteness of an organiser. In a fighting speech at Nadiad, he declared: "This fight will act as a spark which will set the whole country afire." Speaking of Gandhi, he said, "The brave man who has inspired this fight is capable of converting the cowardly into the bravest of persons, and in India, Kheda district is the land of brave men." Patel also told the peasants, "A State ought to be proud of a people who are strong and determined. There is nothing to be gained from the loyalty of a cowardly and cringing public. The loyalty which you get from a fearless and self-respecting people is the loyalty which a Government should welcome

. . . it is only if you are prepared to face hardships now and get the Government to change its policy, that you can remove the source of hardship for all time."[14]

In his public speeches during Gandhi's absence, Patel always struck the same inspiring strain as the Mahatma, attempting to build up his master's image as one who had taught them the new mantra of truth and ahimsa, and who had injected courage and fearlessness into their hearts and minds. Patel told the peasants, "Stick to the path the Mahatma has shown you. You should give up violence; even thought of loot or use of underhand means. Instead, you should take to the path of *dharma*—the path of Truth and justice. Don't misuse your valour. Remain united. March forward in all humility, but fully awake to the situation you face, demanding your rights with firmness. Have no fear of the tehsildar. Even if the heavens fall, you should not forsake your pledge. If you carry it through to success, Kheda's will be the first name in the history of India's freedom struggle."[15]

In the beginning the government thought that by merely taking away their dearly loved cattle, the peasants would be intimidated and pay up the land revenue. This did not work. So, a more drastic step was taken in the confiscation and auctioning of their lands. Lest people's morale crack up under mounting pressures, Gandhi and Patel moved from village to village, injecting into the people a fresh dose of elixir to strengthen their hearts and steel their determination, asking them to honour the pledge they had taken.

In Patel's own village, Karamsad, things were not shaping well. Some non-landholders seemed to be willing to avail themselves of the auctions. Patel was deeply hurt. He implored them: "When I see the condition of this village today, I am reminded of my childhood days, when the elders of the village carried themselves with such dignity that the revenue officers sought their advice and sat most humbly in front of them. Today it is not so. You appear frightened of the officials. This is due to lack of unity amongst yourselves."[16]

Pratt thought of exploiting Gandhi's innate goodness. Since he himself could not reach the boycotting peasants through his officials, he sought Gandhi's help. A meeting of over 2000 peasants was arranged. In order not to embarrass Pratt, Gandhi did not attend the meeting, but sent Patel as an observer.

Pratt exploited the opportunity to gain the upper hand. He attempted to establish a rapport with the peasants by calling Gandhi "Mahatma", and drew loud cheers. Thereafter he appealed to them:

Pray listen to my speech and hear my advice . . . The power to fix assessment is in the hands of the Government and the officers of the Government . . . We are the final arbiters of a legal right you may fight in a court of law. The sole authority to issue orders in the matter rests in the hands of the officials. It is not in the hands of Mr. Gandhi, nor of Mr. Vallabhbhai. You may bear fully in mind that any amount of your effort in this matter is bound to be futile. My words are final orders. They are not my personal orders, but they are the orders of His Excellency Lord Willingdon. I have a letter from His Excellency in which he has been pleased to say that he would confirm whatever orders I may pass in the matter and every word that I may say . . . You may understand that it is not I who say this. It is His Excellency Lord Willingdon.

By mentioning the governor's name, Pratt expected to make the innocent, illiterate villagers fearful of the supreme authority whom he represented. Thereafter, Pratt attempted to deflate Gandhi's influence by deviously paying him a left-handed compliment: "Mahatma Gandhi is an exceedingly good and saintly soul. And whatever advice he gives you, he does with the purest of intentions and in the full consciousness that it is in your interest. His advice is that you should not pay the assessment, because thereby you would safeguard the interests of the poor . . . Do you mean to say that the Government does not protect them? Is not the Government solicitous of their welfare?"

When Pratt went on to add that the Home Rulers would not go to jail, someone from the audience shouted: "Sir, if you send us, we will go." This was an oblique reference to the rumour that Gandhi would be sent to jail. Lest a misunderstanding got hold of the mind of the audience, and they assumed that Gandhi would be jailed, Pratt scotched it by categorically stating: "During the passive resistance campaign in South Africa, Mahatma Gandhi had to go to jail. But under this Government such a thing will not happen . . . The jail is not a fit place for him. I repeat that Mahatma Gandhi is a most saintly character."

Thereafter, ingeniously, Pratt attempted to build his own image with the observation:

The fight of the Government is not with the peasants. If children kick their parents, the latter are pained but not angered . . . I have 28 years of experience of administration of land revenue assessment and of land revenue legislation. Mahatma Gandhi is my friend. He has passed the greater part of his life in South Africa and has been here for only two or three years. In the domain of knowledge, letters and religion, he is a great authority. His advice on these subjects must be right. But in matters of administration and land revenue assessment, his knowledge is limited. I claim better knowledge. I have come here only to give you a final word of advice . . . if you do not pay the assessment, your lands will be confiscated. Many people say, "This won't happen." But I say that it will . . . Those who are contumacious will get no lands in future.[17]

By expressing his willingness to hear people speak out their minds, Pratt disturbed the hornet's nest in the mistaken hope that they would support him. Over a dozen peasants rose, one after another, to express their views in stunningly brutal frankness. By telling a lie about the Ahmedabad millhands calling off their strike, Pratt had provided Patel with a hammer to nail the lie onto him. Mistakenly, he had stated that the vow the peasants had taken had no sanctity, since a similar vow by the millhands had already been broken.

Patel was at the meeting only as an observer. That he was not to speak had given Pratt satisfaction and relief. Unwittingly, he gave Patel an opportunity when he sought his opinion in regard to what Narsinhbhai from Karamsad had said: that their fight was not intended to embarrass the government. Patel jumped at the opportunity and said, "The speaker does not deny that ours is a fight. He admits it is. What he means to say is that it is not intended to embarrass the authorities." Before Patel could proceed further, Pratt, out of nervousness, asked him whether he was going to make a speech. Patel replied that he was going to refer to the question of the millhands' strike only. Pratt remarked rather ruefully: "Well, you may go on. But today is our turn."

Patel, however, observed: "There was no breaking of the millhands' vow . . . Mr. Pratt himself graced the last meeting of the millhands when the terms of the compromise were declared." Thereafter he did not spare Pratt by answering his left-handed compliment to Gandhi with the shrewd observation:

Mr. Pratt says he has great regard for Gandhiji. [The commissioner interjecting: "Yes, of course."] Gandhiji has a great regard for Mr. Pratt, and so have I. But it was Mr. Pratt who said on that occasion that the millhands should always follow Gandhiji's advice and, if they do, they would not fail to get justice. I also say likewise that if you follow Gandhiji's advice in this matter, you are sure to get justice at Mr. Pratt's hands. Here also the Commissioner may, if he so wishes, get a committee appointed and we would willingly accept its decision as not inconsistent with our vow.[18]

Patel netted Pratt nicely. Pratt's discomfiture was complete. It was compounded by some persistent questions from the peasants.

Pratt's threat clearly indicated that the government was poised for action. To counter that, Gandhi told the peasants, "The Commissioner has issued many threats. He has even said that he will see to it that these do not remain empty threats . . . He seems to regard the relationship between the Government and the people as similar to that between parents and children. If that were so, has anyone seen in the whole history of the world an instance of parents having turned their children out of their homes for having resisted them in a non-violent manner?"[19]

Ever willing for a compromise, Gandhi asked the commissioner for an interview. He got a most unhelpful reply: "If you give up all your weapons and come to discuss without conditions, my doors are open to you, but my hands are tied by legal and administrative rules." Gandhi answered, "I am a believer in satyagraha. I would gladly give up my weapons and even my all for the matter of that, but I cannot give up my principles."

The fight went on unabated. It evoked wide response. For the first time women came forward to fight shoulder to shoulder with their menfolk, whom they injected with confidence and courage. They, indeed, displayed unusual bravery. Some even declared: "Let the Government take away our cattle and our ornaments, and confiscate our fields. But our men will not depart from their pledge."

Gandhi had to proceed to New Delhi on an urgent call from the viceroy. Patel assumed command of the satyagraha for the second time. Through his speeches and pamphlets, he kept alive the spark Gandhi had lit. He told the peasants:

A fierce *dharma-yudh* [righteous war] has been going on between the people and blind authority . . . notices of confiscation have been enforced in the case of some leading men's houses. Fines imposed. Standing crops taken possession of. Even threats of arrests held out. But people have remained undaunted, while officers have betrayed their helplessness over their failure. It was then that the Commissioner stepped in, and addressed the peasants at Nadiad. He gave them serious threats; even read out the Governor's letter to impress upon them his authority to act. But the peasants showed rare courage in answering his threats. He was surprised to see such fearlessness for the first time in his 28 years of administrative career. And, no wonder, he left the meeting in sheer desperation.[20]

Patel went on to observe:

The peasants took all this cheerfully. The Government recovered no money at all . . . So the Government gave up confiscations and restarted auctions of movable properties . . . They took charge of milk-giving buffaloes, kept them in the sun, and even separated them from their calves. This reduced the price of the buffalo by half. Even so, the peasants adhered to their pledge patiently and bore whatever hardships they were called upon to bear.

Patel's advice to them was:

> The longer the fight lasts, the stiffer is the test which the people will have to pass. But without such hardships, they cannot have this unique experience . . . If the Government oversteps the limits, is itself angered and harasses us, we, on our part, should not act unreasonably, never be impolite or lose our temper . . . always be peaceful. Even the hardest of hearts can be conquered by love. The more the opponent is stiff, the more should our affection go out to him. Only then shall we be able to win. That is the significance of satyagraha.[21]

Yet, Patel could not surrender his peasant's sturdy independence on some marginal issues. He accepted Gandhi's operational strategy and the principles governing the satyagraha. But he could not subscribe to Gandhi's advice to the peasants to willingly accept suffering by voluntarily surrendering their cattle to the authorities. Although he believed in non-violent protest, his practical nature urged him to get the most out of every situation. He therefore preferred that they should save their cattle from attachment by not letting them remain near their houses.

The struggle continued through April, May, and part of June. Men and women stood firmly behind Gandhi and Patel, willingly suffering any punishment the government imposed on them. Not only were their cattle and standing crops seized, but also their womenfolk's ornaments and household utensils. All the 600 villages showed rare determination and a remarkable solidarity, which surprised many a visitor. The Mumbai newspapers paid glowing tributes to the peasants for their courage and sacrifice.

In the end, the government seemed to have recognised its failure. On 3 June 1918, when Gandhi and Patel reached Uttersanda, a village near Nadiad, they were informed by the *mamlatdar* of the government's decision to suspend assessment till the next year. Upon this, Gandhi and Patel announced termination of the satyagraha from 6 June.

The success sent a wave of jubilation throughout Kheda. Village after village celebrated the victory with gusto. An eyewitness confirmed that the "rejoicings, characterised everywhere by a spirit of moderation and always free from anything like frantic mirth, have unmistakably proved the wonderful hold the Mahatma has secured over the people of Kheda, their deep sense of gratefulness for what has been achieved, as also their appreciation of the moral significance of the campaign. For, everywhere people flocked in their thousands, small villages rocked with their tumultuous rejoicings, and every village that followed tried to vie with the one that preceded in the measure of its reception and in the volume of its gratefulness."[22] At the farewell meeting at Nadiad, Gandhi paid glowing tributes to Patel for the role he had played as his deputy commander: "The choice of my lieutenant was particularly happy . . . without the help of Vallabhbhai we could not have won the campaign. He had a splendid practice, he had his municipal work to do, but he renounced all and threw himself into the campaign."[23]

Patel played a major role in the emergence of Gandhi as an all-India leader in the Kheda satyagraha. Thereafter, Non-cooperation's failure had made Gandhi lie low. It was an hour

of grave crisis in his life. It was Patel—and Patel alone—
who kept alive Gandhi's spirit through three of his satyagrahas:
Nagpur, Borsad, and Bardoli.

Nagpur Satyagraha

The Nagpur satyagraha was fought for the vindication of
the honour of the national flag—the Tricolour, which
had not been allowed to be flown over the Town Hall, along
with the Union Jack, in spite of a resolution passed in its
favour by the municipality. The flag had also been prohibited
from being taken out in a street procession. The satyagraha
started on 1 May 1923 and continued for over three and
a half months till 18 August. Patel took over command
towards the end of July, and emerged victorious in less than
three weeks.

Patel's success at Nagpur lay in ensuring a steady flow of
satyagrahis from different parts of the country. At least fifty
were daily available for arrest. They comprised all classes and
communities: educated, uneducated, High Court lawyers,
school students, *zamindar*s and businessmen. Patel even
planned to draft women volunteers, and had sent a word to
Gandhi's wife, Kasturba, "to be ready to go to jail". The
satyagarha continued unabated. Volunteers daily offered
satyagraha, and filled the Nagpur jail beyond its capacity. The
railway authorities had to restrict the issue of tickets for
Nagpur. Yet, the arrival of volunteers could not be stopped.

The pressure thus built forced the home member of the
Governor's Council, Moropant Joshi, to state in the Provincial
Legislative Assembly that no one would object to the flag
being taken out in a procession if prior permission had been
sought in accordance with the rules laid down. He had come

to realise that the government could not object to the Indian situation especially when the British Bolshevik Party could take out the Red Flag in a procession through London streets, shouting slogans even in front of the British Parliament. The home member, therefore, set the ball rolling by first arranging a meeting between the governor and Patel.

The prohibitory order was to expire on 17 August. Patel stated in true Gandhian spirit: "I desire to make it clear that the Nagpur satyagraha struggle has been started in order to vindicate our elementary right against arbitrary and unjustifiable interference and abuse of law . . . the organisers of the processions never intend to cause annoyance to any section of the public." Nor were the processions organised, he assured, "to offer insult to the Union Jack".[1] With the governor's consent, the home member confirmed the settlement in writing. A victorious Patel announced the termination of the satyagraha.

No fresh order was issued on the seventeenth. But the European members of ICS (Indian Civil Service), ignoring the governor's involvement, raised a storm of protest, and carried their "war" to London. They could directly communicate with the secretary of state over the head of the governor, being directly responsible to him. Patel stood firm. He demanded of the provincial government to honour the agreement reached between him and the home member, and release the volunteers from prison. The provincial government pressed the government of India to authorise their release. It pleaded that its prestige was at stake. A cable came from London agreeing to the release of prisoners.

The volunteers were released on 3 September. A batch of 100 successfully took out the national flag in a victory march through the Civil Lines. The superintendent of police accompanied the mounted police. The processionists halted near the railway bridge which had earned the appellation of the Flag Bridge, and also at the National Flag Square—the venue of satyagraha. Loud slogans rent the air all along the route lined with policemen. Respecting Christian sentiments, complete silence was observed in front of the church in the Civil Lines. The processionists reached their destination without being stopped by the police.

With that success, Patel declared: "The honour of the national flag stands vindicated. Our right to take out processions on public roads in a peaceful and orderly manner has been restored. I regard this as a triumph of Truth, non-violence and suffering. By the grace of God, I am now in a position to announce that the Nagpur satyagraha campaign successfully closes."[2]

Thus ended another successful campaign undertaken by Patel in his capacity as Mahatma Gandhi's deputy commander.

Borsad Satyagraha

The Borsad satyagraha was a fight against dual tyranny. The first involved two dacoits who committed robberies and murders unchecked, even in broad daylight; the second involved the government, which had imposed a punitive tax of over Rs. 2.40 lakh for additional police posted in the villages, allegedly for the protection of villagers. It was to be payable by all over 16 for providing shelter against the dacoits.. That was, however, not the case. In reality, the officials were in collusion with the two dacoits, Babar Deva of village Golel, and Ali, from Borsad town.

Babar Deva was required to report every morning and evening to the police station. For failure to do so one morning, he was arrested and sentenced to six months' imprisonment.

Since he was a scrupulously honest man, his pride was deeply hurt, and on escaping from prison, he turned into an outlaw. Anyone reporting his whereabouts was brutally dealt with. Some had their noses cut off while others were nailed to trees. He did not even spare his wife whom he suspected of betrayal. He committed no less than 22 murders. The police reportedly gave names of informants to Babar Deva. In order to arrest him, the police colluded with the other dacoit, Ali, by supplying him firearms. In return, the police got a share of the booty. Unchecked, Babar Deva and his gang roamed about in the countryside on horseback spreading terror.

Imposition of the punitive tax was a decision of the superintendent of police, not of the collector. The *mamlatdar* had reported that the villagers were too poor to pay the tax. He had also confirmed: "No villager seems willing for the continuance of the additional police in the villages." The collector supported the *mamlatdar* and communicated his concurrence to the commissioner. But the latter overruled both and sided with the superintendent of police. Patel ridiculed the whole affair with the caustic remark:

When Babar could not be got hold of, the police made friends with this new genius [Ali], and sought to get rid of an outlaw with the help of another outlaw, and provided him with arms and ammunition. Oh, the pity and the shame of it! The Government ceased to rule, making room for the outlaw. Who is going to punish the Government for having leagued with this outlaw? God alone! The Government surely knows what number of murders and dacoities Ali has committed, having been armed by the Government itself . . . I hold the Government responsible for all the misdeeds of that miscreant Ali.

Patel added:

> Babar has to his credit twenty-two murders. Not one
> of the victims was a rich man. He did not murder them
> for the mere fun of it. He murdered them as they were
> informants. After twenty-two such informants have
> been murdered, can the Government seriously argue
> that the people do not give information? Shall we ask
> how many policemen were murdered? An informant
> was crucified to a tree by Babar . . . A first-class
> magistrate was waylaid by an outlaw on his way from
> Wasad to Borsad. The outlaw gave a smack on his face,
> and wrested the rifle from his hands. The poor fellow
> had to plead that he was an ordinary clerk and not a
> magistrate in order to escape with his life! A
> Government with such a magistracy has no title to exist,
> and has surely no title to punish a people.

Patel also stated:

> My information is that every petty village officer knows
> the whereabouts of these outlaws, but is afraid of them
> . . . What then should you do? Do not for a moment
> think that you are fighting for the paltry amount of two
> rupees and seven annas . . . You have been fined
> because of your complicity in the crime; because you
> are suspected of sheltering the outlaws and befriending
> them. I ask you to fight only if you are convinced that
> no power on earth has the right to impugn your character
> . . . We shall not recognise the police. Let us have our
> own volunteer corps. I ask you to raise a corps from
> among yourselves.[1]

Patel disclosed that he possessed a secret circular issued by the district superintendent of police, advising all sub-inspectors and head constables "to turn a blind eye to dacoities and offences committed by Ali, as he had undertaken to assist in the arrest of Babar Deva".[2]

Patel drew up the battle line, dividing his volunteer corps into platoons. Each was to non-violently defend a group of villages. He made Borsad his headquarters, from where he conducted his satyagraha. He built up the morale of the people through regular issue of leaflets, which carried his instructions in regard to what they were supposed to do from time to time, what sort of vigilance they were required to maintain, and, above all, how they were to maintain unity among the ranks.

Patel forewarned the villagers:

The Government will confiscate your property, take away your cattle and will have no hesitation in attaching for the recovery of Rs. 2.50 property worth Rs. 25,000. All that you should bear patiently. Under no circumstance should you pay a pie or react violently. The Government has adopted for itself the untruthful and dishonest path. Truth is on your side. If you adhere to the principle of non-violence, you are bound to succeed. Anyone who is honest and who practises non-violence can never lose.[3]

The government started attachment of property in all seriousness. The *mamlatdar* and his staff devoted themselves fulltime to the new task. Non-violent defence organised by Patel's "platoons" reduced official operations to a comic drama. A volunteer was stationed atop a tree at the village entrance. On sighting an attachment party, he would beat a drum, and thereby signal the menfolk to make haste to lock up their houses with womenfolk inside, so as to avoid attachment, and to take their cattle outside the village for grazing. Only present to welcome the attachment party were the urchins, who would follow it shouting and creating all sorts of exasperatingly ludicrous scenes.

Village after village presented a picture of desolation during the day with houses locked. At night, life returned to normal—houses opened and lighted, market place bustling with activity, and women wending their way to fetch water after dark. This was because attachments could not be carried out under law after sunset. The governor, Leslie Wilson, a liberal, felt upset by the allegations of complicity with the dacoits being publicly made against the government. He asked his home member, Maurice Hayward, to conduct an on-the-spot inquiry. Hayward reached Borsad on 4 January 1924. Besides his meetings with the commissioner, the collector, and other officials, he held an open court to which were invited some 150 selected men. After hearing all concerned, and convinced of the righteousness of the fight, he ordered immediate stoppage of attachment of property. On his return to Bombay, the government announced:

The Governor-in-Council has resolved that the cost of the extra police, who have already been enlisted in, shall be met during the current year from general revenues and that the Legislative Council shall be asked to vote funds for the continuance of operations during the next financial year . . . The Governor-in-Council believes that the people of Borsad . . . will respond to this policy of liberality by cordial assistance and cooperation in the further operations necessary for suppressing the violent crimes from which their taluka has so long suffered.[4]

Fully vindicated, Patel ordered immediate withdrawal of the satyagraha, stating:

> Once again there has been a triumph of Truth, non-violence and penance. This victory has been as quick as our struggle was just. It is unique in that both the parties have won. The Government has admitted its mistake openly and with courage . . . We would be failing in our duty if we did not congratulate most sincerely His Excellency the Governor of Bombay, Leslie Wilson, for showing so much moral courage . . . Our victory lies in the Government's withdrawal of the charge made against us.[5]

More than 30,000 people joined the victory celebrations held in Borsad on 12 January. People came even from Ahmedabad and Mumbai. The presence of women electrified the atmosphere. Men added colour of their own: "Patidars, confident of their achievement and of their importance; fine, well-built Baraiyas and Patanwadias with their long sticks and their hubble-bubbles, and Garasias with large turbans." Addressing them, Patel said: "During this short struggle, you have made great sacrifices. You have exhibited great courage, maintained unity, and shown great enthusiasm. We have gained this victory because we walked along the path shown by the great saint who is now in jail."

Gandhi wrote in *Young India*: "These achievements [in Kheda and Borsad] are a great tribute to Vallabhbhai's magnificent organising and administrative ability. And he has collected around him in the process a band of devoted workers of like mind and ability. The Borsad satyagraha is a magnificent example of public activity governed wholly by public consideration."[6]

Lenin of Bardoli

The Bardoli satyagraha occupies a unique position in India's struggle for freedom. Its sole leader, Patel, received rich tributes from Gandhi: "Vallabhbhai found his Vallabh [God] in Bardoli."[1] For leading over 87,000 highly disciplined, non-violent peasants, the British-owned *Times of India* wrote that in Bardoli, Patel had "instituted a Bolshevik regime in which he plays the role of Lenin".[2] As a true Gandhian, he led a weaponless army of satyagrahis with a farmer's staff in hand, wearing a peasant's crude countrymade pair of *chappals*, *jubba* (waistcoat), and *dhoti* made from coarse, handspun *khadi*. His heavy moustache and stern looks gave him the appearance of a Bismarck.

In Bardoli, the unjustified enhancement of land revenue by 30% in 1926 made the peasants seethe with discontent. H. B. Shivdasani (ICS), a former revenue officer, described it as "not fair". The matter could not be taken to the court, as judicial representation was debarred by the Bombay Revenue Jurisdiction Act. A member of the Bombay Legislative Council complained: "So far as the administration of the land revenue system is concerned, the reforms have proved to be a curse. The doors of the law courts are barred . . . by statute; the Government of India's powers of interference are considerably limited . . . Land revenue is a provincial subject and also a reserved subject . . . local Governments possess acknowledged authority of their own."[3]

The revenue settlement of 1926-27 contradicted the assessment of the settlement commissioner in 1896. He had admitted that "the general conclusion from all recorded statistics is that the taluka [of Bardoli] in 1896 was either over assessed or assessed right up to the full limit of half the rental value".[4] In 1900-01, G. V. Joshi had proved that the incidence of land revenue on population in the Bombay Presidency was far heavier than in any other Indian province (as much as Rs. 2.00 per head of population); the incidence on cultivated acreage was the highest in the Gujarat districts (as much as Rs. 4.00 per acre); and that in Surat district, of which Bardoli was a part, it was the highest in Gujarat—as much as Rs. 5.90 per acre.

The revenue settlement of 1926-27 was also in contradiction of what the British Joint Parliamentary Committee had observed in 1919: "The process of revising land revenue assessments ought to be brought under closer regulation by statute as soon as possible . . . the people who are most affected have no voice in the shaping of the system, and the rules are often obscure and imperfectly understood by those who pay the revenue." In 1924 the Bombay Legislative Council likewise recommended: "No revision be proceeded with and no new rates under any revised settlement be introduced till the said legislation is brought into effect."[5] In 1927, the council, by a majority vote (52 against 29) reiterated its 1924 recommendation. The provincial government, however, authorised the action taken by the settlement commissioner. The government of India extended its support to the provincial government. The latter, ultimately, decided on a 22% increase in the revenue, and ordered collection of the enhanced land revenue from 5 February 1928.

Anxious to seek a peaceful settlement, Patel sought a meeting with the governor, Leslie Wilson, whose high praise he had won earlier for outstanding work done during the Gujarat floods. Wilson merely passed on Patel's letter to the revenue department for "official consideration and disposal". Since no ground was left for compromise, Patel took command of the satyagraha but told the peasants:

I still ask you to think twice before you take the plunge. Do not derive comfort from the feeling that you have as your leader a fighter like me. Forget me and forget my companions. Fight, if you feel that you must resist oppression and injustice. Do not take the plunge lightly. If you fail, you will not rise again for several years. If you succeed, you will have done much to lay the foundations of *swaraj*."[6]

Patel added:

We have done everything we could. Now there remains only one way open to us: to oppose force with force. The Government has all the paraphernalia of authority and has the physical strength of the armed forces. You have the strength of Truth and your capacity to endure pain . . . The Government's stand is unjust. It is your duty to oppose it . . . This is not merely a question of an increase of a lakh of rupees or so, or of 37 lakh in 30 years, but a question of Truth and falsehood—a question of self-respect.[7]

The conference passed a resolution, which was supported by representatives of the villages and various communities in the taluka—Patidars, Vanias, Christians, Parsis, Muslims, and backward classes. It stated: "This conference of the people of Bardoli taluka resolves that the revised settlement . . . is arbitrary, unjust and oppressive, and advises all the occupants to refuse payment of the revised assessment until the Government is prepared to accept the amount of the old assessment in full satisfaction of its dues, or until the Government appoints an impartial tribunal to settle the whole question of revision by investigation and inquiry on the spot."[8]

The government was alarmed by the new spirit of rebellion that swept Bardoli. The commissioner of the Northern Division, W. W. Smart, was asked to camp at Surat, so as to be 15 to 20 miles from Bardoli town, while the district collector was asked to reach Bardoli immediately. On arrival, he had a chilling welcome: all the shops were shut and doors of all houses were closed. It was total boycott. He got no conveyance to go to a nearby village, Sarbhon, which he managed to reach with great difficulty. The village *patel* (headman) told him: "The people will not listen to us. They are indifferent to forfeitures and confiscations."[9] Annoyed, he ordered the *talati*s to prepare plans for auction of land and seizure of buffaloes. For implementation, "a number of Pathans of questionable character were brought in from Bombay".

Patel had organised the satyagraha on military lines. As supreme commander or *senapati*, he had under him sector commanders or *vibhagpatis*. Under each commander were volunteers called *sainiks* or soldiers. The battlefield covered about 92 villages. He had horse-riders to bring him messages from the remotest ones. The battle itself involved over 87,000 peasants from the Bardoli taluka and Valod Mahal. Operationwise, there were 18 sectors, 12 being in the former and 6 in the latter. Bardoli was the HQ of the supreme commander, who had, like a general, his personal staff: personal secretary to conduct his correspondence, as also to look after dissemination of war information; master of ceremonies to programme his movements; and editor of publications, *patrikapati*. There was an ambassador, who toured India to brief opinion-builders like Tej Bahadur Sapru, M. R. Jayakar, Srinivasa Sastri and others.

A war bulletin, *Larat-ni-Patrika*, carrying Patel's speeches and satyagraha news, was published daily and distributed among the Bardoli peasants, as also among others outside Bardoli. Hand-written copy would reach Surat before midnight, and the following morning the Tapti Valley railway would carry bundles of printed copies, which volunteers would collect at different stations en route, and take at galloping speed to "the villagers waiting anxiously for the *Patrika* every morning and devouring the contents with avidity".[10] From 5,000 copies at the start, the number soon rose to over 15,000. More than 10,000 copies were distributed in Bardoli alone. Outside Bardoli, every important Gujarat town and village received the war bulletin. To sustain the peasants' enthusiasm, Patel organised a *bhajan mandli*—a troupe of musicians, which went from village to village at night, singing national and religious songs. A story-teller regaled the peasants with inspiring anecdotes and sarcastic jibes. A women workers' unit also moved among the village womenfolk to keep their spirits high.

Peasants, along with their womenfolk, children, and their "beloved cattle" voluntarily locked themselves up in their small, dingy houses for over three months to avoid attachments by officials. K. M. Munshi gave an account of this to the governor:

> As I passed through villages—silent, empty and deserted with sentinels posted at different ends—I saw women peeping through barred windows, and on being reassured they opened the doors. I went inside and I saw the darkness, the stench, the filth, and men, women and children herded together for months in the same room with their beloved cattle—miserable, lacerated and grown pale with disease. As I heard their determination to remain in that condition for months rather than abandon their cattle to the tender mercies of the *japti* [attachment officer], I could not help but

think that the imagination which conceived the dire *japti* methods, the severity with which they were enforced and the inhuman policy they represented were difficult to find outside the pages of a history of medieval times . . . The cheap sneers of lofty bureaucrats, the disproportionately severe sentences for technical offences, the thunders of arrogant proclamations and the official sabre-rattlings have ceased to excite anything but ridicule.

Munshi asked the governor to appreciate the reverence Patel enjoyed of such people. He told him:

Your *japti* officer has to travel miles before he can get a shave. Your officer's car which got stuck would have remained in the mud but for Vallabhbhai, officially styled "agitator living in Bardoli" . . . The Collector gets no conveyance at the railway station without Vallabhbhai's sanction. In the few villages which I visited, not a man, or woman, was either sorry for the step taken or is shaken in his or her faith, and as Vallabhbhai passed through village after village, I saw men, women and children coming out to greet him in spontaneous homage. I saw illiterate women, old and young, in tatters, placing on his forehead the auspicious mark of victory (*kum-kum*), laying at his feet, for their sacred cause, their hard-earned rupee or two and singing in their rustic accents songs of "the misdeeds of the hapless Government".[11]

The modus operandi of Patel's *sainiks* was similar to the one in the Borsad satyagraha. Since law did not permit attachment work after sunset, life returned to the villages after dark. With that would begin Patel's operations. As supreme commander, he moved from village to village, addressing public meetings, or conferring with his sector commanders, or giving his volunteers instructions on the strategy to follow. Each night he covered a distance of 15 miles or more. A friend had placed at his disposal an old Ford motor-car. Roads being unmetalled and dusty, a light rain turned them slushy. Often the car would fail, or get stuck in the mud. Patel, not minding his status or age, would get down, and along with others, push it to make it run again. He would return to his HQ not before daybreak. And before going to bed, he would attend to dispatches received from his sector commanders, and reports brought from government offices by his informants.

Patel's speeches always cast a spell—irresistible and overpowering. To the peasants, he sounded like an oracle who spoke their idiom with the "peculiar flavour of the soil", and his words haunted their minds long afterwards. There was great appeal in the "burning fire in the speaker's eyes and the masculine vigour of his tone".[12] Patel had told them, "I want to inoculate you with fearlessness. I want to galvanise you with new life. I miss in your eyes the flash of indignation against wrong."[13] Mahadev Desai, Gandhi's principal secretary, and others felt that they had never before "heard such brilliance in his language, or seen such indignation in his eyes . . . The villagers were moved by the extraordinary eloquence of his speeches and by his astonishingly simple yet effective popular similes and analogies."[14]

Patel's speeches were torrents of biting sarcasm against the government. He even chastened the peasants for their weakness with well-meaning ridicule. In one of them, he said:

The Government has, like a wild elephant, run amuck. It thinks it can trample anything and everything under its feet . . . priding itself on having trampled in the past even lions and tigers to death, and scorning the little gnat defying him. I am teaching the little gnat today to let the elephant go on in his mad career, and then get into his trunk at the opportune moment. The gnat need not fear the elephant. The elephant can never trample it to death, but the gnat can certainly prove formidable to the elephant.[15]

Officials were alarmed by the revolutionary tone of his speeches. The *Times of India* declared in bold headlines: "Bolshevik Regime in Bardoli; Mr. Vallabhbhai Patel in the Role of Lenin." The newspaper's correspondent wrote: "Iron discipline prevails in Bardoli. Mr. Patel has instituted there a Bolshevik regime in which he plays the role of Lenin. His hold on the population is absolute. The women of Bardoli have been taught amazingly seditious songs with which they incite their men to hate the Government, to obey only the wishes of their Commander-in-Chief, Mr. Patel, and to be ready to die, if need be, in defence of their rights."[16] In the British House of Commons, Lord Winterton admitted that in the Bardoli no-tax campaign Patel had achieved "a measure of success".

As the satyagraha progressed, Patel's tongue became sharper and more biting. He ridiculed the officials and thereby kept up the morale of the people. Addressing women at a public meeting, he tickled them with rustic humour by making fun of English women: "Oh! It seems to me that by remaining in the house all day and night, your buffaloes are fast becoming white like white women!"[17] Since buffaloes were so dear to the women, Patel went further, when "attached" buffaloes started bellowing from inside the nearby police station, by shouting: "Listen to the bellows of these buffaloes. Reporters! Write it down and report that in the police station at Valod, the buffaloes make speeches! . . . Listen to these buffaloes.

They tell you that justice has disappeared from this kingdom."[18]

Mahadev Desai wrote in *Young India*: "As the up-train takes you to Valsad, it is a discussion about Bardoli going on amongst the passengers that wakes you up in the early hours of the morning . . . I had occasion to travel by a day train too. The Bardoli publicity leaflets were in the hands of many passengers. Some of them were reading Vallabhbhai's speeches aloud, and discussing the situation. As I passed through the streets of Navsari with my haversack on my back, a Parsi came running after me to ask if I had the Bardoli leaflets in my haversack!"[19]

Maulana Shaukat Ali (of Khilafat fame) and Maulvi Mahomed Baloch, who visited Bardoli, were "delighted at the wonderful atmosphere of solidarity and unity in Bardoli".[20] Two non-Congress councillors from Mumbai, Joshi and Pataskar, visited Bardoli as critics, but were compelled to admit: "We had come to scorn, but have stayed on to praise."[21] Nine members of the Bombay Legislative Council sent in their resignations to the governor, and demanded an independent inquiry.

As days passed, the satyagraha picked up greater strength. At the same time there were brilliant flashes of Patel's fighting mood. He assured the peasants: "Let there be no mistake. Your land will come back to you knocking at your door . . . The world knows that among the purchasers are *chaprasis* and policemen and a few butchers who were specially persuaded to come from Surat."[22] Speaking on Bardoli Day, celebrated throughout India on 12 June, Patel said, "So long as a square foot of land, belonging to a peasant or to a participant in this fight, remains forfeited, this fight will continue. For the sake of such land, thousands of peasants are ready to die. This is not a charity performance for the Government to hand over land to some kerosene merchant from Broach! He who buys such land drinks the life-blood of the peasants."[23]

Patel was willing to negotiate for an honourable compromise. At the all-India level, Vithalbhai Patel, president of the Central Legislative Assembly, presented the Bardoli case to the viceroy. At the provincial level, K. M. Munshi wrote to the governor about the unconstitutional position of the government, warning him of serious consequences, resulting "either in the elimination of the existing peasants in Bardoli or in bloodshed, and, in either case, will result in deep and lasting embitterment".[24] Other leaders who lent support to the movement included Purushottamdas Thakurdas, Pandit Hridaynath Kunzru, Motilal Nehru, and Tej Bahadur Sapru.

At the district conferences held at Surat, Broach, Nadiad, and Ahmedabad, thousands of peasants pledged their support to the Bardoli satyagraha. In a grim warning to the government, Patel said, "If the Government means to devour land, I warn it that the conflagration will spread over the whole of Gujarat, and it will realise not a farthing in Gujarat next year . . . The Government may think it has far greater strength than Ravana had, but let the mighty Government remember that it has to deal not with one Sita but 87,000 satyagrahis."[25]

On 13 July the viceroy conferred with the governor at Simla. Thereafter, the governor made a statement: "It is His Excellency's obvious duty to uphold the supremacy of the law. But it is also his duty, as representative of the King Emperor, to see that hardship and suffering are not inflicted on so large a number of persons."[26] Following this, the commissioner sent a message to Patel that the governor was arriving at Surat and would like to meet him. Patel met the governor for a total of six hours. No settlement could be reached. The governor insisted on payment of the enhanced assessment, or, alternatively, payment by a third party on behalf of the Bardoli peasants of a deposit equivalent to the enhanced assessment. Patel could not accept such a suggestion, while the governor rejected his terms.

The British-owned *Pioneer* and *Statesman* thought that the government's conditions were unreasonable. The former wrote: "The main point that must be made, and made without delay, is that no impartial observer of the Bardoli dispute, possessed of the plain facts of the case, can resist the conclusion that the peasants have got the right on their side, and that their claim for an examination of the enhanced assessment by an impartial tribunal is just, reasonable and fair."[27] Annie Besant's paper, *New India*, wrote: "If Birkenhead [the secretary of state] remains obstinate, then an agitation should be set up in Parliament to make him change his mind."

Council members from Surat were carrying on negotiations with the government at Pune. Patel's presence there was considered necessary, as they felt that the government was anxious to reach a settlement, but it wanted to preserve its prestige. In this respect, Chunilal Mehta, a senior member of the Governor's Council, played a notable role. In their draft letter, the MLCs told the revenue member: "We are glad to be able to say that we are in a position to inform the Government that the conditions laid down by His Excellency the Governor in his opening speech to the Council, dated 23 July, will be fulfilled." Patel was opposed to this. Mehta, however, assured him: "That is not your concern. If the members are agreeable to addressing the letter, you need not worry as to how, when and by whom the conditions will be fulfilled. You will pay the old assessment after the inquiry is announced."[28] Patel was not to be a party to the offer. Nor was he compromising in any manner. Yet, he agreed to let Mehta play his game on the presumption, to quote Mahadev Desai, that "he knew the mind of the Government better than anyone of us and his patriotism had at this great moment got the better of his officialdom". According to Mahadev Desai, who was one of the negotiators, "If the Government was content with clutching at the shadow of prestige, Vallabhbhai could not be content without the substance. All he wanted was a full, independent, judicial inquiry and restoration of the *status quo*. The Government was perfectly agreeable, provided here too it could have its prestige intact."[29]

In the end, an inquiry committee was appointed, comprising Reginald Maxwell (later home member of the Viceroy's Executive Council) and Robert Broomfield (later a High Court judge). It recommended an increase in the settlement rates of 5.7% as against 22% sanctioned by the government. Following this, the government announced restoration of lands confiscated and sold, release of all prisoners, and reinstatement of *patel*s and *talati*s who had resigned.

Thus ended the Bardoli satyagraha, "pursued by a peaceful peasantry with truth and patient suffering . . . against an enemy who could any day have crushed them to atoms. But the Bardoli peasants demonstrated to the world that Truth and non-violence cannot be crushed".

Mahadev Desai described the Bardoli settlement as

the third of the Sardar's successful campaigns—the third milestone that he had the honour of laying on the road to *swaraj* . . . The Bardoli triumph was unique in that it compelled not only the nation's but the whole Empire's attention, and the justice and moderation of the people's demand won practically the entire nation's sympathy. It was unique in that it was fought by, perhaps, one of the meekest of the *taluka*s in India, in that it affected the Revenue Department, whose dispositions, it was up to now believed, not even the gods may question; and in that it compelled a mighty Government, pledged to crush the movement, to yield within a fortnight of the pledge. It was unique in that the leader of the campaign shed all ideas of personal prestige, and also in that the Governor of the province . . . did all that he personally could to bring about peace.[30]

Patel was flooded with tributes. Gandhi was the first to say, "Without Vallabhbhai's firmness as well as gentleness, the settlement would have been impossible." Motilal Nehru called the satyagraha "a splendid triumph", and described Patel as a "matchless general" and the peasants as "the Balaklava battalion of Bardoli".

Srinivasa Sastri wrote to Gandhi from Johannesburg: "Vallabhbhai Patel has risen to the highest rank. I bow to him in reverence." Lala Lajpat Rai wrote in his newspaper the *People*: "The settlement of the Bardoli dispute . . . is a notable triumph of the popular cause . . . it is a moral victory for truth and justice."

Pandit Madan Mohan Malaviya wrote to Patel: "The first signal triumph of satyagraha was in Champaran. The second and equally great has been in Bardoli." Maulana Shaukat Ali and Shuhib Qureshi wired congratulations to "our brave brothers, their Sardar and co-workers". Subhash Chandra Bose forejudged the Bardoli satyagraha as "the precursor of the larger fight that [Gandhi] was to wage in 1930"[31]—the Dandi March.

According to British historian, Judith Brown, for Gandhi, Bardoli meant "re-evaluation of his public role", dissolving "many of his doubts, born of the debacle and violence of the early 1920s, about the viability of satyagraha in India . . . It revived his faith in the power of non-violence and in the potential for a mass struggle".[32]

John the Baptist in Dandi March

The Dandi March or the salt satyagraha of 1930 was of such astounding success that Gandhi and Patel climbed to new heights of glory in India's freedom struggle—never achieved before or since. Gandhi regained his recognition as apostle of truth and ahimsa; Patel, on his part, played the historic role of John the Baptist. St. John was the forerunner and baptiser of Jesus. Patel's role was similar in the Dandi March. Gandhi was Christ-like: a frail body dominated by hallowed looks, and an oracular voice that inspired an apostle's reverence as well as the hope of resurrection for his people. Patel was John-like: strong-bodied, and a forerunner of Gandhi in the Dandi March, who "baptised" people on the road the master was to follow to Dandi, a small village on Gujarat's west coast near Surat, where Gandhi broke the law prohibiting the manufacture of salt from sea water. It was a simple act which instantly became a symbol of national defiance; even aroused worldwide attention for its revolutionary implications. Like America's historic Boston Tea Party, the Dandi March was a march towards India's independence.

Dandi was Patel's choice. So were the leaders of the March. They were his most trusted lieutenants since his earlier satyagrahas. Patel went ahead of the March as John the Baptist had done in the case of Christ. Gandhi admitted in his speech at Napa that Vallabhbhai had come ahead of him to smoothen his own path.[1] Congress historian Pattabhi Sitaramayya wrote: "While yet Gandhi was making preparations . . . Vallabhbhai went before his master to prime up the villagers of the coming ordeals . . . When Vallabhbhai was moving in advance as Gandhi's forerunner, Government saw in him John the Baptist who was a forerunner of Jesus nineteen hundred years ago."[2]

Patel was arrested at Ras, sentenced to three months' imprisonment and lodged in Sabarmati jail at Ahmedabad.

In his speech at Navagaon, Gandhi admitted that the government had arrested Patel because "it feared that if he were free, he and not the Government would rule over the district".[3] Sitaramayya wrote: "With his arrest and conviction, the whole of Gujarat rose to a man against the Government. 75,000 people gathered on the sands of the Sabarmati to resolve: 'We the citizens of Ahmedabad determine hereby that we shall go the same path where Vallabhbhai has gone'."[4]

A protest day was observed by the Millowners Association, whose members passed a resolution condemning Patel's arrest, and closed down their mills for the day. Businessmen pulled down the shutters of their shops in Ahmedabad and in many other towns of Gujarat. The municipality lodged its protest by keeping offices closed. So did schools in the city. Ras, where Patel had been arrested, surpassed all. Village officers submitted their resignations; landlords surrendered their special rights; a country liquor licensee pledged never to sell alcoholic drinks; and over 500 men and women got themselves registered as satyagrahis. Many villages in the Borsad and Bardoli *taluka*s followed Ras with equal fervour.

In Delhi, Pandit Madan Mohan Malaviya moved a resolution in the Central Legislative Assembly, condemning government action in arresting Patel without trial. Jinnah spoke on the resolution:

> According to the Home Member, Sardar Vallabhbhai Patel had delivered many speeches before he was arrested . . . Were those speeches against law? The point at issue is whether the Sardar committed any breach of law. On that point no information has been given to us. If he had made speeches earlier in which he had committed breaches of law, and was about to deliver

one further speech of the same kind, then the right course for the district authorities was to have taken action against Sardar Vallabhbhai Patel for those earlier offences. It was improper for them to serve upon him an order which cuts at the root of the principle of freedom of speech . . . The Government of India is setting a precedent with very serious implications.[5]

Gandhi began his 241-mile march from Ahmedabad to Dandi on 12 March. He led a batch of 71 satyagrahis. The district superintendent of police confirmed: "Mr. Gandhi appeared calm and collected. He is gathering more strength as he proceeds. His lieutenants like Darbar Gopaldas and Ravishankar Vyas (Maharaj) are getting bolder and arouse the feelings of the people of this taluka by using Vallabhbhai's arrest as their trump-card."[6]

Patel's arrest became the main focus of Gandhi's speeches. At Wasna, Gandhi said, "I may die at any moment, but the future generations will see that my prophecy was correct. Vallabhbhai was not a fit person for arrest. He should have been rewarded by the Government. What wrong did Vallabhbhai do in Bardoli? He befriended the people, which was the duty of the Government. He managed the administration of Ahmedabad; and the Collector and the Commissioner were astounded by his success. I could succeed in Kheda district on account of Vallabhbhai, and it is on account of him that I am here today."[7]

And thus, Gandhi continued his march along the path paved by Patel, amidst overwhelmingly excited crowds. William Shirer, an American correspondent, who witnessed the March, wrote in the *Chicago Tribune*:

The procession soon became a triumphal march. The villages through which the marchers passed were

festooned in their honour. Between the villages, peasants
sprinkled water on the roads to keep the dust down
and threw leaves and flower petals on them to make
the going on foot easier. In nearly every settlement
hundreds abandoned their work and joined the
procession until the original band of less than one
hundred swelled to several thousand by the time the
sea was reached . . . Some of Gandhi's followers began
to compare the March to the journey of Jesus to
Jerusalem, and there was much reading of the New
Testament along the way. To add to the comparison,
someone in the party picked up a donkey to follow in
the wake of Gandhi.[8]

Moving ahead of Gandhi, Patel had delivered a number
of speeches. At Broach, he said, "Within the next eight or
ten or fifteen days, civil disobedience will have begun. There
will take place non-violent breaches of law. Such offences
will be committed by individuals who are devotees of non-
violence, who have no anger, nor any jealousy, and about
whose purity and goodness there can be no two opinions."[9]

Patel said that the British had spread two bogeys in order
to defeat Gandhi's satyagraha. One was Hindu-Muslim
conflict; the other was about the Afghans invading the country
if the British left India. Patel asked the audience:

Have you come across a single Muslim who says the
salt tax is good and should be maintained? Both the
Hindus and Muslims in villages, having identity of
interest, support it, and consider the tax as unjust . . .
The rulers hold out the threat that if they were not
here, the Hindus and Muslims will die fighting. No
matter if some of us die. Let those left behind live in
peace . . . The rulers also threaten us that if they go

away, the Afghans will come in. Oh, the Pathans! And
that not a single unmarried girl's honour will be safe.
Haven't they reduced us to such a helpless state after
150 years of their rule? If 33 crores of us cannot protect
ourselves, then what is left for us to do is to commit
suicide! But to tolerate such talk is a great insult.[10]

Patel ridiculed some other myths spread by the British—
especially the inability of Indians to govern, and the British
claim of being "trustees in India". Sarcastically, he asked,
"But whose trustees? Who had gone to England to crown
them and invite them here? Such talk can no longer be
acceptable. No one will accept their threats . . . The
Government says that it has given us peace. But of what use
is this peace to us when people are suffering from hunger?
There is no blood in our veins, nor lustre in the eyes."

Calling Gandhi the "Saint of Sabarmati", Patel said, "That
man at Sabarmati, with a handful of bones, has shaken the
Empire with his spinning wheel. That is a real wonder. He
has built hopes in you . . . Aren't you going to fulfill them?
Wisdom will dawn on the people just as light follows sunrise
. . . Freedom's first page is being written in Gujarat's history."[11]

Awaiting his arrival at Ras were thousands of enthusiastic
villagers. They had gathered under a large banyan tree outside
Ras to welcome their Sardar. He was not scheduled to speak.
He was to address a public meeting at the nearby village,
Kankapura. It was hurriedly decided by the local leaders that
he should speak to those who had assembled. A sub-inspector
of police, who found out about this from a sweeper, informed
Collector Shillidy, whom Patel had earlier thrown out of the
Ahmedabad municipality. Shillidy looked upon the occasion
as an opportunity to avenge himself by arresting Patel. Patel
had merely said, "Sisters and brothers. Are you ready for the

satyagraha?" A loud "Yes" rent the air. This did not amount to a speech. Yet, Patel was arrested.

A police party escorted Patel to Borsad for a trial. The collector was brought from the travellers' bungalow to the Magistrate's Court. Some pleaders and other gentlemen were cleared out of the court-room. Patel was asked to sit in the adjoining room all by himself with the door closed, whereas in the court-room the collector, the magistrate, and the deputy superintendent of police started the trial. When they had made up their minds, Patel was called in from the other room to hear the judgment. He was asked why he should not be convicted for "disobeying directions given". As a Gandhian he simply said, "I do not want to defend myself. I plead guilty." According to Patel, "The Magistrate did not know under which section he was to convict me. He took about an hour and a half to write out a judgment of eight lines."[12] Further, "as the maximum sentence permissible was only three months and 500 rupees fine, he could not impose a greater punishment."[13] Patel was lodged in the Sabarmati jail in a cell meant for prisoners awarded capital punishment. He was treated "just like an ordinary criminal".

Patel's arrest had no valid ground. According to the home member to the government of India, he had delivered many speeches before he was arrested; whereas Patel had told G. V. Mavalankar:

The only "speech" I made was in reply to the Magistrate's question. I said to him that I would make a speech, and on that expression of my intention I was arrested . . . The District Superintendent of Police gave me no warning . . . I made no attempt to speak, but I simply mentioned my intention, although I would certainly have spoken if I had not been arrested . . . No evidence was recorded in my presence; nor was I examined during the five minutes that I was in the court-room.[14]

Further, neither was a complaint read out to Patel, nor was any witness examined. The lawyers of Ahmedabad, who held him in the highest esteem, were much agitated. The Bar Association passed a resolution, which G. Davis, the district judge, who happened to be a co-student with Patel in Britain for the Bar, dispatched to the High Court.

Ras staged an epic struggle over Patel's arrest. After he had been driven away to Borsad, the assembled audience of young and old, men and women, decided to launch a non-violent, non-cooperation campaign. This involved non-payment of land revenue and closing down of milk dairies and liquor shops in the village, besides boycott of government officials. Gandhi's arrival at Ras on 19 March, on his way to Dandi, was befittingly celebrated with the resignation of village officials—the police *patel (mukhi)*, revenue *patel*, *mamlatdar*, guards, and sweepers.

One late evening, news reached Ras that government officials were coming at night to confiscate property of non-cooperators. The villagers took an unusual decision to abandon the village. By this time it had become dark and the time for the arrival of officials was nearing. In less than half an hour, 400 families packed whatever they could carry on their shoulders, locked their houses, and moved across to the Baroda state territory about a quarter of a mile away. They put up temporary grass-huts for shelter near the villages of Zarola and Vasana. Happily, they called their "march" *hijarat*. The Ras émigrés lived a life of untold hardships for five to six months, even braving unseasonal heavy rains. They bore these with courage, cheer, and determination. According to one of their leaders, Ashabhai Patel: "They were living for Gandhi and their Sardar."

H. N. Brailsford, a British author-journalist, saw how Gandhi and Patel had "mesmerised the crowds". Gandhi "is devotedly loved, and so too is his lieutenant, Vallabhbhai Patel. I asked a group of forty or fifty villagers why they faced the risks and hardships. The women, as usual, answered first, and voiced their feeling of personal loyalty. 'We'll pay no taxes,' they said, 'till Mahatmaji and Vallabhbhai tell us to pay.' Then the men, slowly collecting their thoughts, voiced their economic grievances: 'We won't pay because the tax is unjust' . . . Finally, they added: 'We're doing it to win *swaraj*.'" According to Brailsford:

> Many villages were totally abandoned. I could see through the windows that every stick of property had been removed. In the silent street, nothing moved till a monkey skipped from a roof across the lane . . . the people had moved across the frontier of British India into the territory of independent Baroda. There, close to the boundary, they camped in shelters of matting and palm leaves, the ground cumbered with their chests and their beds, their churns and the great clay-coated baskets that held their grain. In the hot autumn days, life was just tolerable for hardy villagers in these conditions . . . Even in Baroda, these refugees were not always safe. Their camps had more than once been invaded and the Gaekwar's territory was violated by the armed British Indian police under an Indian official, who beat with their *lathis* not only their own people but the Gaekwar's subjects also.[15]

During their absence from Ras, their houses were broken open and looted. The police encamped on the outskirts of the village, and government officials got the crops harvested for sale. Lands were also declared confiscated, and some even sold. Nothing could make the people resile from their resolve. It was only on the conclusion of the Gandhi-Irwin pact that the *hijarat* was over, and the people returned to their houses in Ras. They "entered the village in a procession, happy and gay, led by a band. The village bore a festive look, decorated with colourful flags and buntings".[16]

Much to Patel's regret, the Gandhi-Irwin pact did not provide for the return of lands to the peasants. Patel felt deeply for the villagers and comforted them with the assurance: "Don't worry about your land. It will come back to you knocking at your door." Which it did, after the Congress had assumed power in Bombay Presidency in 1937.

The Dandi March was a historic event greater than the Kheda and Bardoli satyagrahas. For the first time, the satyagrahis faced the merciless blows of armed policemen with unparalleled acts of heroism and dauntless courage, undergoing tremendous suffering. They bore all this with absolute calm. The ferocity of attack attracted worldwide sympathy, especially from the American newspapermen who came to India to witness Gandhi's miracle.

Webb Miller, of the *United Press*, wrote:

Suddenly, at a word of command, scores of native policemen rushed upon the advancing marchers and rained blows on their heads with their steel-shod lathis. Not one of the marchers even raised an arm to fend off the blows. They went down like tenpins. From where I stood, I heard the sickening whack of the clubs on unprotected skulls. The waiting crowd of marchers groaned and sucked in their breath in sympathetic pain at every blow. Those struck down fell sprawling, unconscious or writhing with fractured skulls or broken shoulders . . . The survivors, without breaking ranks, silently and doggedly marched on until struck down . . .

They marched steadily, with heads up, without the encouragement of music or cheering or any possibility that they might escape serious injury or death. The police rushed out and methodically and mechanically beat down the second column. There was no fight, no struggle; the marchers simply walked forward till struck down . . . The police commenced to savagely kick the seated men in the abdomen and testicles and then dragged them by their arms and feet and threw them into the ditches.[17]

Other American journalists saw in the Dandi March a meaningful comparison with the Boston Tea Party which was the harbinger of independence for their country. Like the latter, the former was undertaken in fulfilment of the Independence Resolution passed at the Lahore Congress in December 1929. According to William Shirer: "The day after the Boston Tea Party, John Adams had predicted that it would arouse the country and have 'important consequences'. He considered it 'an Epoch in history'; and so was the Dandi March." In Shirer's estimation: "The struggle in America had been bloody. Gandhi's would be bloodless, but just as relentless."[18]

The Dandi March seemed to have shaken Viceroy Irwin. The witness in Shirer has recorded: "The British authorities at first were flabbergasted. They could not understand it."[19] A compromise was reached in the Gandhi-Irwin Pact, which proved Gandhi's nemesis. At the Round Table Conference in London, he met his Waterloo in the Muslim delegates questioning his credentials to speak on behalf of the Indian Muslims. It was a victory for the British diehards. The defeat

Gandhi suffered undermined the astounding success of the Dandi March. The Round Table Conference proved an anticlimax to Dandi. The Congress suffered such a setback as never to go back to Dandi in spirit or in action. The future looked bleak; and the freedom struggle much harsher, even uncertain of the end—receding far on the horizon.

3

PARTY BOSS

Overcoming Challenges to Congress Unity

The early 1930s witnessed a fundamental change in Congress politics: from Gandhi's non-cooperation to Tilak's responsive cooperation—proposed by Tilak at the Amritsar Congress in April 1919. The change was necessitated by two developments. First, the satyagraha in 1932 had met with failure, and there were no immediate prospects for Gandhi to launch another one. Nehru has written: "It was as if we entered unwillingly to battle. There was a glory about it in 1930, which had faded a little two years later . . . So gradually, the civil disobedience movement declined . . . Progressively, it ceased to be a mass movement."[1]

Second, with the enactment of the Act of 1935, India was entering upon parliamentary form of governance, with promise of provincial autonomy. The Congress considered this the best way to take the country towards independence. A Congress Parliamentary Board was constituted, with Patel as chairman. Since the Ahmedabad Congress of 1921, which was Gandhi's creation, Patel had proved himself a superb party organiser, and a disciplinarian capable of imposing decisions, collectively taken, in a democratic way. He was Gandhi's choice. The Mahatma considered the Congress safe in his hands, with hope of not only getting his policies and programmes implemented, but, at the same time, as Gandhi desired, keeping disunity at bay and warding off challenges to Congress solidarity till India got her freedom.

As chairman, Patel's position was analogous to the general secretary of the Communist Party in the Soviet Union. At the Tripuri Congress in 1939, when Subhash Chandra Bose suffered a defeat at the hands of Patel in his challenge to Gandhi, Patel, in M. N. Roy's apt description, "sat on the dais, a figure of granite, confident of strangulating the ambitious upstart . . . The picture was reminiscent of Stalin when the latter walked up and down in the background of the platform, smoking his pipe with a grim and cynical smile".[2] Patel, however, had none of Stalin's cunning, nor his diabolical designs to capture absolute power. He was there to defend Gandhi's position in the Congress. Equally so, to preserve Congress unity

As chairman, Patel's major responsibility was to watch and guide the Congress ministers, to pull up defaulting partymen, and to smother revolts even by stalwarts. Had Patel not used—judiciously, democratically and promptly—his "muscle power", the Congress would have gone the way of the All-India Trade Union Congress, which had been founded by the Congress in 1920 but slipped into the hands of the Communists manoeuvring under the direction of the Communist International. They had posed a great threat to the Congress during the mid-1930s, which only Patel could tactfully avert on time by securing a change in the minds of the Indian Socialists through whose partnership the Communists designed to capture the Congress.

That was in spite of the Congress being a divided house: the Changers led by Patel, Rajendra Prasad, and

Rajagopalachari, and the No-Changers whose sole voice was Nehru, who had been anti-imperialist since 1928, when, along with Subhash Chandra Bose, he had founded the Independence for India League. It was difficult to reconcile Nehru. It was left to Gandhi to rope him in for support to the Changers. Gandhi did that successfully, leaving Patel to manage the Congress organisation as party boss.

Nehru was away in Germany. Gandhi mollified him by appointing him, without his prior consent, as the next president of the Lucknow Congress in April 1936, thus burdening him with the responsibilities of a president. This veered Nehru away from the path he and Bose had decided upon to follow. On receiving Nehru's consent, Gandhi wrote to him on 3 October 1935:

Your letter about the wearing of the next year's crown was delightful. I was glad to have your consent. I am sure that it would solve many difficulties, and it is the rightest thing that could have happened for the country. Your presidentship at Lahore was totally different from what it would be at Lucknow. In my opinion, it was comparatively plain sailing at Lahore in every respect. It won't be so in any respect at Lucknow. But these circumstances I cannot imagine anybody better able to cope with than you.[3]

Even Rajendra Prasad wrote to Nehru on behalf of the Old Guard on 19 December 1935:

I know that there is a certain difference between your outlook and that of men like Vallabhbhai, Jamnalal [Bajaj] and myself, and it is even of a fundamental character. But, I suppose, that has been there all these years, and yet we have worked together . . . It is not right to put it as if it were a question of acceptance or non-acceptance of offices . . . no one wants to accept offices for their own sake. No one wants to work the Constitution as the Government would like it to be worked. The questions for us are altogether different. What are we to do with this Constitution? Are we to ignore it altogether and go our way? Is it possible to do so? Are we to capture it and use it as we would like to use it and to the extent it lends itself to be used in that way? Are we to fight it from within or from without, and in what way? It is really a question of laying down a positive programme for dealing with the situation created by the introduction of this Constitution in the light of the circumstances as they exist.[4]

Bose, on the other hand, attempted to kindle a "leftist" fire in Nehru by writing to him on 4 March 1936: "Among the front rank leaders of today, you are the only one to whom we can look up to for leading the Congress in a progressive direction. Moreover, your position is unique, and I think that even Mahatma Gandhi will be more accommodating towards you than towards anybody else. I earnestly hope that you will fully utilise the strength of your public position in making decisions."

Bose suggested that Nehru's "immediate task" would be "twofold: (i) to prevent office-acceptance by all possible means; and (ii) to enlarge and broaden the composition of the Cabinet [the working committee]." If he could do that, he would "save the Congress from demoralisation and bring it out of the rut".[5] Bose's efforts were reinforced by those of the Congress Socialists.

Realising that "the presidency did not mean the party's conversion to Socialism", Nehru attempted to wrest power from the Old Guard through radical resolutions. The right-wing leaders under Patel's direction "played their cards most skillfully", allowing the working committee, which was of the new president's choosing, to pass the proposals mooted, but got them rejected by the AICC, whereby the responsibility for rejection was of the Congress as a whole, not of a group of individuals. The radical resolutions were not acceptable even to Gandhi. The proposal to allow collective affiliation of trade unions and peasant leagues with the Congress would have shifted the balance of power into the hands of the Leftists outside the party.

The second proposal, equally radical, was of active Congress participation in agitations in the princely states. Patel was against Congress involvement in the struggle of the states people against their rulers, who were Indians, unless circumstances forced the Congress to do so. Not only were the states people yet incapable of undertaking a struggle, such a step should precede an awakening among them and thus "gradually make them capable of putting up a fight". Nehru's two other resolutions were also rejected. One favoured Congress participation in the "Imperial war" in Ethiopia; and the other, not to contest the provincial elections. The last was a major victory for Patel and other members of the Old Guard.

Nehru's inability in wresting power from the Old Guard was obvious. Yet, he gave expression to his radical views in his address as Congress president at Lucknow on 14 April 1936. He charged the Congress with the "spirit of disunity", which he ascribed to the "gradual divorce of its middle-class leadership from the masses". He even observed: "The Congress must be not only *for* the masses, as it claims to be, but *of* the masses." The peasant satyagrahas of Gandhi and Patel were, on the other hand, totally mass-based.

Gandhi and the Old Guard were upset for another reason too. At the Lahore Congress, Nehru had declared himself a

Socialist and Republican; while at Lucknow, "he reached the logical fulfillment of Socialism—namely, Communism".[6] According to Congress historian Pattabhi Sitaramayya, "the address pleaded for pure Communism in a country which had had its own traditions built up through at least a hundred and thirty centuries of progress".[7] In a letter of 30 April 1936 to Agatha Harrison, Gandhi wrote: "Jawaharlal's way is not my way. I accept his ideal about land, etc. But I do not accept practically any of his methods. I would strain every nerve to prevent a class war."[8]

Gandhi wrote to Nehru on 29 May 1936: "Your statement . . . has given much pain to Rajen Babu, CR and Vallabhbhai. They feel, and I agree with them, that they have tried to act honourably and with perfect loyalty towards you as a colleague. Your statement makes you out to be the injured party."[9] Gandhi wrote again on 15 July: "They have chafed under your rebukes and magisterial manner, and, above all, your arrogation of, what has appeared to them, your infallibility and superior knowledge. They feel that you have treated them with scant courtesy and never defended them from the Socialists' ridicule and even misrepresentation."

Gandhi bluntly told Nehru, "You are in office by their unanimous choice, but you are not in power yet. To put you in office was an attempt to find you in power quicker than you would otherwise have been. Anyway, that was at the back of my mind when I suggested your name for the crown of thorns."[10]

Gandhi's words sobered Nehru. Consequently, the Old Guard withdrew their letter of resignation from Nehru's working committee. They had, however, told Gandhi: "We feel that the preaching and emphasising of Socialism, particularly at this stage, by the President and other Socialist members of the Working Committee, while the Congress has not yet adopted it, is prejudicial to the best interests of the

country and to the success of the national struggle for freedom
. . . We feel the Congress should still follow the ideals, and
the line of action and policy, which it has been following
since 1920."[11] That had been laid down by Gandhi himself.
The Old Guard's apprehensions were not baseless. Nehru
had drafted into the working committee Socialists like
Jayaprakash Narayan, Narendra Deva, and Achyut
Patwardhan, who were soon to become, though unwittingly,
a shadow of the Communist Party.

Patel saw through what was going on. His shrewd sense
of judgment aptly described the Congress Socialists, long
before they had themselves realised, as "sappers and miners"
of the Communist Party. Later, Minoo Masani and some other
Socialists accepted this in their admission that "many of the
gains of the Socialists would ultimately accrue to the
Communists". Patel had correctly sensed that the Communists
sought entry into the Congress through the Congress Socialist
Party. Their own party was banned by the government. Patel
felt worried about "the respectability that the United Front
[formed by the Communists and the Socialists] gave the
Communists and the way it assured them a foothold in Indian
politics, which otherwise would have been difficult".

Masani writes: "Though I used to be annoyed at that time
with Sardar Patel's attacks at the Congress Socialist Party,
looking back I feel that he was justified when he made the
charge of the Socialists being the 'sappers and miners' of the
Communist Party. I myself found it necessary in 1939 to resign
from the Congress Socialist Party over the issue of alliance
with the Communists. In 1941 Jayaprakash Narayan himself
arrived at the same conclusion."[12]

A changed Nehru fell in line with the Old Guard and
strained himself to the utmost in the electioneering work. It
gave him great satisfaction that his performance was superb.

He was overwhelmed by the adulation of the masses. Hereafter, while Nehru managed the platform, Patel built up and controlled the party machine. He emerged as the party's undisputed boss. From his new position, Patel explained to Nehru what the parliamentary programme meant to the Old Guard:

> There is no difference of opinion about the objective. All of us want to destroy the imposed Constitution. How to destroy it from within the legislatures is the question . . . The question of "holding office" is not a live issue today. But I can visualise the occasion when the acceptance of office may be desirable to achieve the common purpose . . . I am no more wedded to the parliamentary programme than to the acceptance of office . . . We might in the course of events be driven to such an acceptance, but it shall never be at the cost of self-respect or through a compromise of our objective.

A mollified Nehru assured Patel: "It would be absurd for me to treat this presidential election as a vote for Socialism or against office acceptance . . . I do believe political independence is the paramount issue before the country, and the necessity for a joint and united action for its achievement is incumbent on all of us."[13]

As chairman of the Parliamentary Board, Patel faced three major confrontations. Two concerned him as chairman; the third was a challenge to Gandhi. The first two were with K. F. Nariman and N. B. Khare; the third was with Bose. In 1936, Nariman, being chairman of the Bombay Provincial Congress Parliamentary Board, expected to be the leader of the legislative party, and by virtue of that, the premier of the

Bombay Presidency. The party, instead, elected B. G. Kher. A campaign of vilification was let loose against Patel by the Parsi-owned Gujarati newspapers and the Parsi-owned *Bombay Sentinel.* The allegation was that Patel had brought to bear improper pressure on the members of the selection committee in the election of Kher.

Patel maintained complete silence in full confidence about his unassailable position. Nariman carried his complaint to the Congress Working Committee, not sparing even Nehru in person. Irritated by his unbecoming conduct, Nehru sarcastically told him that he could "go to the Privy Council or the League of Nations, or any other tribunal in which you have confidence".[14] To end the matter, Gandhi had an inquiry conducted by himself and Justice Bahadurji. Both held Nariman guilty of wrong conduct. Ten years later, Nariman apologised to Patel, and the latter, in his magnanimity, took him back into the Congress.

The Khare episode had graver implications. Nariman's was a party affair; in Khare's case, the British governor of the Central Provinces, of which Dr. N. B. Khare was the premier, had indirect complicity in wanting to exploit the opportunity to damage Congress prestige and power. Khare merely played into his hands. Serious differences arose between Khare and his cabinet colleagues from the Hindi-speaking part of the province, Mahakoshal. Three Ministers submitted their resignations, upon which Patel stepped in to heal the rupture. At a meeting held at Panchmarhi on 24 May 1938, the differences were ironed out and they withdrew their resignations. But Khare had some other plan up his sleeve: his intention to form a ministry, independent of the Congress, with the support of the governor.

On 19 July Khare declared his intention to resign as premier and asked his colleagues to hand over their resignations to him. The three Mahakoshal ministers refused to do so unless instructed by the Parliamentary Board. Ignoring the latter, Khare submitted to the governor his own resignation and the two resignations he had already secured. The governor called the Mahakoshal ministers at midnight, but failed in coaxing them to follow the others. On twenty-first morning he accepted the resignations of Khare and his two colleagues, terminated the office of the other three, and invited Khare to form a new ministry, which he did by taking the oath of office the same day.

Patel called a meeting of the Parliamentary Board on the twenty-second and of the Congress Working Committee the following day. Khare and all his colleagues attended these meetings. Khare was told his conduct did not befit the high position he held. He admitted that they all had committed an error and would set it right by submitting their resignations. They did so. The Congress Working Committee advised Khare to call a meeting of the Congress Legislative Party to consider the resignations and to elect a new leader.

The working committee passed a resolution, which declared Khare "guilty of grave errors of judgment which have exposed the Congress in the Central Provinces to ridicule and lowered its prestige". Further, his action had helped the governor to use his special powers for the first time since the assumption of office by the Congress. Khare was also declared guilty of indiscipline in accepting the governor's invitation to form a new ministry without reference to the Parliamentary Board, thereby proving himself unworthy of holding any position of responsibility in the Congress organisation.

The resolution did not spare even the governor. He was held guilty of forcing a crisis, as "he was anxious to weaken and discredit the Congress insofar as it lay in his power to do so".[15] He was accused of "unseemly haste" in not only accepting the resignations of the ministers, but going so far as to have demanded the resignations of the recalcitrant ministers as well; and, on their refusal to oblige him, dismissing them, and, thereby, helping Khare to form a new ministry.

An anti-Congress campaign was whipped up, particularly in Maharashtra, against Patel who was accused of naked fascism. Gandhi intervened by saying that Khare "should have rushed not to the Governor but to the Working Committee and tendered his resignation. He erred grievously in ignoring or, what is worse, not knowing this simple remedy". Gandhi declared that Khare was "not only guilty of gross indiscipline in flouting the warnings of the Parliamentary Board, but he betrayed incompetence as a leader by allowing himself to be fooled by the Governor, or not knowing that, by his precipitate action, he was compromising the Congress."[16] Gandhi was also critical of the governor's role: "The Governor betrayed a haste which I can only call indecent", and his action "killed the spirit of the tacit compact between the British Government and the Congress."[17]

Supporting Patel's role, Gandhi said, "The Congress must be in the nature of an army . . . the Congress, conceived as a fighting machine, has to centralise control and guide every department and every Congressman, however highly placed, and expected unquestioned obedience. The fight cannot be fought on any other terms."[18] Such centralised control Gandhi had placed in the hands of Patel, and it was Patel's responsibility to shepherd Congress ministers and legislators.

The third confrontation Patel had was with the fiery Subhash Chandra Bose as president of the Faizpur Congress. It was in defence of Gandhi's position. His re-election after Haripura at Tripuri was conceded by Gandhi as a defeat, not so much of Pattabhi Sitaramayya against whom he had won, but a personal defeat. Bose threw two challenges to the Old Guard in a bid to wrest party control. The first was the accusation that the Old Guard was "contemplating to come to some kind of a settlement with the British Government in regard to the Federal scheme". The second was an attempt at reversal of the Congress policy of parliamentary programme by advocating resumption of civil disobedience on a mass scale.

Patel dispelled the confusion Bose was causing by stating: "We have not accepted office in order to carry out a few reforms. We accepted office with a view to moving towards a far greater objective—complete independence, which is the only remedy for all our ills. If by accepting office our ability to move towards that goal is increased, well and good. But if by accepting office we find that our final goal is jeopardised, we must immediately give up office."[19]

As chairman of the Parliamentary Board, Patel objected to Bose's re-election. In a joint statement with six of his working committee colleagues, he argued: "It is a sound policy to adhere to the rule of not re-electing the same President except under very exceptional circumstances . . . The Congress policy and programmes are not determined by its successive Presidents. If it were so, the constitution would not limit the office to one year . . . The position of the President is, therefore, that of a chairman. More than this, the President represents and symbolises, as under a constitutional monarchy, the unity and solidarity of the nation."[20]

Bose remained defiant. In order to malign the Old Guard, he repeated his old charge: "It is widely believed that there may be a compromise on the Federal scheme between the Right Wing of the Congress and the British Government during the coming year. It is imperative in the circumstances to have as President one who will be an anti-Federationist to the core of his heart."[21] Patel was quick to nail the lie: "I can only say that I know of no member who wants the Federation of the Government of India Act. And after all, no single member, not even the President for the time being of the Congress, can decide on such big issues. It is the Congress

alone that can decide . . . even the Working Committee has
no power to depart from the letter and the spirit of the
declared policy of the Congress . . . the matter is not one of
persons but of principles, not of Leftists and Rightists, but
of what is in the best interest of the country."[22] Nehru too
felt that "Subhash Babu should not stand" for presidentship.

Yet, Bose defeated Pattabhi Sitaramayya by 95 votes. In
the *Harijan* of 2 February 1939 Gandhi confessed that "from
the very beginning I was decidedly against his re-election . . .
I do not subscribe to his facts or the arguments in his
manifestoes. I think that his references to his colleagues were
unjustified and unworthy. Nevertheless, I am glad of his
victory. And since I was instrumental in inducing Dr. Pattabhi
not to withdraw his name as a candidate when Maulana Saheb
withdrew, the defeat is more mine than his." Gandhi suggested
that Bose should now "choose a homogeneous Cabinet and
enforce his programme without let or hindrance".[23]

Gandhi's statement had a magical effect on the minds of
the delegates to the Tripuri Congress. Most of them felt, that
had Gandhi expressed himself earlier, Bose might not have
been elected. To Patel, the situation appeared quite serious.
Bose had posed a challenge to Gandhi, which he wanted to
deal with constitutionally—primarily to avenge Gandhi's
defeat. He wanted Bose to prepare resolutions for the Tripuri
Congress in consultation with his supporters and bear
responsibility for the decisions taken. He also thought that
Bose should be allowed a free hand in whatever he wanted to
do. Bose could not attend the working committee meeting at
Wardha owing to high fever. In his absence, 13 members gave
their resignations, which the president-elect accepted.

Amid such an acrimonious atmosphere the Tripuri
Congress was held. On arrival, Bose again took ill, and could
not leave his bed. The presidential procession was taken out
with his portrait placed in a chariot drawn by 52 elephants

symbolising the 52nd session of the party. Owing to the resignation of its 13 members, the working committee could not meet. The session had two resolutions to consider: one by President Bose for the consideration of the AICC; the other by the resigned members of the working committee which the subject committee had accepted by a big majority.

Bose's resolution proposed an ultimatum to be given to the government of civil disobedience to be started at the end of six months. The other resolution, proposed by Govind Ballabh Pant, was supported by about 160 members of the AICC. It proposed: "It is desirable that the AICC should clarify the position and declare its general policy. The committee declares its firm adherence to the fundamental policies of the Congress, which have governed its programme in the past years under the guidance of Mahatma Gandhi . . . the committee regards it imperative that the Congress Executive should command his implicit confidence and requests the President to nominate a Working Committee in accordance with the wishes of Gandhi."[24]

A suggestion to refer Pant's resolution to the AICC was resisted with force by Subhash Chandra Bose's supporters. There was complete pandemonium, "paralysing all proceedings for well nigh an hour". It was "one that had not been witnessed since Surat [1907] or even at Surat".[25] However, Sarat Bose's appeal restored order. Pant's resolution was withdrawn, and the session was postponed. With a view to avoiding repetition of such unseemly scenes, the following day's proceedings were held by keeping visitors out. Finally Pant's resolution was passed.

Subhash Chandra Bose felt "angry and bitter against the Sardar". He had faced many challenges and had to address the issues before him. First: Was he to submit to Gandhi in the selection of his new working committee? Second: How was he to face the prospect of the president's powers being curtailed and those of Patel as chairman of the Parliamentary Board strengthened as per the principle laid down in an AICC resolution of June 1938? The resolution stated that "in administrative matters, the Provincial Congress Committee should not interfere with the discretion of the Ministry, but it is always open to the Executive of the PCC to draw the attention of the Government privately to any particular abuse or difficulty. In matters of policy, if there is a difference between the Ministry and the Provincial Congress Committee, reference should be made to the Parliamentary Board."[26] Third: Gandhi's Congress had categorically rejected Bose's policy of hastening the fight with the government and coming "to grips with the British straightaway".

For nearly a month Bose did not appoint a new working committee. And when he convened a meeting of the AICC in Kolkata, rowdy scenes dominated it. Physical clashes marred the proceedings. To avoid any impression of his influencing AICC members, Patel had not gone to Kolkata. Since he failed to resolve the deadlock, Bose submitted his resignation from the presidentship of the Congress. His place was taken over by Rajendra Prasad, a protégé of Patel.

In M. N. Roy's view, "In 1938, Subhash Bose could have made history, for good or evil. His weakness plus the Sardar's iron-will frustrated his ambition and saved the Gandhian Congress."[27] In Sarat Bose's view, Patel was "the shining light" of the ruling coterie.[28] Even a defeated Subhash Bose acknowledged that "the Gandhian wing had this tactical advantage that it was the only organised party within the Congress, acting under a centralised leadership".[29] Such leadership lay in the hands of Patel as chairman of the Congress Parliamentary Board.

4

ADMINISTRATIVE UNIFIER

Formation of Indian Administrative Service

Patel had no compeer as an administrator. Philip Mason, a distinguished British member of the ICS, called him "a natural administrator who did not seem to need experience". Everything came to him instinctively, instantly, and intuitively. H. V. R. Iengar, his home secretary, once said of him:

> I often used to wonder where exactly lay the strength of the Sardar. There he was, mostly conducting his business from his sick-bed or lying reclined on a chair in his drawing-room, always exquisitely polite and never once raising his voice. His politeness was really impeccable. I believe the truth of the matter was twofold. The first is that he listened patiently to all sides of a case before making up his mind, but once he made up his mind nothing would shake him from his decision. The other is that he had the capacity to say "No" to requests which he felt should not be accepted . . . the Sardar was absolutely firm.[1]

Patel's great assets were a clear vision, a judicious mind, an inflexible determination, and a will that did not allow events to overtake him. This was apparent in October 1946. He was only a home member in Viceroy Wavell's interim government when a communication from the secretary of state conveyed his decision to stop further recruitment to the ICS, suspended during the war years, with indication of the possible termination of his connection with the Services earlier than the date of constitutional changes.

The secretary of state's reported decision had serious implications. In a conflict-torn political situation, a breakdown in administration would have made transfer of power neither smooth nor trouble-free. Patel foresaw administrative chaos descending, but had the boldness to say: "The sooner the Secretary of State's control is ended and the present structure wound up, the better."[2] Patel decided to act on two levels: First, to win over the loyalty of the Indian members of the ICS, and second, to order formation of a new service—the Indian Administrative Service as successor to the ICS. Each was to serve in two different ways: the ICS as implementor of the transfer of power on behalf of the inheritors—the Congress; and the IAS to keep the country bound together, post-independence, through administrative unity of a vast country.

Within two days of the secretary of state's communication, Patel called a conference of chief ministers (then called prime ministers) and announced the formation of the Indian Administrative Service. Patel's decision was not to the liking of the chief ministers who included Gobind Ballabh Pant of United Provinces (later Uttar Pradesh), a leading member of the Congress Working Committee. They favoured a provincial civil service whose members could be under their control "in order to ensure their pliability". According to B. K. Nehru

(ICS), "it was only he [Patel] who could force down the throats of unwilling and very powerful heads of provincial Governments the concept of the all-India Service".[3]

B. K. Nehru opines that Patel, "with his much longer vision and his greater grasp of the essential requisites for the Rule of Law", convinced the Constituent Assembly on 10 October 1949: "The Union [of India] will go, you will not have a united India, if you do not have a good all-India Service which has independence to speak out its mind." Patel considered "an efficient, disciplined, contented Service . . . a *sine qua non* of sound administration under a democratic regime".[4]

Patel was quick to act, losing no time. He addressed the first batch of IAS probationers on 21 April 1947, when transfer of power was yet nearly four months away, and no decision had yet been announced. Patel had the boldness to tell them, "The days of the ICS of the old style are going to be over", and that the formation of the IAS in its place was "both significant and epoch-making—an unmistakable symptom of the transfer of power" from foreign to Indian hands. The IAS "marks the inauguration of an all-India Service officered entirely by Indians and subject completely to Indian control . . . the Service will now be free to, or will have to, adopt its true role of national service without being trammeled by traditions and habits of the past". Offering them paternal advice, he said:

> The days when the Service could be masters are over . . . Perhaps, you are aware of a saying regarding the Indian Civil Service—that, it is neither Indian nor civil, nor imbued with any spirit of service . . . Your predecessors had to serve as agents of an alien rule, and even against their better judgment, had sometimes to execute the biddings of their foreign employers . . .

A Civil Servant cannot afford to, and must not, take part in politics. Nor must he involve himself in communal wrangles. To depart from the path of rectitude in either of these respects is to debase public service and to lower its dignity.[5]

Patel invited about 30 to 40 members of the ICS to his residence and talked to them, much to their surprise, in a manner none had done before—utterly informal and free from the rigid mannerism of their former bosses. His talk was brief, realistic, transparently sincere, and patriotic. Prefacing his talk with a narration as to how he and his colleagues had for years worked with "only one burning desire—to serve the country", Patel invited them "to dedicate themselves equally to the service of the country". He did not promise them "in return anything more than the joy which he himself and his colleagues had experienced through such single-minded devotion to what they regarded as the supreme duty, and which he was certain they too would experience". Patel offered the civil servants "equality" of consideration, "if only they too would respond and work as untiringly and unceasingly as he and his colleagues, whether in or out of Government, had been doing for the people of the country".[6] The response was instant. Patel won over their loyalty; no less their personal love and affection. An emotional bond united them to him.

Patel's concept of the civil service emerged from the belief he held and which he once expressed to his home secretary, Iengar: "It would be a bad day if people did not look up to officials holding high positions. Ministers come and Ministers go, but the permanent machinery [the civil service] must be good and firm, and have the respect of the people."[7] Lord Macaulay had expressed identical views in the British

Parliament over a hundred years ago: "The character of the Governor-General is less important than the character of the Administrator by whom the administration was carried on."[8] The British civil servants were the founders of the empire in India.

Patel realised that in the solution of administrative problems, only the civil servants could act as his faithful agents—not the politicians. Such realism has been admitted by British historian Judith M. Brown: "Patel, as Home Minister in the Interim Government, was well aware that in the turbulent days of 1946-47, the ICS, whatever its previous image in the eyes of Congressmen, was a bastion against chaos and the disintegration of Government." He was "partly instrumental in persuading other Congressmen that continuity in administration must be maintained. Clearly the Service was a source of stability".[9]

Patel looked upon the Services as "partners with him in the task of administration". In his "modesty and profound commonsense", he was ever anxious to make the fullest use of the knowledge and experience which the civil service had acquired. He "selected people, trusted them, and gave them their head, subject to overriding policy being settled by him." He expected of them to think and act independently to the best of their knowledge and ability. On his part, he was open-minded and generous in accepting responsibility for their actions committed in good faith. Once, Iengar was forced to take a decision on a crucial matter. Patel was out of New Delhi and so were other senior ministers, including the prime minister. The decision brooked no delay. Iengar briefed Patel on his return. Iengar writes that Patel "shook his head with evident disapproval, and said that, if I had consulted him beforehand, he would have taken a different decision . . . he patiently explained to me the reasons." He further writes: "I was very unhappy. He asked me not to worry and said that every human being makes mistakes. When the matter subsequently came up before the Cabinet, he told them that the decision was his, and there the matter ended."[10]

Patel saw to it that the civil servants were respected and listened to by those with whom they transacted business on his behalf. He once stated: "My Secretary can write a note opposed to my views. I have given that freedom to all my Secretaries . . . I will never be displeased over a frank expression of opinion." He looked upon the civil servants as "instruments" with whose help he ran the administration; and he argued: "Remove them, and I see nothing but a picture of chaos all over the country."[11]

Patel told the Constituent Assembly: "I need hardly dilate at length on the necessity of maintaining their discipline and morale, and keeping them contented. In no other circumstances we can get out of the Services loyal and efficient service except by trying to appreciate their difficulties and their work . . . It is our duty to see that the machine with which we have to work is kept in good humour and good temper."[12]

Patel built such a status for the civil servants by giving them respect and independence almost as equals. Since Patel operated from his residence and not from office, his home secretary, Iengar, visited him almost daily to transact official business. Even when he had three ministries under his charge—home, states, and information—Patel seldom read a single file, no matter how important. He would hear a brief and give his judgment, which he always stood by.

Iengar was once called upon to undertake an extremely difficult task. The Congress Working Committee had directed the government to take immediate steps towards the formation of a linguistic Andhra Pradesh. As home secretary, an unconvinced Iengar was in a quandary. He asked Patel,

"Sir, the gentlemen who have passed this resolution include Shri Jawaharlal Nehru, Maulana Azad, Dr. Rajendra Prasad and you yourself. All of you are Cabinet Ministers . . . What do you expect me to do about it?" Without a moment's hesitation, Patel asked him: "Are you, or are you not, the Home Secretary?" "Of course, I am," replied Iengar. Patel then said: "Do your duty as Home Secretary. Prepare a note to the Cabinet stating what exactly, in your judgment, are the implications of the proposal and how they should be further examined. It must make no difference to you who are the parties to the Working Committee resolution. You must clearly and frankly analyse the whole problem."

Iengar did exactly that, "subjecting to a cold analysis" the decision which Patel and others had taken. As a result, the proposal to create the state of Andhra Pradesh was postponed, and could not materialise as long as Patel was alive. After the cabinet meeting, Iengar called on Patel and told him in a lighter vein: "I have succeeded in getting you as Home Minister to overrule yourself as Sardar Patel of the Congress Working Committee!" Patel admitted that the formation of linguistic provinces would "unmistakably retard the process of consolidation of our gains, dislocate our administrative, economic and financial structure, let loose . . . forces of disruption and disintegration".[13]

Patel was called the great administrator by none other than Girija Shankar Bajpai, senior-most member of the ICS at the time of Partition in 1947 and secretary-general under Nehru. Presiding over the condolence meeting organised by the ICS Association on 16 December 1950, Bajpai said, "We meet today to mourn the loss and to pay tribute to the memory of a great patriot, a great administrator and a great man. Sardar Vallabhbhai Patel was all three—a rare combination in any historic epoch and in any country." Bajpai referred to the "ties of trust between the Sardar and the Services", as also to the "keenness and warmth of his personal interest in their welfare", and said, "A smaller man might have allowed old-time prejudices to raise a curtain of suspicion between him and those who had served an alien regime . . . That we should deeply mourn the loss of one who gained freedom for us in our time, and sought successfully to impart to it the durability that comes from stable conditions and administrative strength is but natural."[14]

The civil service Patel created proved a strong bond that has held together a diverse people in so many states in a country of India's vast dimensions.

5

PARTITION

Averting Balkanisation of India

Attlee's policy statement of 20 February 1947, and the Indian Independence Act passed by the British Parliament later in July, had grave implications for India. The former, according to H. V. Hodson, was "an open licence for Pakistan in some form or other".[1] The London *Times* too thought that "Muslim separatism is deriving encouragement from the White Paper". The Indian Independence Act had even more serious implications in the provision for creation of Princestan through a "Third Dominion" by transferring power to the states simultaneously with India and Pakistan. Indian foreign secretary, K. P. S. Menon, wrote: "When the British left India, the unity even of divided India was in danger. Some 560 Princely States had been left in the air. It was open to them to adhere to India, to accede to Pakistan, or to remain independent . . . It almost looked as if India was going to be Balkanised. But this danger was averted by the firm handling of the Princes by a man of iron, Sardar Vallabhbhai Patel."[2]

Patel did not allow events to overtake him. He acted with speed and with a decisive, determined mind—in the manner he had earlier, in October 1946, in regard to a single, unified civil service for the country. At his initiative, the Congress Working Committee, at its meeting on 8 March, passed a resolution which asked for "a division of Punjab into two provinces, so that the predominantly Muslim part may be separated from the predominantly non-Muslim part".[3] Patel's was not a call for India's partition, but a forewarning to the Punjabi Muslims of the consequences of the League's demand for Pakistan.

Since Gandhi had not been consulted or forewarned, he felt "as if an abyss had suddenly opened under his feet".[4] He asked Patel for an explanation. Patel's reply was terse and matter-of fact: "It is difficult to explain to you the resolution about Punjab. It was adopted after the deepest deliberation. Nothing has been done in a hurry, or without full thought. That you had expressed your views against it, we learnt only from newspapers. But you are, of course, entitled to say what you feel right."

Even Nehru bluntly told Gandhi that the resolution was "the only answer to Partition as demanded by Jinnah".[5] This amounted to calling for Gandhi's non-interference in crucial national affairs. Patel's fears soon proved true. At his meeting with Mountbatten on 1 April, Gandhi made "an astonishing proposal . . . to dismiss the present Cabinet [interim government] and call on Jinnah to appoint an all-Muslim administration".[6] Gandhi ignored what Jinnah had said in May 1946: "India stands on the brink of a civil war."

Attlee's statement suffered from lack of transparency. It was not a clear-cut plan of action at least in two respects: First, "to whom the powers of the Central Government in British India should be handed over . . . whether as a whole to some form of Central Government . . . or in some areas to the existing provincial Governments." Second, it said, "HMG do not intend to hand over their powers and obligations under Paramountcy to any Government of British India. It is not intended to bring Paramountcy, as a system, to a conclusion earlier than the date of the final transfer of power."

Patel seemed determined not to let the past come in his way, especially at a time when freedom was around the corner. In the early 1920s, Gandhi had given precedence to Khilafat over India's independence by stating: "I would gladly ask for postponement of *swaraj* if thereby we could advance the interests of Khilafat." This time, in March 1947, the story seemed to be repeating itself. To Gandhi, India's unity seemed dearer than India's freedom from the British. That was not acceptable to the realist in Patel. He preferred partition to the unity of India as envisaged in the grouping scheme of the Cabinet Mission.

Patel's analysis of the situation seemed identical to that of Penderel Moon (ICS), an experienced civil servant from Punjab, who has written: "Even if constitution-making had begun, it could hardly have got very far . . . a weak, easily divisible Union of India . . . the price which the League would exact for preserving unity would be too high . . . a weak Federal Centre which would be paralysed by its own internal communal divisions."[7]

Patel had two reasons to influence his decision. First: "the Congress being pledged to non-violence, it was not possible for it to resist Partition." Second: "if Partition were not accepted, there was bound to be long drawn-out communal strife in cities, in some rural areas, and even regiments [of the army] and police forces would be torn by communal dissensions."[8] Further, if not acted upon promptly, prospects for early independence would have receded, and a return might not have been possible for many years to come. Above all, their 30-year freedom struggle was in danger of being reduced to ashes. Patel wanted to grasp the opportunity that appeared within his reach.

Since the Cabinet Mission parleys of mid-1946, Patel had watched with dismay the Congress gradually losing ground to Jinnah. The mission's grouping scheme was a virtual gift to him, with two "Pakistans" on either side of India: Group B comprising undivided Punjab, Sind, and the NWFP on the west, and Group C comprising the whole of Bengal and Hindu majority Assam on the east. In the proposed weak Group A comprising India, Jinnah would have dominated with the support of the Indian Muslims who had been more loyal to him than the Muslims from Punjab, Sind, and Bengal. In their passionate desire to be part of Pakistan, they would have launched another struggle for wresting power in India in order to form Greater Pakistan. Such a hope, the Muslim migrants from India to Pakistan had expressed in the slogan: *Hass ke liya Pakistan, lar ke lenge Hindustan* (we got Pakistan easily; we shall fight for Hindustan). Additionally, Jinnah could have banked upon, as was later proved, the support of some of the Indian princes.

The Congress was a divided house, considerably weak in comparison with the League under Jinnah's sole spokesmanship. Azad, as president, had, on his own, assured the mission of Congress acceptance of the plan. He favoured a federal government "with fully autonomous Provinces with residuary powers vested in the units themselves".[9] He feared that "the creation of Pakistan was to weaken the position of the Muslims in the sub-continent of India".[10]

Gandhi favoured the mission plan since it preserved the unity of India, irrespective of the cost to the non-Muslims. Patel told Wavell that Gandhi "put forward all the arguments for acceptance, but had failed to convince the Working Committee".[11] Whereas Wavell told Arthur Henderson, under secretary of state: "Nehru was ready to give the Mission Plan a chance."[12] Opposed to all of them, Patel, records Wavell, thought that "the proposed solution was 'worse than Pakistan', and he could not recommend it to Congress".[13]

As interim president of the Congress in July 1946, Nehru burst the mission bubble by declaring that Assam could opt out of Group C from the outset. It was a blow to the mission plan; no less it shattered Jinnah's dream. He reacted like a wounded tiger, and declared "war" on the Hindus—starting with the "Great Calcutta Killing" in mid-August. Yet, the mission wanted Wavell to manage the formation of an interim government, unconcerned about whether it would work or not.

Who could have helped Wavell in that? His choice fell on Patel. He felt that none other than Patel was capable of getting it done. He got the secretary of state's approval for approaching him. In his letter to him, Wavell quoted what an "unimpeachable source" had told him: "If Congress were asked to form an Interim Government, Patel would insist on their agreeing . . . convinced that the Congress must enter the Government to prevent chaos spreading in the country."[14] Thus, the interim government was formed on 2 September 1946 with Patel's support, but without Jinnah's League as a participant. Patel, thus, secured a potent weapon in keeping Jinnah out in the cold, with the disadvantage of losing ground for a fight from within the government and even losing the confidence of many Muslims.

It was not in the interest of the British to let Jinnah be thrown into isolation. They wanted him to remain alive and kicking, and counterbalance the Congress. Wavell, therefore, came to Jinnah's rescue for the second time since the Simla

Conference. He asked Nehru, "Would you mind if I invite Jinnah once more and persuade him to join the Interim Government?"[15] Nehru's consent proved to be the nemesis of the Congress since Jinnah was not asked to first cancel his "Direct Action" resolution. Patel had, therefore, correctly told Wavell as early as 12 June: "Jinnah would only use his position in the Interim Government for purely communal and disruptive purposes and to break up India."[16] How prophetic he proved! Jinnah's aide, Ghazanfar Ali, had stated: "We are going into the Interim Government to get a foothold to fight for our cherished goal of Pakistan . . . The Interim Government is one of the fronts of the Direct Action campaign."[17]

With the League's entry, the interim government plunged into a deep crisis. The position of the Congress was very much weakened. Patel still preferred giving a last-ditch fight, both to Jinnah and the British. He told the former, "The sword will be met with the sword", which, however, was not acceptable to Gandhi nor to Nehru. He accused the British of "repeatedly . . . giving way to Jinnah in order to save his face".[18] He publicly declared: "If the Muslim League members were allowed to remain in the Interim Government, the Congress members would resign",[19] in full realisation that Cripps and Pethick-Lawrence believed that "the cooperation of the Congress was vital".[20]

This time Patel was outmanoeuvred by Attlee with his call to Nehru and Jinnah to visit him in London. Patel was against Nehru's going, as he smelt a rat. However, Nehru did go, persuaded by his faith in Attlee's good intentions. A completely disappointed Nehru returned, as Patel commented, like "a broken reed". Even the Congress Working Committee declared that Attlee's verdict over Assam was "full of peril for the future". According to it, Assam would form part of

Group C, along with Muslim majority Bengal, at least for a period of five years; and that Muslim Bengal could frame Hindu Assam's constitution. And thus, the Congress lost its final battle against Jinnah. From then onwards events moved fast to a climax, when, on 20 February, Attlee's policy statement virtually conceded Pakistan to Jinnah. With that, Patel moved away from Gandhi to play an assertive role to save the rest of India. That lay in his asking for a division of Punjab; also of Bengal and Assam by implication.

Mountbatten, the new viceroy, arrived in India on 24 March to implement Attlee's mandate: to transfer power by a date not later than June 1948. But he saw India sliding fast into anarchy. India, to him, appeared "like a ship on fire in mid-ocean with ammunition in the hold". An explosion at any time would leave nothing for Britain to hand over, and would place her in a most precarious situation. He, therefore, turned into a man in a hurry, determined not to let a catastrophe overtake Britain. By early May, he had his transfer plan ready, based on Attlee's statement of 20 February. By 10 May he had it sent to London.

In a somewhat relieved state of mind, and wanting to escape from New Delhi's sweltering heat, Mountbatten retreated to Simla for a cool recess. He took with him Nehru, a personal friend whom he considered the nearest to him of Indian leaders. In utter confidence, he showed the plan document to him. Nehru blasted it, as he saw in it "a direct invitation, at least to the major States, to remain independent kingdoms, presumably as allies or feudatories of Britain"[21], creating thereby many "Ulsters" in India. This had a shattering effect on Mountbatten.

An over-confident, domineering Mountbatten found himself thrown into a deep crisis. Nehru's reaction was "a bombshell of the first order". Of this, Campbell-Johnson writes: "His hair was somewhat dishevelled, but he was still marvellously resilient. He told us that only a hunch on his part had saved him from disaster. Without that hunch, 'Dickie Mountbatten', he said, 'would have been finished and could have packed his bag. We would have looked complete fools with the Government at home', having led them up the garden path to believe that Nehru would accept the Plan."[22]

At that "fateful hour", V. P. Menon came to Mountbatten's rescue with a plan* which he had earlier prepared on his own, when Wavell was the viceroy. The latter had shown no interest, but Menon had secured Patel's general approval of it. Under his plan, transfer of power was to take place on the basis of the creation of India and Pakistan as two dominions. Menon's plan was, on the whole, acceptable to Nehru. But he could not give a commitment on India's membership of the Commonwealth. Throughout his political career he had been an anti-imperialist who favoured severance of the British connection. He believed, with Krishna Menon, that "a link with the Crown was a symbol of oppression".[23] How was he to meet Mountbatten's demand? Nehru telephoned Patel from Simla. Patel told him, "Leave that to me. That is my business."[24]

Mountbatten realised that Patel was not only the party boss, but also the "strongest pillar of the Cabinet" who alone could deliver the goods on behalf of India. He needed his collaboration in the quick, trouble-free transfer of power, with no hurdles blocking his path. He, therefore, reached a six-point understanding with him: an equitable give-and-take arrangement. Mountbatten's three gains were: First, India agreeing to be a member of the Commonwealth without which

---

*Olaf Caroe, governor of the NWFP, appropriately called 3 June plan "Menon" Partition Plan in his review of Hodson's "The Great Divide".

the Labour Government would not have secured Churchill's support to the Indian Independence Bill in the House of Lords. According to Mountbatten, Churchill saw in such membership "the chance of holding on to some vestige of the Empire in the form of the Commonwealth . . . That's how we got the legislation through". Second, the Congress party officially accepting the creation of Pakistan. Third, settlement of division of assets and liabilities between India and Pakistan prior to 15 August, thereby helping transfer to take place on the due date. Patel fulfilled all the three assurances fully and within the specified time-limit.

In return, Patel got from Mountbatten what India needed most. Pyarelal quotes Patel having made a condition that "in two months time power should be transferred and an Act should be passed by Parliament in that time" guaranteeing "that the British Government would not interfere with the question of the Indian States. He said, 'We will deal with that question. Leave it to us. You take no sides. Let Paramountcy be dead'."[25] No matter how opposed this was to Britain's declared states policy, Mountbatten could not go against Patel's wishes. He was conscious of the new winds of change sweeping the country, but more than that, he needed Patel's crucial help in the division of assets and liabilities between India and Pakistan without which transfer of power could not take place by 15 August.

As leader of the Indian team at the Partition Council, Patel's role was historic. Its great success was largely due to his business-like approach: brief, quick, firm and yet accommodating. The Partition Council set up a steering committee of two senior-most ICS officials, representing India and Pakistan. They were assisted by ten expert committees to decide on division of such wide-ranging, purely administrative but highly complex matters as total assets and liabilities, records and personnel, central revenues, currency and exchange, economic controls, trade, foreign relations, and domicile and nationality of inhabitants of British India and the position of Indian nationals abroad.

Patel gave the Indian officials full freedom in their work; even galvanized them with inspiring words of advice at the very start of their work: "We are entrusting you with work of great national importance. It has to be done in a very short time. You will have to work very hard, as you have never done before. All I would like to tell you is that all my life I have enjoyed working for the country, and I have been working very hard. I invite you to share in the same pleasure."[26] He thereby aroused their spirit of patriotism. As for himself, at the Partition Council proceedings, Patel played a superb role. He had "an eye for the essential, and yet no detail escaped his attention. He defended with determination every Indian interest", and had "no difficulty in reconciling it with generosity and goodwill for Pakistan".

Patel infused a similar spirit of compromise, on a give-and-take basis, among the members of the negotiating teams. He made realisation dawn on them: the sooner they reach an agreement, the earlier India and Pakistan would have power transferred to their respective dominions. At the start, when H. M. Patel (India) and Mohammed Ali (Pakistan), leaders of their respective teams, were bogged down by disagreements on almost every issue, Patel's magic worked. He asked the two "to go into an adjoining room at his house . . . the two did not have much difficulty in reaching an understanding on every issue".[27] They were unaffected by the politically vitiated climate outside. Jinnah seemed to have been impressed. He was the keenest to get his Pakistan at the earliest. At the Partition Council meeting, when an issue got stuck in disagreement, he spoke to Patel in a hush-hush tone in his mother tongue, Gujarati: "Can't you and I resolve the issue?"

The Pakistanis were considerably impressed by Patel's approach and outlook—flexible and open-minded. At the concluding session of the Partition Council, the Pakistani representative, Abdur Rab Nishtar, "admired his statesmanship, applauded his constructive approach and affirmed that the Pak Ministers would continue to look upon him as their elder brother".[28]

Patel won rich tributes from Mountbatten as well. He thought that "history would accord to the Sardar great credit for his part in the transfer of power, and that his realistic attitude on the three major issues—Partition, Dominion Status and relations with the Indian Princes—was statesmanship of a high order". [29]

The roles of Patel and Mountbatten were highly complementary. Jointly, Patel and Mountbatten piloted the Indian ship out of stormy seas to safe anchorage, steering India on the path of her new journey as a free nation. Each helped the other in the transfer of power from Britain to India and Pakistan. Patel secured for India her liberation from British rule. Mountbatten, on his part, proved for Britain a liberal decoloniser in not allowing India to turn into another Singapore and suffer an ignominious rout. By converting withdrawal from India into an honourable transfer of power, he proved Britain a generous giver and secured India's membership of the Commonwealth. When Nehru could give Mountbatten no firm assurance on that, Patel told Nehru, "Leave that to me. That's my business."

6

CREATOR OF ONE INDIA

Unification and Consolidation of States

In recognition of Patel's most helpful role in the transfer of power peacefully and within the time-schedule, Mountbatten appointed him minister in charge of states. He strengthened his hands through denial of membership of the Commonwealth to the princes. This killed, for good, the princes' hope of forming a "Third Dominion"—Princestan. Dejected and forlorn, they felt like lost sheep. Patel's wisdom and farsightedness lay in his shepherding them into his pen and offering them kind and large-hearted guardianship.

Lord Curzon had written about the princes to Lord Hamilton in August 1900: "For what are they for the most part, but a set of unruly and ignorant and rather undisciplined schoolboys? What they want more than anything else is to be schooled by a firm, but not unkindly, hand; to be passed through just the sort of discipline that a boy goes through at a public school."[1] Patel proved the ideal schoolmaster. None could have been more firm and kind at the same time than he. Patel's paternalism was the antithesis of the autocracy of the British, or the iron-hand of Bismarck. It was humane, benevolent, and essentially Gandhian.

In appointing Patel minister of states, Mountbatten considered him "essentially a realist and very sensible", one who befriended the princes rather than turning them into enemies. Mountbatten even admitted: "I am glad to say that Nehru has not been put in charge of the new States Department, which would have wrecked everything."[2]

Patel's first address to the princes, immediately after his appointment on 5 July, proved historic: a masterpiece of diplomatic finesse, reflecting his transparent sincerity and political wisdom. He stirred up the princes' nobler sentiments by recalling their proud, glorious past, when ancestors of some of them had played highly patriotic roles in the service of their motherland.

Proudly telling the princes that he was "happy to count many as my personal friends", Patel reminded them: "Our mutual conflicts and internecine quarrels and jealousies have, in the past, been the cause of our downfall and our falling victims to foreign domination a number of times. We cannot afford to fall into those errors or traps again. We are on the threshold of independence . . . The safety and preservation of the States, as well as of India, demand unity and mutual cooperation between its different parts."

Patel urged the princes to consider, that in the exercise of paramountcy, "there has undoubtedly been more of subordination than cooperation", and that "now that British rule is ending, the demand has been made that the States should regain their independence. Insofar as Paramountcy embodied the submission of States to foreign will, I have every sympathy with this demand, but I do not think it can be their desire to utilise this freedom from domination in a manner which is injurious to the common interests of India, or which militates against the ultimate Paramountcy of popular interests and welfare, or which might result in the abandonment of that mutually useful relationship that has developed between British India and Indian States during the last century".

Further: "We are all knit together by bonds of blood and feeling, no less than of self-interest. None can segregate us into segments; no impassible barriers can be set up between us . . . I invite my friends, the Rulers of States, and their people to the councils of the Constituent Assembly in this spirit of friendliness and cooperation in a joint endeavour, inspired by common allegiance to our Motherland for the common good of us all." In a masterly peroration, Patel declared:

> We are at a momentous stage in the history of India. By common endeavour, we can raise the country to a new greatness, while lack of unity will expose us to fresh calamities. I hope the Indian States will bear in mind that the alternative to cooperation in the general interest is anarchy and chaos, which will overwhelm great and small in a common ruin if we are unable to get together in the minimum of common tasks. Let not the future generations curse us for having had the opportunity but failed to turn it to our mutual advantage. Instead, let it be our proud privilege to leave a legacy of mutually beneficial relationship which would raise this sacred land to its proper place amongst the nations of the world and turn it into an abode of peace and prosperity.[3]

Patel was the recipient of many felicitations. Voicing the princes' sentiments, Bikaner said:

May I take this opportunity of sending you my very best wishes in the onerous duties which have fallen upon you . . . The fact that one of the most respected and mature statesmen and leaders of your experience and judgment has been chosen is, I feel, a happy augury. It is most gratifying to recall that you have always shown a realistic and cordial attitude towards the States. The friendly hand that you have so spontaneously extended to the Princes and States . . . is, I need hardly assure you, greatly appreciated by us. We are confident that we may look forward to an association of full cooperation with you and a sympathetic understanding at your hands of the very important problems vitally affecting the States at the present transitional stage, thus enabling the States to take their due and honoured place in the future Union of India, in the making of which we are all proud to give our wholehearted support. I know that the interests of the Princes and States are safe in your hands.[4]

In these dealings, Mountbatten played the honest broker in three ways: First, by placing the states under Patel's charge. Second, by telling the princes at his last conference with them on 25 July: "In India the States Department is under the admirable guidance of Sardar Vallabhbhai Patel . . . You can imagine how relieved I was, and I am sure you will yourselves have been equally relieved, when Sardar Vallabhbhai Patel, on taking over the States Department, made, if I may say so, a most statesmanlike statement of what he considered were the essentials towards agreement between the States and the Dominion of India."[5] And third, by securing Britain's decision that the Indian states would not be given membership of the Commonwealth. This strengthened Patel's hands. He could

settle with the princes individually. A crestfallen Bhopal
resigned from chancellorship; the chamber itself was wound
up; and the dictatorial regime of British diehard residents
and agents came to an end. This was Patel's first great victory.
It threw open new vistas for achieving far greater victories—
one after another, in quick succession, in the next 18 months
or so.

Eastern States
Patel's first brush with the princes

15 August 1947 was epoch-making. People saw the dawn
of freedom after a lapse of over 150 years. Equally
significant was the simultaneous accession of the princely
states to the Indian Union. It was Patel's personal
achievement, for which he was acclaimed as the Bismarck of
India. On this day Patel began his historic march towards the
creation of One India through the unification and
consolidation of princely states as an integral part of India.

Patel's first brush with the princes as a group was in
December 1947, when he reached Cuttack for the proposed
merger of Orissa and Chattisgarh states, numbering 41. The
biggest had an area of 4000 square miles and a population of
10 lakhs; the smallest, 46 square miles and a population of
20,000. Patel was determined to iron out such absurdities—
uneconomic and politically unstable. A former official of the
Political Department described the position as "intractable".
Patel had been warned of the difficult and complex situation.
Keeping that in view, Patel addressed the ruling chiefs'
conference most diplomatically, telling them persuasively: "I
have come to Cuttack to tender friendly advice to the Rulers,

not as a representative of the old Paramountcy or of any foreign power, but as a member of a family trying to solve a family problem." He added that the safety of the rulers, as well as of their people, was in danger and that "the situation demanded immediate solution". Orissa as "a federal unit could only thrive and progress if it was a compact whole and was not torn asunder by multifarious jurisdictions and authorities which ruined its compactness".[1]

Patel encountered rough weather, but was quick to nip the problem in the bud. When a 21-year-old prince started his speech with the words "My people want..." Patel snubbed him with the remark: "They are not your people, Your Highness. They are my people. Leave them to me." Patel delivered a similar snub to a saffron-robed prince who started talking about princely duty with the remark: "Your Holiness [!] is not fit for Princely duties." To the Maharaja of Mayurbhanja, who said he had transferred power to his ministers, Patel administered a snub by leaving him "out of the discussion" with the remark: "I will deal with Your Highness later."[2]

Addressing a public meeting in Cuttack on 14 December, Patel warned the princes with blunt words: "I have met some Rulers today, and I have told them that they cannot carry on in the manner they did in the past. They must transfer their power to the people . . . Today the people of Orissa are agitated over the Rulers. There would be no Rulers if the people as such did not recognise them. They must move with the times. Let them cease to be like frogs in the well. These are the days of democracy, and the Rulers too must put their trust in the people."[3]

The same evening Patel boarded the train for New Delhi. He was unhappy, since his success was not complete. The rulers were more worried over possible repercussions. They sent him a message that he should delay his departure. Patel agreed to stay for an hour. At the end of the hour, they signed the agreement. Two days later, when the princes met Patel in New Delhi, they adopted dilatory tactics. They put forward legal arguments to justify their demand to be left as separate entities and not merged with Orissa. They hinted at taking legal opinion. Patel retorted in anger: "Your Highnesses may consult lawyers, but I make the law." Undeterred, the rulers then shifted their ground with the suggestion that they be allowed to form a Union of their own.

Patel firmly put down this with the remark: "I am prepared to leave each of Your Highnesses as a separate unit, but will not allow Your Highnesses to form a Union. Remember, if any of Your Highnesses wants my help to deal with your people, I will not come to your help."[4] That dampened their spirits, and reduced them to submission.

The governor of Orissa, Dr. K. N. Katju, called the merger of eastern states "a great epoch-making change ushered in in the Indian States by the vision and statesmanship of Sardar Patel. On 14 December 1947, in the Government House at Cuttack, he first set his hand to the wheel of this great revolution".[5] Patel himself looked upon this as "a dramatic beginning", however small, in distant Orissa, which "gradually swept over the whole of the subcontinent". Mountbatten compared Patel's achievement with that of Napoleon in his letter of 23 December 1947: "I personally have for long thought that the principle of mediatisation of States, which was adopted by Napoleon in the Central European principalities in the beginning of the last century, is the right answer for the small and uneconomic States."[6]

Patel had won his first unique victory—so quick and so non-violent was the surrender! His mind went back to the glorious past of the region, and, filled with justifiable pride,

Patel reminded his countrymen: "Centuries ago, it was the proud privilege of Kalinga to arouse awakening in a great monarch . . . Few had dreamt, and none had imagined, that it would be the same land that will usher in a revolutionary change which would achieve for India the same measure of unity, strength and security which India had once attained under that distinguished ruler—Ashoka."[7]

The merger of the eastern states, as Patel correctly claimed, "electrified the whole atmosphere... the Indian States could not long remain citadels of autocracy. The bastions gradually began to give way".[8]

Unification of over 560 princely states took around 18 months. It moved fast with the speed of a soft whirlwind, gently drawing the princes into its warm embrace, hurting none. Patel was watched with wonder and admiration for redrawing the map of India: first with accession, followed by merger of neighbouring states, and, finally, formation of large, viable unions on par with the provinces.

Greater Rajasthan
Maharana Pratap's dream fulfilled

The formation of the Union of Greater Rajasthan in March 1949 was "momentous and historic". Not only did it integrate a divided Rajasthani people, but it was no less strategic from the viewpoint of national security. Rajasthan lay on the Pakistan border and nursed bitter memories of how Jinnah had nearly succeeded in Jodhpur's accession to Pakistan. The occasion was momentous in Patel's unifying into a single, strong block, the states of Bikaner, Jaipur, Jodhpur, and Udaipur by diplomatically overcoming the princes' sensitivities as proud, high-strung, status-conscious, and independent rulers. And it was historic in its being, as Patel claimed, "the fulfillment of the desires and aspirations of Maharana Pratap"[1] who had put up a brave fight for Rajasthan's freedom against the mighty Mughals.

K. M. Panikkar, who had witnessed the whole drama of states integration unfolding itself from close quarters as diwan of Bikaner, paid a most handsome tribute to Patel when he said: "How all these grand and grandiose title-holders were swept under the carpet of history in the twinkling of an eye! Many are amazed that Vallabhbhai Patel was able to sweep them away in so short a time. The *Puranas* say that Parasurama fought twenty-one battles before he could exterminate the Kshatriya princes, but the new Parasurama needed no battle to make a clean sweep of kingship in India. One by one they queued up to sign their Instruments of Accession, collected their pensions and left with good grace."[2]

Travancore
First to revolt

C. P. Ramaswami Aiyar, the non-Travancorean diwan, was the first to have raised the banner of revolt. He declared as early as 9 May 1947 that if it was not possible to frame a constitution for the country as a whole without dividing it, Travancore would have "no alternative but to declare herself a free and independent State, and to take all necessary steps for it".[1]

CP was a stalwart who had occupied centre-stage in politics during the Home Rule movement. He was secretary to its founder, Mrs. Annie Besant, in 1916-17. The seriousness of his revolt lay in Travancore's strategic position: a premier

Hindu state at the southernmost tip of India with a sizeable seaboard and ancient maritime tradition. According to K. M. Munshi, CP's "intransigence gave a new ray of hope to those Princes who had been dreaming of evolving a 'Third Force' out of the States".[2] They were "dreaming of a States League and looking to the wizard of Travancore, who at least has a seaboard for the export of his coconuts and uranium".[3]

Being a super-egoist, CP had isolated himself from major Hindu states, including his neighbour, Cochin, whom Patel had won over earlier. The Maharaja of Cochin had said on 27 April: "The States are subservient autocracies and helpless under the subjugation of a Superior Power." His advice to his brother princes was to play a useful part in the country's future "by willingly assuming the role of constitutional Rulers".[4] But CP derived his inspiration from Bhopal and Conrad Corfield, secretary of the Political Department. In spite of such a discouraging situation, it was diplomatic of Patel to have written to CP a short but sweet letter on 31 May, breathing friendliness, and to time it with CP's visit to New Delhi to see Mountbatten prior to the announcement of the 3 June plan.

Patel wrote: "It is in my nature to be a friend of the friendless. You have become one by choice, and I shall be glad if you will come and have lunch with me tomorrow at 1 p.m." CP replied: "I appreciate your letter, and the kind thought underlying it. It, however, so happens that the 'friendless' person referred to has an engagement with a person for lunch today, and he cannot, therefore, avail himself of your generous invitation. Hoping for better luck later on, and renewing my thanks for the friendliness displayed by you."[5] The person CP was lunching with was Mountbatten.

At the States Negotiating Committee's meeting with Mountbatten on 3 June, CP "pleaded for a loosening or lapse of Paramountcy before the transfer of power, in order to strengthen the bargaining power of the States and enable them to negotiate on equal terms with the prospective Dominion Governments". CP had felt somewhat encouraged by Mountbatten's reply that he would consider "the premature lapse of Paramountcy in special cases if it could be proved that its continuance was a handicap to negotiation".[6]

On 10 June, CP boldly announced Travancore's decision to declare itself independent on 15 August. He asked the people of the state to stand "solidly by His Highness" on "a matter of life and death". He urged them "to cogitate and decide whether they wished to cherish their freedom and independence, or preferred to be submerged and absorbed as an adjunct to a Dominion in a divided India, or be a colony or dependency." Travancore, he said, was "destined to be the saviour of South India".[7] CP raised the slogan "Travancore for the Travancoreans", even when he himself was not one. He told them, "The future for the next hundred years, at least of Travancore, is in the making . . . The Maharaja does not act, has not acted, will not act as an autocrat. He conceives himself as the trustee and the spearpoint of Travancore's activities and of Travancore's will, and I am making this appeal on behalf of the Maharaja and with his special permission, and on behalf of the dynasty he represents."

He asserted: "There is no question that Travancore is ever going to enter the Constituent Assembly. There is no question that Travancore is now going to join the Indian Union. Travancore will be an independent State, and will function as an independent State from 15 August . . . from the 15 August no power on earth, short of an open war for which we are prepared, can prevent Travancore from declaring its independence . . . from 15 August Travancore will be an international entity."[8] CP even announced his intention to appoint a trade agent in Pakistan.

Jinnah was quick to lend his support to CP by stating, on 17 June, that "constitutionally and legally, the Indian States will be independent sovereign States on the termination of Paramountcy and they will be free to decide for themselves to adopt any course they like; it is open to them to join the Hindustan Constituent Assembly or the Pakistan Constituent Assembly, or decide to remain independent . . . Neither the British Government, nor the British Parliament, nor any other power or body, can compel them to do anything contrary to their free will and accord".[9]

R. K. Shanmukham Chetty, a former diwan of Cochin, voiced his grave concern over CP's stand on 22 June, stating:

> The most disquieting feature of the Indian political situation is not so much the fact of division or the potentialities of communal troubles, but the declaration of some of the Indian States that they intend to remain as independent sovereign States on the termination of the British Paramountcy . . . the creation of the separate State of Pakistan may not be a damaging blow to India's prestige or influence . . . The real danger to the unity and prestige of India is the attitude of certain Indian States. If a considerable number of Indian States choose to follow the example of Travancore and Hyderabad, it would mean the Balkanisation of India.

Shanmukham Chetty regretted: "It is one of the ironies of fate that the Diwan of Travancore, who has been the champion of pure Indian nationalism and a strong Central Government, should now make an alliance with Jinnah."[10]

Gandhi too expressed his concern: "If the Travancore Diwan were allowed to have his way and his example were followed by others, India would be split up into several States—a disaster too dreadful to contemplate. Those many

States would need an Emperor, and the Emperor who was leaving might even return with redoubled force."[11]

Patel was more categorical in his statement: "So long as the Congress continued to have a foothold in Travancore, there is no question of independence and sovereignty."[12]

CP indulged in sabre-rattling again on 23 June and continued doing so almost throughout July. K. P. S. Menon, India's foreign secretary, thought that CP had declared Travancore independent "in a moment of megalomania", especially when "he expressed his intention to establish diplomatic relations between Travancore and Pakistan, and even selected a retired police officer for the post of ambassador of Travancore in Karachi".[13]

On 10 July, Pattom A. Thanu Pillai, president of the Travancore State Congress, cabled Patel: "Terrorist organisations composed of goondas formed throughout State under control of police and other Government agencies to wreck public meetings and assault public men . . . Life of public men in danger. Members of [these] organisations parade public streets armed with lathis, knives and other weapons . . . Life and property insecure . . . Conditions rapidly degenerating into widespread violence . . . Travancore subjected to unbridled dictatorship by an irresponsible non-Travancorean Diwan."[14]

With CP's "rogue elephant politics" getting worse, Keralite K. M. Panikkar felt emotionally stirred and decided to jump into the fray to fight CP face to face. Patel stopped him with the advice that there was no need for him "to do any such thing and he would solve the Travancore problem himself".[15] Patel was "furious and determined, if necessary, to deal severely with Travancore". He directly telephoned the Maharaja and asked him in a voice that was soft, firm but blunt, "Who's standing in your way?" The Maharaja felt rattled. He communicated to Mountbatten his decision to accede to India. Simultaneously, on 25 July, there was an attempt on CP's life by the Communists, whose party workers had been brutally treated in their struggle in Punnapara and Vayalas. This rattled CP. Realising his time was up, he resigned from diwanship. A mollified CP wrote to Patel on 11 November from his retirement at Ootacamund: "May I take this opportunity to convey to you my sincere felicitations over the forthright and unequivocal policy adopted and maintained by you during the present time of crises and momentous decisions. I have differed from you on several occasions, but cannot refrain from paying my tribute to the consummate talents of leadership manifested by you and Pandit Jawaharlal Nehru at this juncture." With his characteristic magnanimity, Patel replied: "We both know how much we have differed in the past. But, in spite of those differences, I have always regretted that we could not make use of your undoubted talents in a wider sphere of activities."[16]

CP's praise for Patel increased as time passed. He wrote to Purushottam Tricumdas on 27 March 1948: "Generally speaking, all the great Kshatriya rulers—descendants of the Sun and Moon—behave like mendicants and sycophants, and have no more spirit than a parcel of frightened rabbits or sheep. They deserve [their] fate, and I congratulate Patel on the brilliant results of his downright policy".[17]

The United State of Travancore and Cochin was inaugurated on 1 July 1949 in Trivandrum. Patel could not attend the function owing to ill-health. But his message described the union as "the culminating point of the policy of consolidation of States which was inaugurated not more than eighteen months ago; and which, with the cooperation and assistance of the Rulers and the support and consent of the people of the States, has been my proud privilege to

implement". He further said, "It has also been my unique
pleasure to find among the Princes and the people a willingness
to make sacrifices in the cause of the country."[18]

Mountbatten said of Patel's success, "The adherence of
Travancore, after all CP's declaration of independence, has
had a profound effect on all the other States and is sure to
shake the Nizam."[19]

Jodhpur
Jinnah's failure to entice the Maharaja

In Jodhpur's accession to India, rather than allowing it to
fall into the lap of Pakistan, lay a unique victory for Patel.
At the same time it was an ignominious defeat for Jinnah: an
end to his diabolical plans to weaken India in Rajasthan on
the Indo-Pak border. In H. V. Hodson's view: "The case of
Jodhpur illustrates the lengths to which Jinnah was prepared
to go in order to wean States from India."[1] After winning his
Pakistan, Jinnah had cast his eyes on some of the strategic
Indian states in order to secure their association, if not
accession, with Pakistan.

Events in Jodhpur took a dramatic turn with the sudden
demise of Maharaja Umed Singh in June 1947 and the
succession to the throne of his son, Hanwant Singh, who
was young, rash, headstrong, and given to irresponsible
emotional outbursts. The father had cast his lot with India,
and was among the first few princes whose representatives
took their seats in the Constituent Assembly on 28 April 1947.
The son was to prove different.

On the occasion of the *rajtilak* (crowning ceremony) on
21 June, the new Maharaja announced that Jodhpur would
continue to be associated with the Constituent Assembly of

India, and would work wholeheartedly for the formation of a Union of India. But the presence of the Nawab of Bhopal in Jodhpur forebode ill. As an emissary of Jinnah, he was to arrange a few meetings for him with the young Maharaja in New Delhi—at Jinnah's residence, at which Bhopal, along with his legal adviser, Mohammed Zafrullah, was to be present to assist Jinnah in weaning the Maharaja from India.

Jinnah planned to build a Karachi-Jodhpur-Bhopal axis, which, according to Patel, would be "a dagger thrust into the very heart of India". This way Jinnah wanted to avenge the truncated Pakistan forced on him by Patel—a Pakistan minus East Punjab, West Bengal, and Assam, all Hindu majority areas. All of these had been assured to him both under the Cabinet Mission plan and Attlee's policy statement on transfer of power to India and Pakistan. But to Jinnah's utter frustration, Patel upset his applecart.

C. S. Venkatachar, prime minister of Jodhpur, came to know of Bhopal's secret mission in Jodhpur from whispers floating around the palace. He sent H. V. R. Iengar, the home secretary to the government of India, a hand-written note giving news of the "utmost gravity for the very stability of India. The Ruler has been approached by Jinnah and has been persuaded to stay out of the Indian Dominion".[2] Iengar took the note to Patel and apprised him of the "gravity of the situation." Had Jinnah succeeded, this would have led to Bhopal, Indore, and a few other Central Indian states forming an independent federation under Bhopal's leadership with ultimate accession to Pakistan. Bhopal expected Baroda to join his group on Jinnah's promise that he would be allowed to exercise control over his port of Bedi Bandar on the Saurashtra coast. Jinnah was hopeful of roping in the Jamsaheb of Nawanagar as well.

Jodhpur was hesitant to see Jinnah alone. He took with him the Maharajkumar of Jaisalmer, besides his ADC, Col.

Thakur Kesari Singh. Jinnah told Jodhpur: "As long as the Central Government in India is weak, we are both strong . . . Your Highness, I sign on the dotted line, and you fill in the conditions."[3] Jinnah tempted the Maharaja with five good offers: a sea-outlet through the use of Karachi as a free port; free import of arms; continuance of manufacture of firearms in his state; jurisdiction over the Jodhpur-Hyderabad (Sind) railway; and a large supply of grain for famine relief. This was Jinnah's "basket of apples", which Bhopal had already tempted Jodhpur with. The Maharaja seemed to be happy with the offer. Not to be alone in accepting it, he invited the Maharana of Udaipur to join the Bhopal plan. Udaipur's reply was: "My choice was made by my ancestors. If they had faltered, they would have left us a kingdom as large as Hyderabad. They did not. Neither shall I. I am with India."[4] Bikaner also refused Jodhpur's offer to join Jinnah.

Anxious not to let him slip out of his net, Jinnah "signed a blank sheet of paper and gave it to Maharaja Hanwant Singh along with his own fountain pen, saying, 'You can fill in all your conditions' ". The Maharaja asked Jaisalmer whether he too would sign. Jaisalmer laid down the condition that if there was any trouble between the Hindus and the Muslims, he would not side with the Muslims against the Hindus. This was "a bombshell that took Maharaja Hanwant Singh completely by surprise".[5] Zafrullah tried to make light of the whole affair and pressed Jodhpur to sign the instrument. The Maharaja could not make up his mind. Taking advantage of his vacillation, his ADC, Col. Thakur Kesari Singh, whispered into his ear: "Your Highness, before you sign, you must ask your mother." The Maharaja greatly respected his mother. She was "a woman of great character, power and influence".[6] The Maharaja suggested to Jinnah that he would go back to Jodhpur and return the next day.

Since Britain had not yet transferred power to India, Patel exercised no direct authority to deal with the princes officially. His approach to Bhopal could only be through Mountbatten as the Crown representative. Mountbatten took up the matter with Bhopal, telling him that Patel had received information that "His Highness had made contact with the young Maharaja of Jodhpur and induced him to come with him to Jinnah. He also added that at this meeting Jinnah had offered extremely favourable terms on condition that he did not sign the Instrument of Accession, and that he had even gone so far as to turn round and say to the Maharaja of Jodhpur: 'Here's my fountain pen. Write your terms and I will sign it'." Bhopal gave an evasive version of the story. But Mountbatten warned Bhopal: "I pointed out to His Highness that no amount of friendship would enable me to protect either himself or his State or the new Ruler of the State, if the future Government of India thought that he was acting in a manner hostile to that Government by trying to induce an all-Hindu State to join Pakistan."[7]

The Maharaja returned to New Delhi three days later for his final meeting with Jinnah. He did not appear to be his earlier self—apparently subdued by his mother's talk, as also by what his guru, a swami, had reportedly told him: "How could a Hindu State like Jodhpur agree to accede to Pakistan which will be a Muslim State?" Yet, V. P. Menon feared that unless the Maharaja was handled "quickly, the chances were that he might accede to Pakistan".[8] Mountbatten was persuaded to handle the Maharaja.

Menon drove the Maharaja to the viceroy's house. Mountbatten explained to the Maharaja that from a purely legal standpoint, there could be no objection to Jodhpur's acceding to Pakistan, but he should not overlook the fact that his was a predominantly Hindu state: if acceded to

Pakistan, "his action would surely be in conflict with the principle underlying the partition of India on the basis of Muslim and non-Muslim majority areas; and serious communal trouble inside the State would be the inevitable consequence of such affiliation".[9]

The Maharaja remained non-committal. He tried to put off Mountbatten by asking for "impossible concessions". Mountbatten admitted his failure: "I could not get the Maharaja to agree then and there, although I had obviously shaken him, and I then conceived the idea of getting V. P. Menon to take him to see Sardar Patel before returning to Jodhpur."[10] At their meeting, Patel was "extremely polite, exceedingly courteous, but firm in tone". The conversation between the two was very brief. But the awe-inspiring looks of Patel, and his sternness, made the Maharaja shaky. He faltered in tone. Patel told him, "Your Highness is free to stay out, if you like. But if there is trouble in your State as a result of your decision, you will not get the slightest support from the Government of India."[11]

According to Iengar, "there was a clear warning that there *would* be trouble in the State", and Patel "left the Ruler in no doubt that the move initiated by Jinnah was dangerous not only to India, but to the Ruler himself".[12] Patel closed the conversation with a mild admonition by saying that the Maharaja's father, who was his friend, had left him to his care as a ward; and if he did not behave as he should, Patel would have to act as a guardian to discipline him. The Maharaja felt rattled. He got up from his seat and told Patel in a mollified voice, "Well, Sir, I have decided to go back to Lord Mountbatten and sign the Instrument of Accession right now."[13]

In the settlement of the Jodhpur affair, a great calamity was averted. Patel's greatest gain was in winning over the abiding loyalty of the Maharaja. He gave Patel the reverence he would have shown to his late father. His devotion led him to serve Patel as an "errand boy" who happily flew in his aircraft from prince to prince and from state to state carrying Patel's messages. The Maharaja proved to be the most lovable of the princes, whose courage and patriotism flowered under Patel's paternal affection.

Kathiawar
Jinnah suffers a rebuff

Simultaneously with developments in Jodhpur, Jinnah had cast his eyes on Kathiawar, whose strategic importance lay in its seaboard overlooking the Arabian Sea. Further, the position of the Jamsaheb of Nawanagar in Kathiawar was more important than that of the Maharaja of Jodhpur in Rajasthan. He enjoyed great respect and influence among the princes of Kathiawar. On him largely depended the unification of the Kathiawar states.

A situation similar to that in Jodhpur was developing in Jamnagar around May-June 1947. On 1 July, B. L. Mitter, diwan of Baroda, wrote to Nehru: "The Jamsaheb is reported to be negotiating with Jinnah regarding his port of Bedi Bandar. If this port and Veraval, the Junagadh port, come into the orbit of Karachi, Bombay will be seriously affected."[1] Much earlier, on 22 November 1946, Mitter had informed Patel: "The Princes Chamber is playing Jinnah's game . . . The Jamsaheb has bought his immunity by selling his soul to the Political Department. His confederation plan is sponsored by the department."[2] Mitter wrote to Patel on 26 March 1947 that the chief of Wadia (in Kathiawar) had told him, "The Jamsaheb was strengthening his armed forces . . . was aspiring to be the overlord of Kathiawar."[3]

A gathering of Kathiawar rulers, with the Jamsaheb as leader, had met in a secret conference at Mount Abu under the presidentship of the resident. The view propagated was that "if Travancore can declare its independence, the Kathiawar States, being maritime States, can do likewise . . . they can rule without any interference from Delhi and develop their ports and they need not depend upon India for anything".

The conference decided to form a Union of Kathiawar, comprising the seven states of Jamnagar, Bhavnagar, Gondal, Porbandar, Morvi, Dhrangadhra, and Junagadh. In the event of its accession to Pakistan, Junagadh "would enter into an offensive and defensive treaty" with the union. Mitter also told Patel, "The Resident is helping and the Jamsaheb has promised to put up a crore of rupees in furtherance of the scheme . . . The Resident and the Political Agent are out to Balkanise India." There was something sinister in granting Junagadh the right to "either declare separate independence or to join Pakistan".[4] The move unmistakably implied severance of links with India.

Patel watched the developments with deep concern but with equanimity, waiting for an opportunity to act. Such an opportunity arrived on 11 May. The Jamsaheb was passing through Delhi on his way to Central India to meet some of the princes there. Patel lost no time. He acted boldly and decisively, even when he then exercised no authority, as transfer of power was two months away. He lent his car to Col. Himatsinhji, the Jamsaheb's brother, and sent him to the airport to bring the Jamsaheb to his residence. Accompanied by Her Highness, the Jamsaheb lunched with Patel. The meeting proved momentous. It changed the course of events. Patel's influence on the Jamsaheb worked and he was won over. A happy Mitter wrote to Patel on 14 May: "You have converted the Jamsaheb. Now you will have to fashion the Kathiawar and Gujarat units for the Union."[5]

Patel was cautious in expressing his opinion to a co-worker from Kathiawar: "The Jamsaheb had come here yesterday [11 May] . . . He is still hopeful of his confederation scheme succeeding, and he has gone to Kotah for that purpose . . . From his talk I understood that all the Kathiawar States, except for Junagadh and Bhavnagar, have joined the [proposed] confederation. I have, of course, expressed no opinion about the merits of this scheme."[6] Patel had, however, made the Jamsaheb appreciate the dangers India faced, from Pakistan all along the border from Rajasthan to Kathiawar. Events in Jodhpur and Junagadh seemed to have convinced the Jamsaheb of Patel's logic in checkmating Jinnah's designs. A hopeful indicator of the Jamsaheb's mind, as also of the Maharaja of Dhrangadhra, was what they told V. P. Menon: "With Shah Nawaz [Bhutto] in the saddle, there was a possibility of Junagadh going over to Pakistan."[7]

Since Gandhi came from Porbandar, he was "intensely interested" in the unification of the Kathiawar states. Its achievement was the fulfillment of Gandhi's dream. For Patel, there was an additional consideration: it would contribute in a big way to the political consolidation of the country. The unification was highly necessary like the unification of the Rajput states. It was complex too, as it involved 222 states of great diversity and covering an area of over 22,000 square miles. As many as 46 states had an area of 2 or less than 2 square miles; the smallest had an area of 0.29 square miles, a population of 206 souls and an income of Rs. 500 a year. Many of the states had scattered pockets of territory outside their own boundaries. Such a chaotic state of affairs rendered law and order poor and even unmanageable, hampered trade, and encouraged extensive smuggling. In fact, "all the worst effects of political fragmentation were to be seen in Kathiawar".

Patel inaugurated the United State of Kathiawar on 15 February 1948. Paying tributes to the Jamsaheb and other rulers, he said, "But for their vision, wisdom and patriotism, the happy result you are seeing today would not have fructified. It was Mahatma Gandhi's dream that Kathiawar should be united, and it gladdens my heart that the dream of such unification has come true."[8] In his reply, the Jamsaheb significantly observed: "It is not as if we were tired monarchs who were fanned to rest. It is not as if we have been bullied into submission. We have by our own free volition pooled our sovereignties and covenanted to create this new State so that the United State of Kathiawar and the unity of India may be more fully achieved."

Nehru described the event as "a great step forward . . . one of the most notable in contemporary Indian history". He called it "a far-sighted act of statesmanship".[9] Nehru was more specific when he wrote to the provincial chief ministers on 20 February:

> Six months ago, it would have been considered an idle dream to think of an administrative merger of the hundreds of Kathiawar States, let alone such a merger accompanied by full responsible government. The peninsula was ridden by factions and jealousies; and it was a crazy patchwork of States of varying degrees of sovereignty with only one thing common, namely, autocratic rule. On 15 February, the whole of the peninsula became one unit under one responsible Government. This is an achievement for which Sardar Patel has deservedly won high tribute.[10]

Mountbatten wrote to Patel: "It appears that you have again scored a brilliant success in your handling of the Kathiawar States problem."[11]

Bhopal
Jinnah's emissary surrenders to Patel

The Nawab of Bhopal, Hamidullah Khan, was a Muslim ruler whom the British had deliberately invested with greater influence than his position deserved. His territory was small, and his subjects were predominantly Hindus. He proved the most troublesome prince. As Jinnah's emissary in India, he conspired to secure accession or association of Indian princes to Pakistan. He caused more headaches to Patel than Corfield, secretary of the Political Department. The latter worked silently from behind the scenes, while Bhopal openly played his game, exploiting his position as chancellor of the Chamber of Princes.

Patel complained to Gandhi on 11 August: "For the last fifteen days I have been occupied with the Princes. It is so taxing. There seems to be no end to the Nawab of Bhopal's intrigues. He is working day and night to cause a split among the Princes and to keep them out of the Indian Union."[1] Bhopal was sly and aggressive, surreptitiously but swiftly moving from one prince to another, tempting them to join hands with him in torpedoing Patel's dream of India's unification.

Bhopal had two objectives to achieve: first, to establish the princes as a potential "Third Force" and thus build a third dominion; and, two, to achieve the task Jinnah had entrusted him with: to persuade the Hamlets among the princes to form independent confederations outside the Indian Union. As Jinnah's emissary and one of his "closest advisers", Bhopal was "not averse to playing an important role in the higher politics of Pakistan"[2]—and to succeed Jinnah after his death. The crafty shepherd in Bhopal was confident of satisfying both Corfield and Jinnah by driving the fear-stricken, bewildered lambs among the princes into the pens each was building to rope them in.

Bhopal's importance was due to his being a dynamic, articulate, and crafty ruler, who had forged himself to the forefront of the princely order as a Muslim ruler who could be a most trusted ally of the British. Ascending to the throne in May 1926, he had been in prominence since the Round Table Conference in 1931. With British support, he became chancellor of the Chamber of Princes, first from 1931 to 1932, and again from 1943 till his resignation under force of circumstances in 1947.

K. M. Panikkar, who was secretary to the chamber during 1931-32, writes: "One year's stay in Bhopal had taught me that Hamidullah was a Muslim partisan and an enemy of the Hindus. I was certain that he manoeuvred to gain the Chancellorship at this time [1943] to strengthen the voice of the Muslims and to weaken the Hindu claims with the instrumentality of the Hindu Princes"[3], who, looking upon the political department as "their patron saint, became tools of Bhopal".[4] In 1947, Panikkar, as prime minister of Bikaner, tilted scales against Bhopal by his Maharaja's decision to participate in the Indian Constituent Assembly.

In a circular letter of 1 April 1947, the Maharaja of Bikaner told his brother princes, "The only safe policy for the States is to work fully with the stabilising elements in British India to create a Centre . . . which would safeguard both the States and British India in the vacuum that would be created by the withdrawal of the British Government." His appeal to them was: "Let the Princes of India rise to the occasion to be hailed as co-architects of the structure of India's independence and greatness."

In the proceedings of the States Negotiating Committee on the issue of princes joining the Constituent Assembly,

Bhopal's was an anti-Indian role: browbeating weak, vacillating princes by prophesising "bloodshed and chaos" in the states if a time-limit on their joining the Constituent Assembly were imposed. He tried to influence them by word of mouth, besides pressing into service his chancellor's Pakistani-dominated secretariat, to make them adopt a policy of "wait and see".

Patel outmanoeuvred Bhopal, and made him suffer a humiliating defeat at the hands of the Maharajas of Bikaner and Patiala. Equally so through a vocal opposition built up within and outside the chamber by the states prime ministers—diwans Mirza Ismail of Mysore, V. T. Krishnamachari of Udaipur, Panikkar of Bikaner, and B. L. Mitter of Baroda. This resulted in the weakening of Bhopal's position. Yet, because of Corfield's support, and inspiration from Jinnah, Bhopal continued, undeterred, to persuade the princes sitting on the fence to keep off the Bikaner-Patiala group.

Panikkar and some other diwans believed that Bhopal was "acting as an agent of Pakistan"; and that "Bhopal came forward as the standard-bearer for Hyderabad", having entered into "a compact with the Nizam whereby the former [Bhopal] agreed to use the Chamber to rally Hindu Princes to undermine Hindu power in India and the Government of Hyderabad was to finance this devious scheme".[5]

Bhopal believed, like Jinnah, that "a government in India, weakened by the hostility of the Hindu Princes to the Congress, would not dare to offend Muslim public opinion and impose its will on the Nizam". He was of the firm opinion that Hyderabad, as large as England and having a population of 17 million and revenue of Rs. 20 crore, would survive; and his "tiny island in a Hindu ocean" could do so "in association with Hyderabad".[6]

The 3 June plan delivered a shattering blow to Bhopal's dreams. With its announcement he resigned from the chancellorship of the Chamber of Princes, but clung to the hope that "Bhopal State would, as soon as Paramountcy is withdrawn, be assuming an independent status".[7] He went so far as to say that Bhopal would negotiate directly with the successor governments of India and Pakistan. Bhopal felt so embittered by the 3 June plan that he did not attend the meeting of the rulers and states representatives called by Mountbatten on 25 July in his capacity as the Crown representative. Bhopal dismissed it with the contemptuous remark that the rulers had been "invited like the Oysters to attend the tea-party with the Walrus and the Carpenter". Mountbatten regretted his attitude with the remark: "I have spent more time on Bhopal's case than on all the other States put together . . . it would be a tragedy if he were to wreck the State by failing to come in now."[8]

As 15 August drew nearer, Bhopal realised that his game was up. He also realised that in losing the battle to Patel, and not to Mountbatten, he might lose all in the end. He found himself in "an anomalous and difficult position". He approached Mountbatten to find out whether he could sign a standstill agreement without acceding to India. He perhaps wanted to see how strong Patel would be after the transfer of power. He wanted to formulate his strategy accordingly. He was told this was not possible. Thereupon, he sent his constitutional adviser, Zafrullah, to V. P. Menon to seek clarification of the terms of accession. Menon told him that Bhopal could not be an exception. Bhopal met Mountbatten on 11 August, four days prior to the transfer of power, and sought his help to save face. Could his accession be announced ten days after the transfer of power, i.e. by 25 August? Patel was generous to grant Bhopal's request.

Since accession had to precede, not follow, transference of power, Bhopal's was an unconstitutional request. No other prince had asked for it. Patel was, however, gracious to a pro-Pakistani Muslim ruler in granting him grace-time to find out his chances of succeeding Jinnah in Pakistan. Bhopal's claim lay in his having served Jinnah as a faithful emissary in his efforts to wean strategically located Indian states to his side. In many cases he had nearly succeeded but for Patel playing a Chanakya. As a devout Muslim, Bhopal aspired, according to Wavell, "to fight to the death for the Muslim cause".[9] This, he thought, he could do best from Pakistan as head of state.

According to Hodson, "three days before the period of grace expired", Bhopal, after a long talk with Patel, saw Mountbatten and explained the reasons for his hesitation: "he had ambitions to play a big role in the Muslim world in the future, and he feared that if he acceded, Jinnah would denounce him as a traitor to the Muslim cause".[10] Bhopal had flown to Karachi to meet Jinnah, who, though "sufficiently magnanimous" towards the Nawab, must have by then seen opposition from Liaquat Ali and other Muslim leaders. It was thereafter, on his return from Pakistan, that the state of Bhopal acceded to India.

After his accession on 25 August, Bhopal wrote to Patel on the twenty-sixth:

By the time you receive this letter, you will have heard the news that I have decided to join the Union of India . . . I do not disguise the fact that while the struggle was on, I used every means in my power to preserve the independence and neutrality of my State. Now that I have conceded defeat, I hope that you will find that I can be as staunch a friend as I have been an inveterate opponent . . . I now wish to tell you that so long as you maintain your present firm stand against the disruptive forces in the country and continue to be a friend of the States as you have shown you are, you will find in me a loyal and faithful ally.

Patel was generous in his reply:

Quite candidly, I do not look upon the accession of your State to the Indian Dominion as either a victory for us or a defeat for you. It is only right and propriety which have triumphed in the end, and in that triumph, you and I have played our respective roles. You deserve full credit for having recognised the soundness of the position and for the courage, the honesty and the boldness of having given up your earlier stand, which, according to us, was entirely antagonistic to the interests as much of India as of your own State.[11]

With this, the anti-Indian front of the princes, that Bhopal had built, collapsed. There followed total confusion among the rulers of his group. They were completely "routed" and were so crestfallen that they sought interviews with Patel, looking for some saving-grace in his forgiveness. One such ruler was the Maharaja of Indore, Bhopal's closest ally. Erratic and bad-mannered, he did not, like Bhopal, attend the rulers' meeting Mountbatten had called on 25 July. On the thirtieth, Mountbatten sent six of his fellow Maratha princes, headed by Baroda, to Indore with "a personal letter from the Viceroy urging the Ruler of Indore to come to Delhi".[12] The Maharaja insulted his brother princes by declining to see them. Baroda told Menon that "all of them were waiting in the Maharaja's drawing-room when he came in and went past them on his way upstairs as though they did not exist".[13] With Bhopal's having fallen from his earlier "high" position, Indore realised his position too was no longer safe. Along with Bhopal, he saw Mountbatten on 4 August, and was given "a dressing-down of painful severity".[14] Thereafter, Indore called upon Patel. He had a similar dressing down—and an abject surrender.

Bhopal's surrender was a great victory for Patel. It brought to an end the Political Department's plans to balkanise the country through the creation of a "Third Dominion". Patel also gave burial to the Churchillian proposal to create Princestan: a confederation of over 560 princely states.

Junagadh
Nawab's accession to Pakistan

In Junagadh's accession to Pakistan on 15 August, Patel saw "the first danger sign for splitting India again". He stated: "After Partition, we had a huge problem. Those who partitioned the country had mental reservations. They thought that this Partition was not the last word, and they started the game immediately thereafter. Among Kathiawar States, they went to Junagadh and got its accession to Pakistan . . . We woke up in time and those who tried to play that game saw that we were not sleeping."[1]

In Junagadh, Patel was presented with a fait accompli. Mountbatten recognised Junagadh as "Pakistan territory" in his report to the king: "My chief concern as Governor-General was to prevent the Government of India from committing itself on the Junagadh issue to an act of war against what was now Pakistan territory . . . my own physical presence as Governor-General of India was the best insurance against an

actual outbreak of war with Pakistan."[2] Mountbatten
confessed to Nehru: "Pakistan is in no position even to
declare war, since I happen to know that their military
commanders have put it to them in writing that a declaration
of war with India can only end in the inevitable and ultimate
defeat of Pakistan."[3]

Mountbatten's role in Junagadh was against India's interest.
He had no control over Junagadh's actions, nor over
Pakistan's. He, nevertheless, assumed that he could use his
position as governor-general in averting a war with Pakistan
by binding India to three conditions: reference of Junagadh
to the UNO; preventing Indian troops from entering Junagadh
territory; and an offer of holding a plebiscite in Junagadh.
Reluctantly, Patel agreed to a plebiscite, even when Jinnah
had not asked for it. He rejected the first two. The first would
have given Pakistan locus standi in Junagadh, and thereby
internationalised the issue, as it happened later in the case
of Kashmir.

Mountbatten failed to consider that in Junagadh's accession
to Pakistan would lie "Jinnah's tactical shrewdness. He must
have seen—or, if he did not, it certainly turned out—that
the accession of Junagadh to Pakistan placed India in an acute
dilemma from which any escape could be turned to the
advantage of Pakistan".[4] There was also the danger of
Pakistan securing a foothold in Junagadh by landing troops
through its port of Veraval. Once on Junagadh soil, India
could not have dislodged Pakistan from there. Mountbatten
faced opposition, not from Nehru, but from Patel, with
unfailing determination.

Patel refused to oblige Mountbatten in two respects. He
objected to "forcible dragging of our 80 percent of Hindu
population of Junagadh into Pakistan by accession in defiance
of all democratic principles".[5] He was also concerned about
accession setting up a dangerous precedent. Junagadh's

accession, according to Campbell-Johnson, was "a direct challenge to the essential validity of the whole accession policy, with disastrous effects both upon the Kathiawar States and upon the Hyderabad negotiations".[6]

What supported India's claim was that Junagadh, unlike Jodhpur, had no contiguity with Pakistan by land, though it could establish a direct link with Karachi through its port of Veraval—just 300 miles away. Landlocked Junagadh was separated from Pakistan by the territories of Kutch, Baroda, Nawanagar, Porbandar, and Gondal. Junagadh's map, according to H. V. Hodson, had "absurd complexity . . . fragments of other States were embedded in Junagadh, and fragments of Junagadh were embedded in other States, while an arm of Junagadh separated one substantial outlying portion of the Maratha State of Baroda from another and from the sea".[7]

Patel called Junagadh's accession to Pakistan an act of perfidy. As early as 11 April 1947, the Muslim ruler had camouflaged his real intentions by stating that "what Junagadh pre-eminently stands for is the solidarity of Kathiawar, and would welcome the formation of a self-contained group of Kathiawar States".[8] He deliberately omitted any reference to Pakistan. His diwan, Abdul Kadir Mohammed Hussain, categorically repudiated, on 22 April, allegations that Junagadh was thinking of joining Pakistan. He left for Europe in May for medical treatment, handing over charge to Shah Nawaz Bhutto, whose son, Zulfikar Ali Bhutto, later became prime minister of Pakistan.

Nabi Baksh, Junagadh's representative at the rulers' conference on 25 July, told Mountbatten that his intention was to advise the Nawab to accede to India. He had also given a similar impression to Patel when he called upon him, as also to the Jamsaheb of Nawanagar, his neighbour. Junagadh had, on the other hand, secretly recruited to the state forces, Baluchis and Hurs from Pakistan, and a decision had been taken that the local Bahauddin College was to be affiliated to the Sind University in Karachi.

According to H. V. Hodson, handling of Junagadh was "full of traps, and there was good reason to suspect that some of those traps had been deliberately laid by Pakistan". Hodson believes that Bhutto obeyed Jinnah's advice, given on 16 July, "to keep out under all circumstances until 15 August".[9] With the termination of paramountcy, Bhutto would have been entitled to take an independent decision. Meanwhile, Jinnah assured Bhutto that he would not allow Junagadh to starve as "Veraval is not far from Karachi". This was in response to Bhutto's fears that "Junagadh stands all alone surrounded by Hindu Rulers' territories and British Indian Congress provinces".

Bhutto's hopes lay in his belief: "We are, of course, connected by sea with Pakistan. If geographical position by land was fairly considered, Kutch, Jamnagar and other territories adjoining Junagadh geographically should be considered connected with Pakistan, as they once in the past actually formed part of Sind. Though the Muslim population of Junagadh is nearly 20% and non-Muslims form 80%, seven lakh Muslims of Kathiawar survived because of Junagadh. I consider that no sacrifice is too great to preserve the prestige, honour and rule of His Highness and to protect Islam and the Muslims of Kathiawar."[10]

The Jinnah-Bhutto conspiracy had dangerous implications. If Junagadh were allowed to accede to Pakistan, V. P. Menon thought that "its detachment would turn it into a hothouse plant with no powers of survival". What worried Menon most was "the immediate potentialities for turmoil when stability was the crying need of the hour. The Nawab's action would have undesirable effects on law and order in Kathiawar as a whole. It would extend the communal trouble to areas where at present there was peace. There was also the fear that it would encourage the intractable elements in Hyderabad".[11]

Junagadh's accession to Pakistan had been kept a closely guarded secret. Even Mountbatten as the Crown representative was kept in the dark by the Political Department, the residents and agents keeping mum. The government of India, which had no inkling about it, found out on 17 August from newspaper reports. On enquiry, Junagadh simply confirmed the news. Pakistan having not yet formally accepted the accession, India moved into the matter constitutionally by inviting the attention of the Pakistan high commissioner to India to the invalidity of accession on grounds of Junagadh's geographical contiguity to India, the composition of its population, and the need for consulting the views of the people. Pakistan remained discreetly silent. Even a reminder sent on 6 September evoked no response.

Jinnah expected that Mountbatten would not let India take precipitate action, while Nehru would show hesitancy in taking a firm decision, pursuing his usual policy of soft peddling. On Nehru's suggestion, a telegram addressed to the Pakistan prime minister, Liaquat Ali, indicated India's willingness to abide by the people's verdict. Lest India's message was ignored like the earlier ones, the telegram was personally carried by Ismay to Karachi. He also carried Mountbatten's message to Jinnah, that if Pakistan accepted Junagadh's accession, it would lead to a dispute between the two dominions, and that if Jinnah wanted any state to accede to Pakistan, he could not have chosen a worse state. Pakistan merely telegraphed on 13 September confirming acceptance of Junagadh's accession.

The Junagadh crisis, according to Campbell-Johnson, erupted as if from "a wholly unexpected quarter", and "in the welter of great events immediately before and after the transfer of power, Junagadh was simply overlooked".[12] Patel rejected Nehru's suggestion that "it would be desirable for us to send a message to the British Government about the Junagadh affair" with the polite comment: "I am not quite sure whether we need say anything to the British Government at this stage."[13]

Junagadh's decision sent a wave of indignation and protest among the people and rulers of Kathiawar—Nawanagar, Bhavnagar, Morvi, Gondal, Porbandar, and Wankaner—all of whom strongly condemned it. The Junagadh affair made the rulers turn to Patel to handle the situation. The Maharaja of Dhrangadhra asked the Nawab of Junagadh, in a personal letter, to reconsider the decision as it was opposed to geographical compulsions and was against the wishes of the people, adding that failure to reverse it would cause disruption of Kathiawar.

The Nawab's reply was: "The Indian Independence Act did not, and does not, require a Ruler to consult his people before deciding on accession. I think we are making an unnecessary fetish of the argument of geographical contiguity. Even then, this is sufficiently provided by Junagadh's sea coast with several ports which can keep connection with Pakistan."[14]

The Jamsaheb rushed to New Delhi to tell Patel that the rulers and people of Kathiawar were greatly agitated over Pakistan's attempt to encroach on Indian territory, that it would be difficult to restrain the people of Kathiawar from retaliating, and that, if the government of India did not take "immediate and effective steps", the Kathiawar states would "lose faith in the will and ability of the Indian Dominion to carry out all the obligations arising from their accession to India".[15]

Mountbatten and Ismay seemed concerned not so much with Pakistan's perfidy as with how to deter India from any physical action. Mountbatten had long talks with Nehru and

Patel. He easily carried conviction with Nehru; with Patel he could not. According to Campbell-Johnson, Mountbatten "reiterated Ismay's thesis that the whole manoeuvre was almost certainly a trap and part of a wider campaign which Jinnah might be expected to launch for the express purpose of presenting Pakistan to the world as the innocent weak State threatened by the ruthless aggressor".[16]

This did not impress Patel. World opinion, though important, did not weigh much with him. He was concerned with saving Junagadh from falling into the hands of Jinnah. If he withheld action, it was in deference to the wishes of Mountbatten and Nehru.

Two developments hastened the crisis. One was Liaquat Ali's reassertion on 25 September that the Nawab had every right to accede to Pakistan regardless of the state's territorial location. The other related to the Nawab's declaration of accession of Babariawad and Mangrol to India as invalid, claiming both as integral parts of Junagadh territory. Junagadh refused to withdraw its troops sent to Babariawad. For Patel, it was "an act of aggression, which must be met by a show of strength, with readiness in the last resort to use it".[17]

Mountbatten suggested reference to the UNO. Patel rejected it on the ground that Junagadh was not a disputed matter, but was a case of blatant interference on the part of Pakistan. Reference to the UNO would have internationalised the issue, as happened in the case of Kashmir later. Patel also rejected Mountbatten's other suggestion that the Central Reserve Police, and not the Indian Army, should be entrusted with the task of occupation of Babariawad and Mangrol. To Patel, this meant "taking unnecessary risks; he was firm that the operation should be handled by the Indian Army".[18] In the Maharaja of Gondal's view, the worsening situation posed a threat to "the peace and tranquillity of the whole of

Kathiawar". Without violation of Junagadh territory, Indian troops, under a newly created command, the Kathiawar Defence Force, were deployed in the adjoining states with a view to "creating [a] steadying effect all over Kathiawar". Babariawad and Mangrol were occupied on 1 November. At the same time, under the leadership of Samaldas Gandhi, a provisional government was formed with headquarters at Rajkot. Over two and a half months' political stalemate and economic stagnation had reduced Junagadh to near bankruptcy, resulting in a steep fall in the state's revenues and leading to a fast deteriorating food situation. Since no help arrived from Pakistan, the Nawab was forced to flee to Karachi "together with his family, many of his dogs, and all the cash and negotiable assets of the State Treasury".[19]

From Karachi, the Nawab authorised Bhutto to use his "judicious discrimination as the situation demanded, and to negotiate with the proper authorities".[20] Bhutto wrote to Jinnah on 27 October, telling him of "the fading of Muslim ardour for accession". He also said, "Today our brethren are indifferent and cold. Muslims of Kathiawar seem to have lost all enthusiasm for Pakistan."[21] Bhutto called a meeting of the Junagadh State Council on 5 November, which decided: "The position arising out of the economic blockade, interstatal complications, external agitation and internal administrative difficulties make its necessary to have a complete reorientation of the State policy and a readjustment of the relations with the two Dominions, even if it involves a reversal of the earlier decision to accede to Pakistan."

In pursuance of the state council resolution, Bhutto started negotiations with Samaldas Gandhi on 7 November for handing over power. It was supported by the Muslim Jamiat of Junagadh. Bhutto, therefore, told the Indian regional commissioner in Kathiawar, N. M. Buch, that the government of India could take over the administration. At that point, Liaquat Ali, the Pakistan prime minister, threw a spanner in the works with the statement that since Junagadh had acceded to Pakistan, neither the diwan nor the ruler could negotiate a temporary or permanent settlement with India, and that it was a violation of Pakistan territory and a breach of international law.

Mountbatten and his advisers had hoped that "Patel would be satisfied for a decision on the occupation of Junagadh itself to lie in the pending tray until greater problems were safely resolved". Patel played his game. Mountbatten was "tactfully left in the dark". By the time he discovered what was happening, troops were already on the move. According to Campbell-Johnson: "All these developments were only brought to Mountbatten's notice late in the evening. It is the first time since the transfer of power that the Government has carried out a major act of policy without fully consulting or notifying him in advance of the event. He feels this may be due to Patel's and VP's [Menon's] desire to spare him embarrassment."[22]

Due to Patel's firm handling of the Junagadh crisis, the storm blew over in no time. India took over the Junagadh administration on 9 November. On the thirteenth, Patel visited Junagadh. Addressing a mammoth public meeting, he assured the people that India would abide by their wishes. And then, dramatically, "by way of oratorical flourish, he asked the audience to indicate whether they wished the State to accede to India or Pakistan. Over ten thousand hands were immediately raised in favour of accession to India."[23] Patel also did some plain-speaking: "The action of the Nawab of Junagadh would be a lesson to those who are persisting in their chimera of attachment to an authority with which they have no natural ties . . . The State is no property of a single individual. Paramountcy has lapsed—certainly not by the efforts of the Princes, but by those of the people."[24]

A plebiscite, as Patel had promised, was held on 20 February 1948. Out of a total of 201,457 registered voters, 190,870 exercised their franchise. Only 91 cast their vote in favour of accession to Pakistan. A referendum was held at the same time in Mangrol, Manavadar, Babariawad, Bantwa, and Sardargarh, which showed that out of 31,434 votes cast in these areas, only 39 went in favour of Pakistan. Jossleyn Hennessy, of the *Sunday Times*, London, and Douglas Brown, of the *Daily Telegraph*, who were in Junagadh at that time, confirmed that "they could find little fault with the manner in which the referendum was conducted".[25]

Patel was the recipient of congratulations from many quarters for his "crowning success", especially the princes who eulogised his "noble efforts" in achieving "a unique victory over Junagadh without causing loss of life and property". All the Kathiawar princes and people felt grateful to Patel for "preserving the integrity and unity of Kathiawar by his timely action".[26]

Hyderabad
Mountbatten's pro-Nizam role

In Hyderabad, India faced a situation far more serious than in any other Indian state. Situated as it was in India's belly, Patel asked, "How can the belly breathe if it is cut off from the main body?"[1] It was a question of survival for India. A frightening situation was rapidly developing in Pakistan-dominated Hyderabad. Mountbatten's press attaché, Alan Campbell-Johnson, saw Hyderabad's various "sponsored" acts as "acts to display her status as an independent nation".

CREATOR OF ONE INDIA

Such acts related to "moral and physical violations of the Standstill Agreement": a loan of Rs. 20 crore to Pakistan, and the state Congress leaders' imprisonment without trial. The "most provocative was the activity of Kasim Razvi".[2] Further, Hyderabad's prime minister, Mir Laik Ali, was, till September 1947, Pakistan's representative at the United Nations. Far more disquieting was Jinnah's statement: "I require Hyderabad as an active ally, not as a neutral in such a war"[3]—a war against none other than India.

Patel's most formidable obstacle lay in Mountbatten's outlook and his conversion of Nehru to his point of view: to prevent the Indian Army from moving into Hyderabad. Further, Walter Monckton, the Nizam's constitutional adviser, was a friend of Mountbatten whose services Mountbatten had secured for the Nizam for conducting negotiations with India. Monckton had stated that "he felt there was no fundamental difference of approach between Mountbatten and himself. He would continue to look for the formula which would allow statutory independence for Hyderabad, and which, while containing no direct reference to the word 'accession', would incorporate it on a *de facto* basis".[4] Both Mountbatten and Monckton wanted the Nizam to have an "association" with India, not accession. Accession, as Monckton explained to the Nizam, could not be abrogated, whereas association could.

Patel failed to understand why Mountbatten asked India alone "to adopt ethical and correct behaviour towards Hyderabad and to act in such a way as could be defended before the bar of world opinion".[5] Such moralisation had little value for Patel when others were not reciprocating. The Nizam showed no qualms in trampling all codes of moral conduct. Campbell-Johnson admitted that "both the Nizam and his Government are very volatile statesmen, pursuing a very inconsistent and wavering line of policy."[6] In such a situation, Mountbatten naturally found in Patel "a much sterner and less conciliatory leader than Pandit Nehru".[7]

Patel had turned sterner and less conciliatory by the anti-Indian activities of the British secretary of the Political Department, Conrad Corfield, and his British diehard residents and agents in the states. Added to this was Monckton's highly intriguing role. "Even before Attlee's February statement, Monckton [who was in touch with Jinnah through Bhopal] was testing the possibility of Conservative Party support for appeals by Jinnah and the Muslim princes for separate membership of the Commonwealth. In mid-January he was in touch with the chief creator of the 1935 Act, Samuel Hoare [Lord Templewood], and was 'much encouraged' by their measure of agreement." In April 1947, Monckton was "in touch with Templewood about the acquisition of port facilities at Marmagoa, in Portuguese Goa, with a rail linkage to be built from the State to the sea". One Alexander Roger, a businessman, who had "important contacts among the Portuguese authorities, was employed as intermediary". Monckton himself is reported to have visited Portugal in April before reaching India. He is quoted to have stated that "for the Nizam to join India would be political suicide"; and "if we go warily, we shall very likely outlast them [the Indian government]". Monckton was "sanguine of Hyderabad's survival", and believed that "if HMG would maintain relations with Hyderabad, then Pakistan would recognise it, as would Egypt and Saudi Arabia".[8]

Monckton's presence in Hyderabad from April onwards was sufficient encouragement to the Nizam to step up his activities aimed at achieving independence. Even before Britain's transference of power, plans were hatched for the transfer of Bastar to Hyderabad. Panikkar wrote to Patel on

19 May: "A very serious and extremely dangerous intrigue is taking place" in Bastar, where the Nizam's government had been given a mining lease, the right to extend the Nizam's railway to Bastar and to acquire 15,000 square miles of rich mineral deposits. Panikkar stated: "It is a part of the dangerous intrigue to strengthen the Nizam in every possible way, e.g. by the sale of the Bren gun factory . . . This intrigue with the Nizam has to be scotched, otherwise the whole of Hindustan will be undermined." Even Nehru wrote to Patel: "The Hyderabad Government has come to an arrangement with the Birmingham Small Arms Company for supply of arms . . . an order for four crores of rupees worth ammunition with Mr. Kral, calling himself representative of the Czechoslovakian Government."[9]

On 12 June, after the announcement of the 3 June plan, the Nizam issued a *firman* which declared that "the departure of the Paramount power . . . will mean that I shall become entitled to resume the status of an independent sovereign". The Nizam had "set his heart on becoming a 'Third Dominion' of the British Commonwealth".[10] Early in June, the Nizam had been advised not only to declare his "independence" but also to "recruit Britishers to the state forces, to ask for Goa as part of his state, to demand a corridor between Hyderabad and Goa and apply for membership of the United Nations."[11]

The Nizam, on whom the king had conferred the titles "Most Exalted Highness" and "Faithful Ally to the British Government", was disappointed to find that the Indian Independence Bill did not provide for dominion status to Indian states. He protested against "the way in which my State is being abandoned by its old ally, the British Government, and the ties which have bound me in loyal devotion to the King Emperor are being severed".[12] Mountbatten dispelled all doubts when he told the Nizam's delegation on 11 July that HMG would not agree to Hyderabad becoming a member of the British Commonwealth except through either of the two dominions of India or Pakistan. This humbled the Nizam's pride, but did not dishearten him as he had other plans up his sleeve: to gain time by engaging India in prolonged constitutional negotiations through Monckton; to make preparations for a military confrontation with India by purchase of arms through foreign sources; and to build up the Ittehad-ul-Mussalmeen so as "to arm himself with a view to crushing the Hindu subjects"[13]—even to encourage migration of Muslims from some of the Indian provinces and states to Hyderabad.

On Monckton's advice, the Nizam wrote to Mountbatten on 8 August that "he could not contemplate bringing Hyderabad into organic union with either Pakistan or India", but was prepared to enter into a treaty which guaranteed the integrity and independent identity of his state under three conditions: in the event of a war between India and Pakistan, Hyderabad would remain neutral; Hyderabad should have the right to appoint agents-general wherever it thought fit; and if India seceded from the Commonwealth, Hyderabad would be free to review the situation de novo.

Patel told Mountbatten rather sternly on 24 August:

I wish to let Your Excellency know my mind before you meet the [Nizam's] delegation. I see no alternative but to insist on the Nizam's accession to the Dominion of India. The least variations in the Instrument of Accession, or arrangement regarding the State's association with the Dominion in regard to the three subjects, would not only expose me to the charge of breach of faith with the States that have already joined the Dominion, but would create the impression that advantage lay in holding out rather than coming in, and that, while no special merit attached to accession, a beneficial position could be secured by keeping out. This is bound to have most unfortunate consequences in our future negotiations for accession to the Union.

Patel also informed Mountbatten: "I have authentic information that the recent activities of the Ittehad-ul-Mussalmeen are designed almost to create a feeling of terror amongst the non-Muslim population, so that its agitation in favour of the independence of Hyderabad, with possible alliance with Pakistan, should flourish."[14]

What role was Monckton playing? He himself disclosed that in his note of 15 September to the Nizam's Executive Council:

My object has been to advise a course calculated to obtain for Hyderabad the maximum degree of real, practical independence, compatible with its prosperity and security . . . that Hyderabad is landlocked in the belly of Hindustan; that Pakistan is not yet in a sufficiently established State to be able to give effective help; that, if Hyderabad is to remain independent, she must stand on her own feet . . . The guiding principle has been to avoid executing an Instrument of Accession.

According to Monckton, an agreement of "association", as opposed to "accession", meant that "a treaty or agreement, short of accession, preserves independence in law, whereas accession destroys it and involves merger or organic union; that, when circumstances change, e.g. if Pakistan and Hyderabad grew strong enough to warrant it, the treaty can be denounced . . . once a State has acceded to the Dominion, it will find it hard to extricate itself".

Monckton further explained:

> I wanted the negotiations to continue for Hyderabad as long as possible after 15 August . . . the longer they continued the better for us . . . we have a breathing space to get ready for the economic and political conflict if it comes . . . I know that Patel was, and is, against any extension of time to Hyderabad and that the Governor-General prevailed over the Cabinet of the Dominion to allow him personally two months' time to see whether he and I, who had known each other intimately for many years publicly and privately, could find a compromise satisfactory to both sides.[15]

Encouraged by Monckton's note, the Nizam wrote to Mountbatten on 18 September, that short of accession, Hyderabad was "ready and willing" to make a treaty of association with India. "Simultaneously with this approach to us," writes V. P. Menon, "the Nizam got into contact with Jinnah with a view to securing the services of Zafrullah Khan as the President of his Executive Council." Zafrullah could not be spared as he was to lead the Pakistan delegation to the UNO.

Following this, an uncertainty hung over Hyderabad, with the result that delegation after delegation, with leaders and members changing now and again, began visiting New Delhi for negotiations with Mountbatten. These were almost endless, with no agreement in sight. About mid-October Patel got completely fed up and wanted to break off the negotiations. This upset Mountbatten, who pleaded: "It would be a great pity if the negotiations were to break down." He ignored what the Nizam wrote towards the end of October: that "if the negotiations with the Government of India were to break down, he would immediately negotiate and conclude an agreement with Pakistan". Patel was much annoyed. He told Menon, "The only decent course for us is to send back the new delegation by the very same plane by which it has arrived."[16]

Meanwhile, the situation within Hyderabad worsened. There was serious communal rioting in Secunderabad on 25 August. The police were entirely manned by Muslims. A member of the Nizam's Executive Council, Arvamudh Aiyangar, wrote that the Muslim police were "unwilling to protect the life or property of a Hindu", and "armed Pathans, Rohillas and Arabs are allowed to roam about without let or hindrance, terrorising the people". This caused an exodus of the Hindus. According to Aiyangar, "The local Muslim League, which has been well organised and supplied with arms, is only waiting for an opportunity to attack the Hindus *en masse* . . . if Hyderabad joins the Union, there will be mass slaughter on a large scale." Again he reported on 23 October: "One Lancaster landed at Begumpet aerodrome direct from Pakistan. It is suspected that it contained arms and ammunition."[17]

Earlier on 19 September, Patel had told Mountbatten, "The Nizam has mortgaged his future to his own Frankenstein, Ittehad-ul-Mussalmeen."[18] The Razakar leader, Kasim Razvi, had mounted a vitriolic tirade against Patel. He said on 14 October: "Patel belongs to the class of Hitler . . . Our Government is temperamentally like Chamberlain . . . what is there to prevent carrying on negotiations with Pakistan and other Muslim and non-Muslim countries?"[19]

Mountbatten saved the situation for the Nizam by agreeing to reach a standstill agreement with Hyderabad on

25 November. Nehru wrote to Patel: "I have just heard on the radio that the Hyderabad agreement has been signed. Congratulations. Whether this puts an end to the trouble there or not is a matter of doubt." Patel's reply was pragmatic: "It gives us breathing time and gives the Nizam plenty of scope to think over and to deal with the Frankenstein which he has created in his Ittehad-ul-Mussalmeen."[20] A year later India had to resort to "Police Action" in Hyderabad. Patel had seen its inevitability from the beginning. He could not carry it out because of Mountbatten's opposition. By the time the Police Action was taken, Mountbatten had left India. It was now Nehru whose opposition Patel had to encounter.

Earlier, the proposed standstill agreement had given the Nizam time to conspire for his independence through back-door diplomacy. He demanded that India's newly appointed agent-general to Hyderabad, K. M. Munshi, should be only a trade agent. The Nizam seemed to be planning to have ambassadors between India and Hyderabad, indicating that Hyderabad was an independent country. His second demand was withdrawal of Indian troops and supply of arms and ammunition for the Hyderabad army and police. And further, he wanted Hyderabad to be able to appoint agents in several foreign countries. Hyderabad had already appointed a public relations officer to Pakistan without reference to India.

The Nizam was buying time. He explained this in a cable of 6 January 1948 to Monckton in London: "I agree with your opinion that there is no good of our hurrying up making long-term agreement with the Indian Union at the beginning of the year, but to wait and see what further developments arise before we do it, namely, towards the end of the year. Besides, we must see how Kashmir and Junagadh's case is going to be settled by UNO. After that we can think about our own affair."[21] The Nizam wanted time to further build his

Gandhi's GOC: In Vinoba Bhave's words, Patel was "the accurate bowman of Gandhi's struggle, his disciple and GOC. He knew no retreat". Extreme right: Maniben, Sardar's devoted daughter who sacrificed all in the national cause by serving her father, not only by running his house and looking after visitors, but also by acting as his secretary.

Rebel Student Leader who organised strikes for securing justice for the wrongs done to fellow students.

Borsad Lawyer who led a successful satyagraha to fight dacoits.

Kheda Satyagraha (1918): Gandhi paid glowing tributes to Patel: "The choice of my lieutenant was particularly happy . . . without the help of Vallabhbhai we could not have won the campaign. He had a splendid [legal] practice, he had his municipal work to do, but he renounced all and threw himself into the campaign."

Ladbai: Mother who gave birth to two illustrious sons of India—Vithalbhai and Vallabhbhai.

A proud mother with her five sons (L to R): Vithalbhai, Somabhai, Narsibhai, Vallabhbhai, and Kashibhai (standing).

With family members on his 74th birthday on 31 October 1949.

Barrister Patel: He stood first in Roamn Law and passed the final with honours.

Sardar with elder brother Vithalbhai (left): In obedience to his elder brother, Sardar surrendered to him his passport and other documents as also his money, to enable him to go to the UK and become a barrister first.

Hero of Bardoli called Lenin: Patel commanded 87,000 absolutely non-violent, highly disciplined satyagrahis. The *Times of India* wrote that Patel had "instituted there a Bolshevik regime in which he plays the role of Lenin".

Saviour of Kashmir: Patel at Srinagar airport on 4 November 1947. Sheikh Abdullah and Bakshi Ghulam Mohammad pleaded for more military support to save Srinagar from falling into the hands of Pakistani raiders. Patel's prompt action saved the situation.

On Kashmir, Patel bluntly told **Arthur Henderson, British under secretary of state**, "We should never have gone to the UNO . . . not only has the dispute been prolonged but the merits of our case have been completely lost in the interaction of power politics . . . we were so terribly disappointed at the attitude of your delegation . . . it was, we maintain, the attitude of Noel Baker that tilted the balance against us. But for his lead, I doubt if the USA and some other powers would have gone against us."

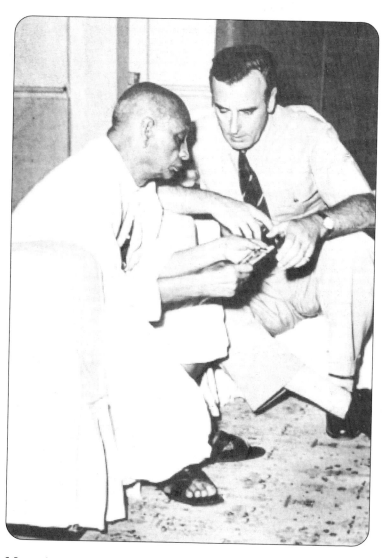

Mountbatten and Patel in discussion on a six-point deal on transfer of power. Mountbatten conceded Patel's demand in regard to the princes: "We will deal with that question. Leave it to us. You take no sides. Let paramountcy be dead."

Maharaja of Bikaner's appeal to the princes in April 1947 when the 3 June plan on transfer of power was yet two months away: "The only safe policy for the States is to work fully with the stabilising elements in British India to create a Centre . . . which would safeguard both the States and British India in the vacuum that would be created by the withdrawal of the British Government . . . Let the Princes of India rise to the occasion to be hailed as co-architects of the structure of India's independence and greatness."

The Maharaja of Jaipur being administered the oath as Rajpramukh of Greater Rajasthan. This was the fulfillment of Maharana Pratap's dream and a barrier to any "mischief" by Pakistan from across the border.

The Jamsaheb of Nawanagar being sworn in as Rajpramukh of
the United State of Kathiawar. The Jamsaheb spoke on the occasion,
"It is not as if we were tired monarchs who were fanned to rest. It is
not as if we have been bullied into submission. We have by our own
free volition pooled our sovereignties and covenanted to create this
new State so that the United State of Kathiawar and the unity of
India may be more fully achieved."

The Maharana of Udaipur with Patel. The Maharana said, on being invited by the Maharaja of Jodhpur to join the Bhopal plan: "My choice [to accede to India] was made by my ancestors. If they had faltered, they would have left us a kingdom as large as Hyderabad. They did not. Neither shall I. I am with India."

His Exalted Highness the Nizam of Hyderabad never received visitors at the airport. Sardar was an exception. He is seen being received by the Nizam at Begumpet airport.

The Maharaja of Gwalior (Scindia) said of Patel: "Here is the man whom I once hated. Here is the man of whom I was later afraid. Here is the man whom I admire and love." The Maharaja confessed to General S. P. P. Thorat: "If we Princes have to have our throats cut again, we will undoubtedly choose the Sardar and VP [Menon] to do it."

V. P. Menon: On unification of states with the Dominion of India, Mountbatten wrote to Patel, "I feel no one has given you adequate recognition for the miracle you and your faithful VP have introduced." H. V. Hodson has written in *The Great Divide: Britain-India-Pakistan:* "Rao Bahadur V. P. Menon was a remarkable man in many ways... It was by sheer merit that he won his way to the top in an administrative system controlled by the brahminical ICS."

H. M. Patel: His arduous task of division of assets and liabilities between India and Pakistan, to be completed before 15 August, was crowned with remarkable success. The issues involved were complex and sensitive, and their number was large. His ability lay in resolving them as a negotiator and reaching satisfactory solutions under the large-hearted and mature guidance of Sardar.

Churchill's message to Patel through Anthony Eden: "He should not confine himself within the limits of India, but the world was entitled to see and hear more of him."

A Gandhian to the tips of his fingers, Patel used to spin regularly at the Bardoli Ashram.

The Troika: Nehru-Gandhi-Patel, who led the last phase of India's freedom struggle from 1921 to 1947.

Patel sharing a lighthearted moment with the Mahatma.

Patel's message to Nehru on the latter's birthday on 14 November 1950, a month prior to Patel's demise: "My affectionate greetings on your birthday. Relations between us transcend boundaries, and I need hardly say anything more than this: It is my fervent and heartfelt prayer that you may live long and work to lead this country through all difficulties, and establish in it an era of peace, happiness and prosperity."

Highly complementary companionship: Patel contributed the strength of Shiva; Nehru, the softness of Vishnu. Such companionship helped India overcome the many problems of a newborn nation. By the time Patel passed away, India was on her feet as a great nation—united as never before. (*Photograph courtesy Mrs. Homai Vyarawalla, eminent photographer pre and post Partition in 1947*)

Gandhi's "muscle man": Congress success lay in Patel lending his "muscle" power as a great organiser to Gandhi's "soul" force. The *Manchester Guardian* wrote: "Without Patel, Gandhi's ideas would have had less practical influence, and Nehru's idealism less scope."

The Great Administrator: On his demise on 15 December 1950, on behalf of the ICS Association, Secretary-General Girija Shankar Bajpai said: "We meet today to mourn the loss and to pay tribute to the memory of a great patriot, a great administrator, and a great man. Sardar Vallabhbhai Patel was all the three - a rare combination in any historic epoch and in any country . . . That we should deeply mourn the loss of one who gained freedom for us in our time and sought successfully to impart to it the durability that comes from stable conditions and administrative strength is but natural."
Photo: Henri Cartier-Bresson

armed strength through acquisition of more arms, completion of new airfields and to initiate "a large-scale programme of converting Harijans to Islam,"[22]—besides giving the Ittehad-ul-Mussalmeen time "to get Muslims to migrate to Hyderabad" and even "induce ex-army Muslims or those in active service to join the Hyderabad army".[23]

Patel had to tell Mountbatten that "the period of two months, which we have agreed to give the State to make up its mind, is being utilised for preparations rather than for negotiations . . . I am convinced that it would neither be proper nor polite for us to agree to any arrangement other than the Instrument of Accession already settled between us and the other States".[24] The Nizam, realising that Patel would "not be bamboozled into a surrender even to the slightest extent", changed his strategy: to bank on Nehru who was "more accommodating than Sardar Patel", and to pin his "faith to the chance of having a better reception when CR [Rajagopalachari] becomes Governor-General".[25] The Nizam's expectations from the latter were due to his having, in 1944, sponsored the Gandhi-Jinnah talks, and subsequently advocated the conceding of Pakistan.

From his sick-bed at Dehra Dun, where he had retired after his heart-attack in March 1948, Patel watched with exasperating helplessness the increasing intransigence of the Nizam, failure of Mountbatten's efforts, and a growing feeling in Hyderabad that India was "not in dead earnest to take action". When Laik Ali called on him on 16 April at Dehra Dun, Patel told him with stunning bluntness, "You know as well as I do where power resides and with whom the fate of the negotiations must finally lie in Hyderabad. The gentleman [Kasim Razvi], who seems to dominate Hyderabad, has given his answer. He has categorically stated that, if the Indian Dominion comes to Hyderabad, it will find nothing but the bones and ashes of one and a half crores of Hindus. If that is the position, then it seriously undermines the whole future of the Nizam and his dynasty."

Patel made it clear:

The Hyderabad problem will have to be settled as has been done in the case of other States. No other way is possible. We cannot agree to the continuance of an isolated spot which would destroy the very Union which we have built up with our blood and toil. At the same time, we do wish to maintain friendly relations and to seek a friendly solution. This does not mean that we shall ever agree to Hyderabad's independence. If its demand to maintain an independent status is persisted in, it is bound to fail.

Many reasons hardened Patel's attitude. On 26 March, Laik Ali had told Munshi that "the Nizam was willing to die a martyr and that he and lakhs of Muslims were willing to be killed". Immediately thereafter, Razvi, in a speech on 31 March, "indulged in a good deal of sabre-rattling and urged the Muslims of Hyderabad not to sheathe their swords until their objective of Islamic supremacy had been achieved". He exhorted the Muslims "to march forward with the Koran in one hand and the sword in the other to hound out the enemy". He even declared: "The forty-five million Muslims in the Indian Union would be our fifth columnists in any showdown." Still worse, he asserted on 12 April: "The day is not far off when the waves of the Bay of Bengal will be washing the feet of our Sovereign", and that he would "hoist the Asaf Jahi flag on the Red Fort in Delhi."[26]

Mountbatten was to say good-bye to India in a month's time. He felt worried whether, after he had gone, Patel could be restrained from sending troops into Hyderabad. He was anxious "to make one final effort to bring about agreement between Hyderabad and India" so as "to end his fateful career in India in a blaze of glory by presenting an association with Hyderabad whatever form it took". With a plan for Patel's acceptance, he flew to Dehra Dun early in June, taking with him Nehru, Rajendra Prasad, Gopalaswami Ayyangar, and Baldev Singh—all of whom were "confident he [Patel] would not agree" to the plan. Monckton, who had drafted it, admitted to Mountbatten that "the terms were now so heavily weighed in Hyderabad's favour that it would be a miracle if India accepted".

Mountbatten's meeting with Patel was momentous. "Soon after arrival," records Mountbatten, "I gave the paper to Patel to read. He grunted: 'Impertinence—I will never initial it.' I then dropped the subject . . . After lunch Sardarji became quite emotional, and spoke of the debt India owed me. 'How can we prove to you our love and gratitude? Whatever you ask for, if your wish is in my power, it will be granted.' I hardened my heart, for I too was affected, and replied, 'If you are sincere, sign this document.' Sardarji was visibly taken aback. 'Does agreement with Hyderabad mean so much to you?' he asked in a low voice. 'Yes.' Patel initialed the draft . . . The others, although astonished, accepted this, and I flew to Delhi very elated at my success . . . Monckton could hardly believe his luck and flew back at once to Hyderabad with it . . . Then an astonishing thing happened. The Nizam and his advisers now rejected their own draft."

Monckton was told by Laik Ali: "We shall fight to the last man." To this, Monckton retorted: "You will be in the first aeroplane to Karachi." An unhappy Mountbatten recorded: "The situation was indeed 'lost' by Hyderabad through the intervention of Kasim Razvi . . . But for India, it spelt 'victory'. Now their conscience would be clear if they had to intervene in Hyderabad."[27]

With Mountbatten's departure, a major roadblock seemed to have been removed from Patel's path. He did gain a free hand; but not full freedom. Nehru and he differed. Not so much on what India was to do—Police Action—but when to do it. With Patel it was *now*; with Nehru it was *later*. Nehru told the chief ministers on 1 July, "We are ready at short notice to invade Hyderabad. But we propose to wait for developments and to avoid such invasion if we can help it, because of the other consequences that it is bound to bring in its train."[28] In contrast, Patel was categorical, unwavering and assertive. In his speech at the inauguration of the Patiala and East Punjab Union on 15 July, he declared: "If Hyderabad did not behave properly, it would have to go the way that Junagadh did. The former Governor-General, Lord Mountbatten, thought that he would be able to secure a peaceful settlement . . . Although I was doubtful whether the efforts would succeed, I let him try."[29]

Patel was now in a new mood, buoyant and cheerful. This was reflected by what he told Munshi over the telephone. Munshi records: "Next day [after Mountbatten's departure] I heard Sardar's voice over the phone, vibrating with good cheer. 'Well Munshi! How are you? Is everything all right? What about your Nizam?' 'Oh, he is all right,' I said. Then I told him about Zaheer's suggestion. 'Settlement!'—as if he had never heard of any such thing. 'What settlement?' His jocose queries were a sure sign of his mood. He now felt himself the master of the game. 'The Mountbatten settlement,' I said. 'Tell him that the settlement has gone to England,' he replied caustically and laughed."[30]

Patel also publicly stated: "The terms and the talks which Lord Mountbatten had have gone with him. Now the settlement with the Nizam will have to be on the lines of other settlements with the States. No help from outside, on which he seems to rest his pathetic hopes, would avail him."[31]

Patel's path was not yet all clear. Mountbatten's policy seemed to be dominating Nehru's mind. Four days prior to Mountbatten's departure, he had stated: "We will pursue an open door policy so far as these proposals [offered by Mountbatten] are concerned, and the Nizam is welcome to accept them any time he chooses."[32] This was not acceptable to Patel. It was a policy of drift, which the Nizam had successfully managed so far with the support of Mountbatten.

In a letter of 21 June to N. V. Gadgil, Patel wrote: "I am rather worried about Hyderabad. This is the time when we should take firm and definite action. There should be no vacillation; and the more public the action is the greater effect it will have on the morale of our people, both here and in Hyderabad, and will convince our opponents that we mean business . . . If, even now, we relax, we shall not only be doing a disservice to the country, but would be digging our own grave."[33]

The situation was climaxing towards confrontation. On 2 August, Laik Ali told the State Legislature: "Hyderabad has decided to refer its case to the United Nations . . . The Indians may coerce us. They may subject us to any ordeals. They may overrun us by their military strength. We cannot give up our stand. We shall not give up our freedom." Earlier he had told a Muslim deputation that "if the Union Government takes any action against Hyderabad, a hundred thousand men are ready to join our army. We also have a hundred bombers in Saudi Arabia ready to bomb Bombay."[34] Munshi reported to Patel on 3 August: "During the last fortnight, the atrocities of the Razakars have become utterly irresponsible, and loot, murder and rape are going on in more than one district."[35]

By early July, Hyderabad "bore the appearance of a war camp". Gun-running from Goa by land and from Karachi by air had been accelerated. On 6 July, India's secretary-general, Girija Shankar Bajpai, informed India's high commissioner in London, Krishna Menon, "of gun-running by air into Hyderabad from airfields near Karachi". Engaged in these operations was an Australian, Sidney Cotton, who smuggled arms and ammunition into Hyderabad by night, landing his aircraft either at Bidar or Warangal. Thomas Elmhirst, the commander-in-chief of the Indian Air Force, warned the defence minister, Baldev Singh, that "if these gun-running aircraft (six Lancasters) were loaded up with bombs, he could be powerless to intercept them with the aircraft at his disposal".[36]

Pakistan's complicity was clear from what Pakistan's General Gracey told India's General Bucher on 30 August: "Any coercion of Hyderabad would put Pakistan in an impossible position, should civil disorder breaks out in India."[37] Pakistan's hostility was seen in her cashing a portion of the Rs. 20 crore government of India securities which the Nizam had offered Pakistan as a loan. Further, the Nizam's UN delegation had first visited Karachi prior to proceeding to the USA. Reference to the UNO had been made on Monckton's advice in the expectation that it would delay Police Action; and that even "the UNO might get India to accept the modifications to the rejected Mountbatten drafts".[38]

Patel called to Dehra Dun, Major-General J. N. Chaudhuri, who was to lead the operations, and subjected him to a cross-examination for his personal assurance before giving the army the go-ahead. Chaudhuri records what Patel told him: "If I did well, I would take the credit; but if things went wrong, I would be blamed. But whatever I did, I would be supported. This was the wonderful thing about working with Sardar Patel.

He gave a feeling of intimacy."[39] His wholehearted backing and unflinching faith in men under him not only spurred them into action but helped them to attain final victory; never to retreat, as he himself had never done.

In a democratic set-up, cabinet sanction was essential for Police Action. Patel faced a formidable task in overcoming Nehru's reluctance. At one of the meetings of the defence committee, of which Nehru was the chairman, "there was so much bitterness that Sardar Patel walked out. Seeing his seat vacant," V. P. Menon told a Rotary meeting in Bombay, "I too walked out five minutes later." This seemed to have shaken Nehru out of his complacent mood, and mellowed his opposition. Later, at a meeting attended by the governor-general (Rajagopalachari), the prime minister, the home minister (Patel), and secretary to the states ministry (Menon), "it was decided to order troops into Hyderabad".[40]

Patel had yet to face the Hamlet in Nehru. The British commander-in-chief of the Indian Army, General Roy Bucher, persuaded Nehru that "even at that late stage the campaign should be called off, as militarily risky and hazardous on grounds of internal security in the whole country".[41] About midnight on 12 September, after he had spoken to Nehru, Bucher attempted "a rare feat" in pulling Patel "out of bed at that hour" and advised him to at least postpone action for fear of air attacks on Bombay and Ahmedabad. Patel reminded Bucher "how London had suffered during the Great War, and coolly assured him that Ahmedabad and Bombay both could stand up to an attack if it came".

Bucher, Munshi writes, "was hesitant throughout. He overestimated the capacity of the Hyderabad army, underestimated that of his own troops, and knew not the ability of the Sardar . . . to deal with the problems of internal law and order. Like most Englishmen, he was unable to realise that no price was too high to be paid for eliminating the

Razakar menace which threatened the very existence of India".[42] In H. V. R. Iengar's view, "the verdict of history will be that the Sardar was right"[43]—a verdict with which Nehru wholeheartedly agreed later.

Indian troops marched into Hyderabad on 13 September. The campaign was named "Operation Polo". It lasted barely 108 hours! Patel replied to the Jamsaheb's congratulations: "The whole operation went through like a machine."[44]

The army earned a handsome tribute from Patel, who wrote to Bucher:

> I should like to send you and officers and men under your command my sincerest felicitations on the successful conclusion of the Hyderabad operations. The speed and the skill of these operations cannot fail to extort admiration even from our severest critics, and I have no doubt that history will record these operations as a masterpiece of efficiency, organisation and all-round cooperation. The Indian Army has added one more chapter to its glorious record of achievements, and I should like to convey to you and through you to all those who have had a hand in these operations my personal thanks for the part which each one has played in it. We are really proud of them all.[45]

Bucher had admitted to his sister in a letter of 4 April 1948: "The real trouble there [Hyderabad] seems to be that the Nizam has become bound hand and foot to the Ittehad-ul-Mussalmeen . . . The Indian policy is one of reasonableness insofar as this is practicable."[46]

Congratulatory messages poured in. From Switzerland, the Jamsaheb wrote to Patel: "Here I am just rejoicing on your splendid success over Hyderabad, and in fact over the Security Council." Muslim Leaguer H. S. Suhrawardy, who was responsible for the "Great Calcutta Killing", congratulated Patel: "I take the liberty of offering you most sincerely my very best thanks and congratulations on the speech that you made just before the Hyderabad surrender. It has been widely appreciated by the Muslims in India."

Even Monckton couldn't help writing to Nehru: "I want to tell you how relieved I am that the action which you were eventually driven to take did not result in large-scale communal troubles. I know how anxious you were not to take the action at all, and how hard you struggled to avoid it . . . everyone who wants to see a peaceful and prosperous India will rejoice, as I do, that the episode is quietly finished."[47]

Nehru was most happy with the outcome. His fears and doubts had been set at rest. He wrote to the chief ministers on 21 September: "What has happened in Hyderabad has created a situation which should lead to a stabilisation of the communal situation in India, or rather to a progressive elimination of the communal sentiment." He again wrote on 4 October: "I have a feeling that India has turned the corner more specially since these Hyderabad operations. We are on the upgrade now. The atmosphere is different and better."[48]

Patel visited Hyderabad in the last week of February 1949. His courteous treatment of the defeated Nizam not only dispelled the latter's fears, but cemented a friendship between the two. The Nizam wrote to Patel: "I was glad to get an opportunity of making my acquaintance with you . . . and hope that this will prove to be a happy augury for the future of the premier State of Hyderabad." Patel's large-hearted reply was: "I was happy to learn that Your Exalted Highness had adapted yourself so readily to changed conditions. As I told Your Exalted Highness, while error is a human failing and divine injunctions all point to forgetting and forgiving, it is the duty of human beings to contribute their share to this process by sincere repentance and by employing the period that is left in discharging their duties to their people and to their God." A grateful Nizam again wrote to Patel on 12 May: "Your great personality is a valuable asset for India at this critical period when the whole world is in turmoil."[49]

Bucher, who had opposed the operations, paid glowing tributes to Patel in his admission: "I take no credit to myself for the success of the Hyderabad operation. In all the circumstances from beginning to end, I was not prepared to say 'Go' until every possible development had been thought out and guarded against. The Sardar is, in my opinion, a very great man indeed . . . Undoubtedly, he was right when he decided that either the Government of Hyderabad must accept the Indian Government's conditions, or else the State would have to be entered in order to eliminate the Razakars."[50]

Writing in the *Christian Science Monitor*, W. Gordon Graham called Patel the man "who by his decisiveness resolved the great Hyderabad crisis . . . Hyderabad, a State covering 80,000 square miles in the heart of peninsular India, was at that time in the grip of an unscrupulous minority, which aimed at secession from India. Had the bid succeeded, India might not have survived as a political unit. This situation needed a man of iron who would not balk at coercive action, and in the Sardar India had at that vital moment just the man".[51]

7

DEMOLISHER OF PRINCELY ORDER

Patel vs. Wellesley

Patel's unification and consolidation of over 560 princely states, in a country of continental size and diverse people, was epoch-making—of greater importance than Bismarck's role in Germany. In India, his creation can be comparable, though in contrast, with Lord Wellesley's princely order that laid the foundations of Britain's Indian Empire. That order, nevertheless, met with its peaceful demise at the hands of Patel. The replacement was most democratic, taking care of the interests of both, the princes and their subjects. Wellesley's policy was aggressive imperialism that reduced the once proud princes to mere puppets and sycophants. Patel didn't do that. His integration was a bloodless revolution, in the achievement of which the princes were his equal partners. He was generous to them to a fault, allowing them to live, as before, in their royal palaces and to enjoy handsome privy purses to live happily in the style they were used to. He even offered them opportunities to serve their country in dignified positions.

Wellesley, governor-general of India (1798-1805), built the empire on the basis of two Indias—British India and princely

India, each independent of the other, but the latter served as a bulwark against the former. During his seven years in India, Wellesley concluded as many as 100 treaties with Indian princes, making them subservient to British rule under his policy of subsidiary alliances—an umbrella of "defensive alliance and mutual guarantee".

India was passing through chaotic times. Princes faced danger from their neighbours, small and big. Wellesley offered them guarantee of protection by stationing British troops within a state, for which payment was made "either in cash or by alienating a portion of his territory to British control". By such arrangement, the prince was "secure against his Indian enemies, but also irrevocably attached to his British friends. The Princely fly was firmly enmeshed in the British political web, and any hope of escape was idle".[1]

The princes responded to Wellesley's offer in their own interest. To them, his offer of alliances was a beacon of hope, guaranteeing them a continuation of their rule, integrity of their territories and the prospect of their leading a carefree, luxurious life, in many cases licentious, in the seclusion of their palaces. For all this, the princes mortgaged their freedom, and were reduced to powerless stooges—impotent potentates.

In 1947, the departing British left the princes forlorn—indeed orphaned—by terminating paramountcy prior to the transfer of power. They feared being swept off by the new winds of a revolutionary change in the wake of the transfer of power. Earlier, the princes had faced threats from their *jagirdars* and neighbouring princes; now they faced them from their restive subjects, who were determined to wipe off their autocratic rule—an anachronism in the new climate—in their overwhelming desire to join the mainstream of national life pulsating with the soaring aspirations of a free people. At such a critical moment, Patel came to the princes' rescue by offering them a new honourable life in a democratic India as equal members of a free nation. He freed them from slavery in the proposed "Third Dominion" under the patronage of the Political Department.

Like a kind shepherd, Patel brought them under his umbrella and adopted them as his own flock. His winning over their hearts was a great achievement at a personal level. His wisdom and far-sightedness were reflected in his directive to his aides: "Do not question the extent of the personal wealth claimed by them, and never ever confront the ladies of the household. I want their States—not their wealth."[2] Such was Patel's judicious benevolence towards the princes. He had won their goodwill; even earned their gratitude and admiration.

Mountbatten had special pride in telling Patel: "By far the most important achievement of the present Government is the unification of the States into the Dominion of India. Had you failed in this, the results would have been disastrous . . . Nothing has so added to the prestige of the present Government than the brilliant policy you have followed with the States."[3] During his visit to India in 1956, Soviet leader Khrushchev felt so overwhelmed by Patel's achievement as to observe: "You Indians are an amazing people! How on earth did you manage to liquidate the Princely rule without liquidating the Princes?"[4]

Patel was a democrat, very unlike the British imperialists who had built and ruled over their Indian Empire. One of them, Charles Napier, had declared in one of his "typical outbursts": "No Indian Prince should exist. The Nizam should no more be heard of . . . Nepal would be ours."[5] Such Churchillian viciousness was alien to Patel's Gandhian mind. Its loftiness lay in its purity of mind and actions: frank, judicious, and straightforward. He was equally inflexible, firm, and determined when the country's interests were at stake. At the same time, none could have been gentler than he, to both, the Nawab of Bhopal who had conspired against India on behalf of Jinnah, and the Nizam of Hyderabad who waged a war, even when their subjects were predominantly Hindu. He liberated their people, without liquidating them. Rather, he welcomed them as honoured citizens of the new India he built.

History will one day rank him with Ashoka and Akbar. Theirs were benevolent empires. Patel's was a democratic people's republic. A leading Socialist leader, Yusuf Meherally, had opined: "The Mahatma had found a lieutenant that those Emperors would have given a kingdom to get."[6]

Part II
SUPPORTIVE ROLE

8

KASHMIR, TIBET AND NEPAL

Mature and Farsighted Advice

This section covers such subjects as were under Nehru's direct charge and to which he was passionately devoted—even considering them his close preserve. Yet, Patel often rushed to Nehru's aid whenever he needed his advice. That happened in the case of Kashmir, in spite of the state having been taken away from his charge; as also Tibet and Nepal. In all these, Patel's advice proved mature and farsighted. Later-day developments convinced many that had such advice been followed, history might have been different.

Patel went to Nehru's help in April 1950 at the cost of his health, during his visit to Kolkata to calm down the storm of protest by the Bengalis over the atrocities committed on the Hindus in East Pakistan (now Bangladesh). Muslim rowdies had "plundered and burnt houses and attacked men, women and children . . . accompanied by the abduction and forcible conversion of Hindu women to Islam and desecration of Hindu places of worship . . . What happened in Dacca was repeated in many districts of East Bengal."[1]

In April 1950, Kolkata was seething with anger. Nehru could not have faced the people after signing a No-War Pact with the Pakistan prime minister, Liaquat Ali. Patel told Nehru, "We have had sufficient experience of the implementation of agreements with Pakistan. We have also a bitter taste of the protection which it affords to minorities . . . all preparations for war are being made."[2] At such a critical moment in Nehru's life, Mountbatten pleaded with Patel: "You have for years been the 'strong man' of India. With your support Jawaharlal cannot fail. I do not believe there is one man in the country who would stand up to you when you make up your mind, so that the support which you are in a position to give him is a matter of highest international importance."[3]

Patel's visit to Kolkata had a most soothing effect. It calmed down rebellious Bengalis. Nehru was saved from a crisis. Patel had ignored Nehru's words, casting aspersions on the usefulness of their association, in his letter of 26 March 1950: "Lately, new developments . . . have made me doubt seriously whether this attempt at joint working serves a useful purpose, or whether it merely hinders the proper functioning of Government." Patel had felt "personally pained and hurt".[4] Yet, that did not deter him from visiting Kolkata, where he had resounding success, much to Nehru's relief. On his return began his last journey of life, which ended in his demise eight months later on 15 December 1950.

Irrespective of Nehru's doubts about his usefulness as a colleague, Patel, whom Mountbatten called the strongest pillar of the cabinet, never held himself back in offering Nehru his honest, pragmatic advice whenever sought, and rushed to his side whenever Nehru was in trouble. It mattered little to him if his advice was not implemented; he merely discharged his duty to his country. If he could surrender to

Gandhi's will in nominating Nehru as India's first prime minister (discussed later), other things were trivial, of no consequence to him. For Patel, his country was uppermost; and his dedication, supreme.

Saviour of Kashmir from Pakistani Raiders

It was the beginning of November 1947. Extreme wintry conditions gripped the valley. The people of Srinagar could ward off biting cold by remaining indoors, and warming themselves with burning coal in their *kangaris* under their woollen overalls. But they faced another, far worse fate. Four miles outside the city limits, the Pakistan-backed tribal raiders were amassing for their final assault. People shivered with fear, awaiting with certainty the fate that had befallen Baramulla a few days earlier: large-scale looting, indiscriminate burning, brutal murder and rape of innocent women. All the victims were Muslims. Confident of the capture of Srinagar, Jinnah was at Abbotabad "expecting to ride in triumph into Kashmir".[1] A "personally outraged" Sheikh Abdullah felt tormented by "ancestral recollections of previous incursions up the same route".[2] Was history repeating itself? It would have, but for Patel's timely help.

At such a critical moment in Kashmir's history, Patel arrived in Srinagar on 4 November to save the people from the ordeal they faced. He had brought with him the defence minister, Baldev Singh, so that his decisions could be given effect to without delay. The journey was hazardous. Weather was cruel. Conditions could deteriorate to render visibility poor. The plane could have moved into Pakistani territory, the air-passage between Jammu and Srinagar being so narrow. Consequences could have been serious. However, the landing was safe, and Patel immediately plunged into the job for which he had come: to assess the military requirements of the army. Conflicting reports from the valley had confounded New Delhi. This had upset Nehru so much as to make him say that "to receive two diverse reports on the situation in the Kashmir Valley over a matter of hours was more than he could tolerate".[3]

Patel moved to the control room for a briefing by Brigadier L. P. Sen, in charge of the 161 Brigade engaged in the operations. Sen has an interesting story to tell: "Sardar Patel had closed his eyes soon after I had begun the briefing, and I assumed that he was feeling the effects of air journey and had fallen asleep. The briefing completed, I looked at Sardar Baldev Singh and asked him a direct question, 'Am I expected to eject the tribesmen from the Valley regardless of the fate that may befall Srinagar, or is the town to be saved?' Sardar Patel stirred. The Tiger had not been asleep, and had heard every word of the briefing. A strong and determined man and one of few words. 'Of course, Srinagar must be saved,' he snapped. 'Then I must have more troops, and very quickly . . . some artillery (as well).' 'I am returning to Delhi immediately,' he said, 'and you will get what you want as quickly as I can get them to you.' . . . That evening I got a message that two battalions of infantry, one squadron of armoured cars and a battery of field artillery were being despatched to the Valley by road . . . Sardar Patel had lived up to his reputation as a man of action."[4] And, thus, Srinagar and the valley were saved from falling into the hands of the raiders.

General Roy Bucher, the British commander-in-chief of the Indian Army, was opposed to Patel's taking a great risk by flying to Srinagar. But Patel simply "ordered an aircraft . . . to be placed at his disposal." Bucher conceded: "This

flight did result in reinforcements being sent to Kashmir."[5]
Earlier, immediately after the Maharaja's accession to India
on 26 October, the cabinet had to sanction airlifting of troops
to Srinagar. Nehru, as usual, vacillated, worried by
international opinion.

According to Field Marshal Sam Manekshaw, then a
brigadier in charge of military operations: "Panditji's long
exposition about accession of the State and the United
Nations was cut short by the impatient Sardar Patel with the
question: 'Jawahar, do you care for Kashmir, or not?' 'Of
course, I do,' thundered Panditji. Sardar turned to me and
said, 'Go, you have your orders'."[6] And thus Patel put an end
to such vacillation, and the airlifting took place the very next
morning of the twenty-seventh. Delay would have helped
Pakistan, not only to capture Srinagar, but to take over the
whole state as constituted before the transfer of power. She
would have had international support, as later events proved.

The threat to the valley had thus been averted, though
not Pakistan's adventure. Patel was anxious to end that too.
In November 1948, Patel was acting as prime minister while
Nehru was away in Europe. He sent for Air Marshal Thomas
Elmhirst, chairman of the Chiefs of Staff Committee, "to
discuss a point relating to the Kashmir war", and spoke to
him thus: "If all the decisions rested on me, I think that I
would be in favour of extending this little affair in Kashmir
to a full-scale war with Pakistan . . . Let us get it over once
and for all, and settle down as a united continent."[7]

A war between India and Pakistan was not in
Mountbatten's interest, nor in Britain's. Both had a big hand
in Pakistan's creation; and they wanted its stability in order
to keep alive balance of power in the sub-continent. Pre-
Partition such balance was between the two communities—
Hindus and Muslims; post-Partition, it was to be between

the two independent countries—India and Pakistan. Mountbatten had warned Jinnah of the dangers he faced, when he told him, at his meeting with him in Lahore on 1 November 1947, that "war, whilst admittedly very harmful for India, would be completely disastrous for Pakistan and himself".[8] He had no plenipotentiary powers to act on his own. Yet, he did, sure of the unstinting support of Nehru in the two steps he took: offer of plebiscite in Kashmir, and reference of Kashmir to the UNO.

As Mountbatten admitted, the plebiscite idea was "entirely his". He specially flew to Lahore on 1 November to make a personal offer to Jinnah. He was accompanied by no Indian leader. His only companion was Ismay, whom he wanted as a witness to his offer. Mountbatten had "drafted out" the proposal in the aeroplane during his flight to Lahore. He has also admitted that it was an offer that "I had not yet shown to my Government, but to which I thought they might agree".[9] This was despite the fact that earlier, at the cabinet meeting on 28 October, there was "strong resistance to the whole idea . . . comparisons were made with Neville Chamberlain's visit to Hitler at Godesberg in 1938. Vallabhbhai Patel, in particular, made his opposition clear to the Governor-General".[10] Yet, an "unbriefed and unauthorised" Mountbatten offered plebiscite to Jinnah, and talked as "an ex-Viceroy who had a major hand in partitioning the country".[11] Jinnah called Mountbatten's offer "redundant and undesirable . . . objected strongly to a plebiscite."[12] Yet, Mountbatten forced Nehru to honour his offer of plebiscite to Jinnah.

Mountbatten's forcing Nehru to refer Kashmir to the UNO early in January 1948 was far more serious than his offer of plebiscite to Jinnah. It sucked India into the vortex of international politics, making a solution far more complex and difficult. Mountbatten had a purpose in hastening Nehru

to act. It had to be done before Patel's return to New Delhi
to avoid a repeat of Junagadh.

On his return, Patel's unofficial comment was: "Even a
District Court pleader will not go as a complainant." Later,
he did not hesitate in telling the British under secretary of
state, Arthur Henderson:

> Unfortunately, it is my experience that the attitude of
> an average Englishman in India is instinctively against
> us . . . we should never have gone to the UNO . . . at
> the UNO, not only has the dispute been prolonged but
> the merits of our case have been completely lost in the
> interaction of power politics . . . we were so terribly
> disappointed at the attitude of your delegation . . . it
> was, we maintain, the attitude of Noel Baker that tilted
> the balance against us. But for his lead, I doubt if the
> USA and some other powers would have gone
> against us.[13]

In January itself, Nehru regretted to Patel that Kashmir
"has been raised to an international level . . . by reference to
the Security Council of the UN and most of the great powers
are intensely interested in what happens in Kashmir".[14] A
month later, Nehru admitted that the Kashmir issue "has
given us a great deal of trouble . . . the attitude of the great
powers has been astonishing. Some of them have shown active
partisanship for Pakistan".[15] In May, Nehru wrote to Patel
again: "We feel that we have not been given a square deal."[16]
Kashmir worried Nehru so much that he lamented to Patel
from Paris on 27 October: "This business of a plebiscite and
the conditions governing it fills the people's minds . . . people
cannot get rid of the idea that Kashmir is predominantly
Muslim and, therefore, likely to side with Muslim Pakistan."[17]

Even from his retirement in London, Mountbatten's influence on Nehru worked: a cease-fire, which was kept a closely guarded secret, was ordered. Even the army commanders engaged in the Kashmir operations were kept in the dark. That was not so with the Pakistan army commanders, who, having been briefed, moved up their troops to occupy some of the more strategic heights vacated during extreme cold.

Haji Peer was one such commanding peak of great strategic value, linking Poonch and Pakistan. India could have asked for its return under the cease-fire agreement. But India failed to do so. An answer to that may be sought in General S. P. P. Thorat's complaint: "Our forces might have succeeded in evicting the invaders, if the Prime Minister had not held them in check, and later ordered the cease-fire . . . Obviously, great pressure must have been brought to bear on him by the Governor-General . . . Panditji was a great personal and family friend of Lord Mountbatten."[18]

In the 1965 Indo-Pak war, India captured Haji Peer. Influenced by Nehruvian vacillation, Lal Bahadur Shastri, India's prime minister, could not resist Soviet pressure for a compromise—status quo under the Tashkent Agreement in January 1966. Haji Peer remained with Pakistan.

Equally inexplicable was Nehru's blind faith in Sheikh Abdullah. His biographer, S. Gopal, alleges that he was Nehru's "old friend and colleague and blood-brother".[19] According to his other biographer, Stanley Wolpert, Nehru believed "the fate of Kashmir was tied to the fate of the Nehru family— their intertwined destiny". He quotes Nehru as having said, "Kashmir is of the most vital significance to India . . . We have to see this through to the end."[20] Nehru somehow believed that only Abdullah—and none else—could help him achieve that. He was Nehru's anchor of hope in the Muslim-dominated valley.

In the bargain, Nehru mortgaged to Abdullah not only the freedom of the Dogra Hindus of Jammu and the Buddhists of Ladakh, but even that of the ethnically different Muslims of the state—the border Muslims, the Bakarwals, the Gujjars, and the Paharis. Besides, Jammu and Ladakh had half the state's population and over 89% of the area. Worse still, Nehru bluntly told the Kashmiri Pandits at the annual session of the National Conference at Sopore in 1945, "If non-Muslims want to live in Kashmir, they should join the National Conference [of Abdullah], or bid good-bye to the country [Kashmir] . . . If the Pandits do not join it, no safeguards and weightages will protect them."[21] The Pandits' wholehearted cooperation with the valley Muslims could not give them any protection. In 1991, they were driven out of the valley.

In May 1946, Nehru's blind support to Abdullah in his Quit Kashmir movement—in imitation of Gandhi's Quit India movement of 1942—boosted Abdullah's ego sky-high. After his visit to Srinagar, Acharya Kripalani declared that the Quit Kashmir movement was "abusive and mischievous . . . The Maharaja was a son of the State . . . absurd to ask him to quit . . . there could be no comparison between the 'Quit Kashmir' agitation and the 'Quit India' movement".[22]

During the Quit Kashmir agitation, Abdullah had been arrested. Nehru got him released through Patel's mediation with the Maharaja. On coming out of prison, he called upon the Maharaja, and offered him a *nazarana* as a token of his loyalty. He wrote to him: "In spite of what has happened in the past, I assure Your Highness that myself and my party have never harboured any sentiment of disloyalty towards Your Highness's person, throne or dynasty . . . I assure Your Highness the fullest and loyal support of myself and my organisation."[23] After his assumption of power, he cast to the winds the faithfulness he had promised, and demanded of the Maharaja "to quit the Valley bag and baggage and leave the Kashmiris alone to decide their future by themselves".

The task seemed not so easy. He had to have two major roadblocks removed from his path—Patel and the Maharaja—and thereafter to gain independence under Article 370 of the Constitution.

In December 1947, Nehru took away Kashmir from Patel's charge and placed it under the charge of Gopalaswami Ayyangar. Such an affront hurt Patel deeply. He wrote to Nehru: "Your letter of today [23 December 1947] has been received just now at 7 p.m. and I am writing immediately to tell you that it has caused me considerable pain . . . your letter makes it clear to me that I must not, or at least cannot, continue as a member of Government, and, hence, I am hereby tendering my resignation."[24] The letter seemed to have remained undelivered at Gandhi's intervention on Mountbatten's persuasion that without Patel the Government could not be run.

Abdullah's next target was the Maharaja, who, he demanded, should leave the state for good. The demand seemed totally unconstitutional in its denial of justice to the Maharaja, whom the British, under the Indian Independence Act of the British Parliament, had given the right to accede to India or Pakistan, or to choose to remain independent. It did injustice to the Dogras of Jammu as well, who wanted the Maharaja to stay on. Nehru refused to accept two basic truths: that the Maharaja's position was the same as that of other Indian princes, and that the Maharaja was as much a son of the soil as was Abdullah. Yet, at Nehru's request, Patel persuaded the Maharaja to leave the state.

After gaining his "freedom" from Patel, as also from the Maharaja, Abdullah moved towards his bigger objective—to secure "freedom" for his state through its separate

Constitution, beginning with Article 370 of the Indian Constitution. In November 1948, Nehru was to leave for Europe, and was under great pressure of time. At such a hectic time, Abdullah arrived in New Delhi and pressurised Nehru for immediate action. Nehru left for Europe, entrusting the drafting of the Article to K. M. Munshi, a constitutional expert, and Gopalaswami Ayyangar, an administrator. According to Munshi, "Abdullah was unhappy with the Article [370] as we drafted" and Munshi feared that "though he was scheduled to support the Article in the Constituent Assembly, he might absent himself from the proceedings".[25]

Article 370 created an uproar at a Congress Parliamentary Party meeting. Ayyangar was helpless to restore order. He called for Patel's support. Patel had the draft unanimously accepted the very next day. During the discussion on the draft in the Constituent Assembly, Abdullah's pride was hurt and he staged a walk-out in protest. Patel, who was officiating for Nehru, was much displeased. Abdullah decided to leave for Srinagar the same night. He had hardly settled down in the train when Mahavir Tyagi entered the compartment to deliver Patel's stern message: "Sheikh Sahib, the Sardar says you could leave the House, but you cannot leave Delhi."[26] More out of fear than respect, Abdullah got down from the train. That made some believe that Kashmir would have been different had the state remained under Patel's charge, like Hyderabad. Abdullah feared Patel, not Nehru.

Could Patel have settled the Kashmir problem for good? He once told H. V. Kamath that "if Jawaharlal and Gopalaswami [Ayyangar] had not made Kashmir their close preserve, separating it from my portfolio of Home and States", he would have "tackled the problem as purposefully as he had already done in Hyderabad".[27] He seemed more confident in telling M. R. Masani that "but for Nehru, he could settle the Kashmir issue in no time by arranging that the Kashmir Valley go to Pakistan and East Pakistan to India. Both countries would benefit from such an arrangement".[28]

Field Marshal Auchinleck held a similar view. He had stated: "Pakistan should let East Pakistan go. They will always be a millstone round their necks and a great danger, or more. Jinnah made a big mistake when he fought for their inclusion . . . Punjabis and Pathans will never mix with Bengalis. They are like oil and water. They differ so in every way except religion, and I always think a Bengali is a Bengali first and a Muslim second! I think myself that they should agree to separate."[29]

Once, Dr. Rajendra Prasad told Jayaprakash Narayan, "The Sardar used to evade an answer with the remark that he had left the problem for Jawaharlal to tackle. But once he did say that when we had given away Punjab, Sind and the NWFP, of what value could the small valley of Kashmir have for us? Will the people there ever agree to live happily with us?"[30] M. N. Roy speculated over Patel's attitude towards Kashmir: "I am inclined to believe that it was as realistic as his attitude towards Pakistan. Nevertheless, once the dice were cast by the gambler's megalomania, the Sardar had no choice but to play the game. But one could be sure that he loathed the stupidity clothed in the glamour of popular heroes."[31]

Patel's Proposals to Save Tibet

The Himalayas are a god-given gift to India—the abode of the *rishis,* and the origin of her rivers. The Himalayas are not only India's crown of glory, but they have also served her for centuries as a protecting shield extending right across her northern borders—from the Nanga Parbat (26,629 feet)

in Kashmir to the Namcha Barwa (25,000 feet) in eastern
India. But in 1962, the Himalaya's impregnability was breached
by the Chinese. None could have imagined that they would
invade India from across her northern borders. Nehru suffered
the rudest shock, because of his implicit faith in Chinese
friendship. In deep anguish, he said, "How I worked for
friendship between India and China, fought for Chinese
legitimate interests in the world . . . and aggression was my
reward."[1]

Could that have been avoided? Patel had answered that
as early as in 1950, when China threatened India's territorial
integrity in her Himalayan states. Thousands of copies of a
map were distributed in Sikkim and other Himalayan regions.
The map showed Tibet and China as "the palm of a human
hand, and Ladakh, Nepal, Sikkim, Bhutan and NEFA as its
five fingers".[2] Patel had foreseen China's designs as far back
as June 1949 when he wrote to Nehru: "We have to strengthen
our position in Sikkim as well as in Tibet. The farther we
keep away the Communist forces, the better. Tibet has long
been detached from China. I anticipate that, as soon as the
Communists have established themselves in the rest of China,
they will try to destroy its [Tibet's] autonomous existence."
His advice to Nehru was: "You have to consider carefully
your policy towards Tibet in such circumstances and prepare
from now for that eventuality."[3]

In November 1950, a month prior to his demise, Patel
attended a cabinet meeting called to discuss Tibet. Nehru's
mood was petulant. He snubbed N. V. Gadgil with the remark:
"Don't you realise that the Himalayas are there?" Whereupon
K. M. Munshi ventured to say, that "in the seventh century,
Tibetans had crossed the Himalayas and invaded Kanauj".
Nehru dismissed this as nonsense. Immediately after the
meeting, Patel left for Ahmedabad, but he continued

"anxiously thinking" over the problem. On his return to New Delhi, he wrote a letter to Nehru on 7 November, which, according to Munshi, showed Patel's "uncanny vision" in discerning "as far back as 1950 the portents across our north-eastern border and the dangerous implications of our foreign policy in that direction . . . Every word of what he wrote has been proved true by the developments of the past seventeen years".[4] Patel had written to Nehru:

> The Chinese Government has tried to delude us by professions of peaceful intentions. My own feeling is that at a crucial period they managed to instil into our Ambassador a false sense of confidence in their so-called desire to settle the Tibetan problem by peaceful means . . . The final action of the Chinese, in my judgment, is little short of perfidy. The tragedy of it is that the Tibetans put faith in us . . . we have been unable to get them out of the meshes of Chinese diplomacy or Chinese malevolence . . . it appears that we shall not be able to rescue the Dalai Lama.

Patel tried to convince Nehru that "the Chinese do not regard us as their friends" and "their last telegram to us is an act of gross discourtesy not only in the summary way it disposes of our protest against the entry of Chinese forces into Tibet, but also in the wild insinuation that our attitude is determined by foreign influences. It looks as though it is not a friend speaking in that language but a potential enemy".

Patel further warned Nehru:

> Very soon they [the Chinese] will disown all the stipulations which Tibet has entered into with us in the past. That throws into the melting pot all frontier and commercial settlements with Tibet on which we have

been functioning and acting during the last half a century. China is no longer divided. It is united and strong. All along the Himalayas in the north and north-east, we have on our side of the frontier, a population ethnologically and culturally not different from Tibetans or Mongoloids. The undefined state of the frontier, and the existence on our side of a population with its affinities to Tibetans or Chinese, have all the elements of potential trouble between China and ourselves . . . Chinese ambitions in this respect not only cover the Himalayan slopes on our side, but also include important parts of Assam . . . The danger from the north and north-east, therefore, becomes both communist and imperialist.

Patel suggested a number of positive steps, which included: improvement of road, rail, air, and wireless communications with Nepal, Bhutan, Sikkim, Darjeeling, and the tribal areas in Assam; building of defensive lines; policing and intelligence of frontier posts to stop infiltration of spies, fifth columnists and Communists; and fully manning the outposts, and ensuring loyalty of people inhabiting the regions concerned.

Patel further suggested redisposition of forces with a view to guarding important routes or areas which are likely to be the subject of dispute, and an appraisal of the strength of our forces. With regard to Chinese entry into the UNO, he felt that "in view of the rebuff which China has given us and the method which she has followed in dealing with Tibet, I am doubtful whether we can advocate her claims any longer". Patel's warning was: "Any faltering or lack of decisiveness in formulating our objectives, or in pursuing our policy to attain those objectives, is bound to weaken us and increase the threats which are so evident."[5]

Earlier, in 1901, India's confrontation over Tibet had been with Russia; now it was with China. Curzon, the viceroy, had firmly clarified the British position which approximated Patel's thinking, though Curzon's language was of an imperialist and empire-builder. Like Curzon, Patel did not desire occupation of Tibetan territory; and his view was that of Curzon's, who had stated: "Of course we do not want their country. It would be madness for us to cross the Himalayas and occupy it. But it is important that no one else should seize it; and that it should be turned into a sort of buffer State between the Russian and Indian Empires. If Russia were to come down to the big mountains, she would at once begin intriguing with Nepal . . . Tibet itself, not Nepal, must be the buffer that we endeavour to create."[6]

Unpreparedness and vacillation on Nehru's part, lasting more than a decade, could not rescue the Dalai Lama, nor could he avoid humiliation in his ignominious defeat in the Indo-Chinese war in 1962.

Nepal: Patel's Lasting Solution

The deteriorating situation in Nepal since 1950 threw Nepal into a deepening crisis in 2005. There was murder of democracy with the king's assumption of absolute monarchy, heightening dangers for Nepal, as well as for India, from the Maoist guerrillas—and even from China. According to reports, during 2005, the monarch received from China, 18 truck-loads of arms and ammunition, adding anxiety and complications to India's stake in Nepal.

In 1950, trouble in Nepal had forced the infant king to seek asylum in the Indian embassy in Kathmandu. He was shifted to New Delhi for security reasons. The Foreign Affairs

Committee of the Indian cabinet met to discuss whether India should give recognition to the infant ruler. According to K. P. S. Menon, foreign secretary, Nehru felt that "the King's espousal of the popular cause should be taken at its face value and that he should be enabled to go back to Nepal as King". Patel differed. He thought of the future, and observed that "Nepal is a frontier State, that stability is the paramount consideration there, and that the Ranas are in a better position to ensure stability than anyone else." Nehru's view prevailed but "Patel stood primarily for stability and Nehru for freedom".[1]

From Patel's point of view, such freedom under a hereditary and autocratic rule was an anachronism; even contradictory to Nehru's socialist thinking. Patel hoped to establish people's supremacy in Nepal through the Ranas, not through the king. Being an incarnation of Lord Vishnu, nobody could assail him, least of all remove him. Patel's support for the Ranas seemed to have been influenced by his democratic spirit that had led him to replace the princely order in India by people's raj. Similar rule in Nepal would have brought the people of India and Nepal closer to each other, impelled by cultural and religious affinities. In such a climate of commonality of relations, built on mutual interests, regards and goodwill, Nepal might not have suffered the later-day isolation, and become a hotbed of world power intrigue. The two people of the same stock, faith, and language would have lived in a climate of trust and brotherhood.

In 1956, the king attempted to loosen Nepal's traditional ties with India by negotiating a treaty of peace and friendship with China; also inviting the Russians and the Americans to Kathmandu. Nehru was so irked over the Nepal-China affair that he informed the Chinese government that "a treaty of friendship with Nepal would, from India's view-point, be inopportune . . . They are perfectly free to go their own way, and we shall go our own".[2] It was a surrender without confrontation or a diplomatic manoeuvre.

During 2004, Nepal's politics had reached its nadir. With his direct rule having failed, the king found it difficult to find a prime minister to run his government. The streets of Kathmandu witnessed the spectacle of protesters shouting anti-king slogans. The picture in the countryside looked still grimmer. With Nepal in a state of turmoil, could India legally interfere to stop Nepal drifting into total chaos? Not so easily, if judged by India's earlier bad experience in Sri Lanka. Yet, since the two people are the same, one could hope that sooner or later the Nepalese themselves would rise to seek India's help to put their house in order.

Looking back, in 1950, Nepal posed no problem for India. India could lord over Nepal's destiny and help shape her future—as a people's democracy. But not so in 2005, after the king's installation of absolute monarchy in a coup on 1 February. Over the years, India had allowed herself to be reduced to the status of a helpless spectator, with practically no option left, except to support the king. India faced multiple dangers. The countryside in Nepal was not ruled by the government but was under the domination of the Maoist guerrillas. Since 1996, they had killed some 11,000 people. They controlled 68 out of 75 districts. Out of 1,135 police stations, only 100 were functioning.

The anarchy in Nepal led to the spilling of Maoists into the Indian states of Uttarakhand, Uttar Pradesh, Bihar, Andhra Pradesh, Orissa, Jharkhand, and West Bengal. The Maoists and the Naxalites, it was feared, might jointly create terror in these states and beyond. Some even feared that a desperate king could play the China card and that China's role might be facilitated with the improvement of the existing roads:

Kathmandu-Lhasa through the Kodari Pass, and Kathmandu-Tibet through the Rasuwagadhi-Kerung pass; as also with the construction of new roads, one through the Koshi-Kimathanka corridor in the east, and the other, Jomsom-Lumanthang, in the west.

Terror looked down upon India from the Himalayas' 1,754 km open border. It posed a danger far greater than Kashmir, whose LOC is 778 km long, and protected by fencing. Nepal and the adjoining regions sat right on India's head, whereas Kashmir was tucked away in a corner of India. Further, Nepal was an independent kingdom unlike Kashmir, which made matters far more difficult. China had stirred up moves to beat India by offering the king liberal military and monetary support, without, of course, ignoring Nepalese Maoists. It was necessary for India to pursue carefully worked-out tightrope diplomacy.

In April 2006, when Kathmandu was rocked by protest marches, the London *Economist* wrote: "Few conventional observers feel qualified to peep far into Nepal's future."[3] Patel, nevertheles, did that in 1950, as mentioned earlier, by openly advocating parliamentary democracy in Nepal through the Ranas, in the same manner as the Indian princely states by "dethroning" hereditary rulers. Nehru, however, favoured the king, which sowed the seeds of the later-day trouble in Nepal. Patel had desired a people-to-people relationship between Nepal and India.

In the abolition of monarchy in December 2007 and Nepal's becoming a republic in May 2008 lay a solution Patel had suggested to Nehru in 1950. It was the one he had himself implemented in India in the demolition of the princely order.

Part III
APPENDICES

9

A CHURCHILLIAN PLAN

Partition of India

Winston Churchill, as prime minister of Britain, had favoured, in March 1945, India's "partition into Pakistan, Hindustan and Princestan".[1] He had won the war, but was losing the empire. Britain had neither manpower nor money to rule over a restive India. Churchill saw in a complete withdrawal "serious implications for Britain's communications and bases between the Middle East and South-East Asia". His plan, therefore, was to ensure continuation of British hold over India through a division of the sub-continent into three independent constituents under British hegemony in one form or another. It was called imperial strategy.

Churchill agreed with Wavell that the Congress, under the influence of a pro-Soviet Nehru, was "unlikely to cooperate with Britain in military matters and foreign policy", whereas the Muslim League would be "willing to do so".[2] Western Pakistan would, therefore, agree to have "defence ties with Britain"[3] for her control over borders with Afghanistan and Russia. For effective implementation of such policy, it was considered imperative to create a Pakistan that would have "political stability" and "economic viability" through a larger, untruncated Pakistan. The two Pakistans were to be complementary to each other: the east economically strong; the west militarily. This was to serve, essentially, British interests in the north-west. Equally so, between Baluchistan and Chittagong on either ends, the British would have maintained the Indian Ocean as a zone of peace under their control. All this was part of imperial strategy.

The British had decided on Pakistan's creation earlier in 1942. On 2 March, the secretary of state, Amery, wrote to A. Harding: "Here is the Document as drafted by the India Committee under Attlee's chairmanship . . . what Linlithgow* and I were agreed upon in July 1940 . . . This is the first public admission of the possibility of Pakistan, i.e. an India divided between the Muslim and Hindu parties."[4] Further, on 24 March, Amery wrote to Linlithgow: "Jinnah, I should have thought, will be content to realise that he has now got Pakistan in essence, whether as something substantial or as a beginning point."[5]

Partition of India was, thus, part of the imperial strategy Churchill had ordered to be prepared immediately on the surrender of Germany on 5 May 1945. It was to meet the grave apprehensions Russia was causing. Stalin had earlier told Hitler's foreign minister, Ribbentrop, that it was "ridiculous that a few hundred Englishmen should dominate India". And Churchill had concurred with his chief of staff, Ismay, that "if we evacuate India, nothing would remain to prevent Russian infiltration".[6] Churchill's "long-term policy required to safeguard the strategic interests of the British

---

Linlithgow's support for Pakistan came four months after the Lahore Resolution on Pakistan on 23 March 1940.

Empire in India and the Indian Ocean".[7] Russia had come to be looked upon as "our most probable potential enemy".[8]

Britain's first priority was defence of India's western and north-western borders, adjoining Afghanistan and Russia. The former through Pakistan presented no problem, as Pakistan was totally dependent on Britain in military matters. The latter posed a problem, as the territory was part of the Kashmir state, whose Hindu Maharaja, the British feared, might accede to India. They played a clever ruse through the Gilgit Scouts, who were British and who contolled the region. On 30 July 1947, when India and Pakistan were yet to become independent, all the British officers of the Gilgit Scouts "opted to serve Pakistan"; on 31 October 1947, the Gilgit Scouts installed a provisional government; on 4 November, Major Brown "hoisted the Pakistan flag in the lines of his command; and on 12 November, an official styling himself as political agent arrived from Pakistan and established himself in Gilgit".[9]

Implementation of imperial strategy comprised: a) reinforcing defence installations on Pakistan's north-western borders; b) "detaching Baluchistan from India" for purposes of developing the Indian Ocean as a zone of peace; c) ensuring fuel supplies for naval vessels in the Indian Ocean, for which purpose Mountbatten had proposed to the foreign oil companies operating in India to consider the building of two oil refineries, one each on the west and the east coasts of India; d) a common governor-general for India and Pakistan for effective coordination and control of the sub-continent; and e) an undivided army under the command of a British supreme commander in order to keep effective power in British hands.

The imperial strategy did not take off. Patel was the first to kill it by not allowing the British to arbitrarily hand over to Jinnah the whole of Punjab and Bengal. Jinnah was the second killer. In his greed for power and status, he refused to accept a common governor-general for India and Pakistan, and an undivided army under a British supreme commander. No less a contributory factor was Churchill's exit as prime minister on losing the election. Attlee, his successor, lacked the force of his personality: the courage, the tenacity, and the daredevilry of the bulldog that Churchill possessed.

Partition of India was, therefore, a Churchillian plan. Jinnah was its implementor. There were "confidential" Churchill-Jinnah links before India's independence.[10] As part of his imperial strategy, Churchill had even directed Jinnah's role at the Simla Conference in June-July 1945. Jinnah had wrecked the conference, confessing to Durga Das of the *Statesman*: "Am I a fool to accept this [compromise], when I am offered Pakistan on a platter?" He seemed to have been told that if he "stepped out of the talks, he would be rewarded with Pakistan".[11]

Wavell was Churchill's hatchet man. It was he who gave shape to the Churchillian plan at the Simla Conference, leading ultimately to the break-up of India, as Churchill desired, into Hindustan and Pakistan. It was Patel who did not allow the creation of Princestan. Against heavy odds, Wavell built Jinnah's position, as Churchill desired, both at the provincial and all-India levels. Since Punjab held the key to the creation of Pakistan, Wavell caused the demise of the powerful Muslim-dominated Unionist Party, which had ruled over the province successfully since 1926 in collaboration with Hindus and Sikhs.

For Jinnah's all-India spokesmanship of the Muslims, Wavell held the general elections by the year-end: just six months after the termination of the war, without updating the voters' list and allowing the Congress leaders time for preparations. They had been in prison for nearly 3 years since August 1942. They were totally out of touch with the voters and the world outside. Wavell even tacitly allowed Jinnah to appeal to the Muslim voters in the name of Islam. A former governor of Punjab, Bertrand Glancy, warned of "a very serious danger of the elections being fought, so far as Muslims are concerned, on an entirely false issue . . . The uninformed Muslim will be told that the question he is called on to answer at the polls is: are you a true believer or an infidel and a traitor?"[12] By not boycotting the communally-surcharged elections, the Congress helped Jinnah move faster towards his goal of Pakistan than he would otherwise have.

Partition would have foundered on what was most dear to the Punjabi Muslims: their united Punjab. According to Ayesha Jalal, "once Punjabi Muslims realised" that Partition meant partition of their province, they would "think twice before blindly following Jinnah".[13] Not to let that happen, and at the same time smoothen Jinnah's path, an undivided Punjab was conceived to be part of both the Cabinet Mission plan of May 1946 and Attlee's policy statement of 20 February 1947.

The Simla Conference, held in June-July 1945, laid the foundation for Jinnah's rise as the sole spokesman of the Muslims through two steps: first, by bringing Punjab under Jinnah's control; and second, in securing equality of status for the League with the Congress through parity between the caste Hindus and Muslims. That built the latter's faith in Jinnah even when he did not enjoy the provincial leaders' confidence and their support. Jinnah received added strength with Congress president Azad's tacit acceptance of parity. The Congress failed to realise that parity would, in the end, lead to Partition. It was far more pernicious than separate representation granted to the Muslims under the Morley-Minto Reforms of 1909.

When Jinnah faced a challenge to his authority to nominate Muslims on the viceroy's proposed Executive Council, he appealed to Wavell: "I am at the end of my tether . . . I ask you not to wreck the League." The challenge came from powerful non-League Muslims including not only the prime ministers of the NWFP and Punjab—Dr. Khan Sahib and Khizar Hyat Khan Tiwana—but also independent influencial Muslims like Sultan Ahmed and others. They shared former Punjab premier Sikander Hyat Khan's vision for his province: "If Pakistan meant Muslim raj in Punjab, he would have nothing to do with it. He wanted a free Punjab in which all communities would share self-government."[14] In 1945, Sikander Hyat Khan was no more to oppose Jinnah.

Wavell responded to Jinnah's call by taking two steps, both drastic and arbitrary. He called off the Simla conference. H. V. Hodson, a former reforms commissioner, called it "a capitulation to Jinnah", and opined: "If the Viceroy had been as adamant as Jinnah, the latter would have obliged himself to give in . . . Jinnah's control of the Muslim League was at that time far from complete . . . There were still many uncommitted Muslims in the country."[15] Wavell's second step, in refusing a Muslim nominee of the Unionist Party on his proposed Executive Council, resulted in "the destruction of the Unionist Party, which paved the way for partition of Punjab".[16] Jinnah's solid position, nevertheless, depended on the Muslim voters. At the elections held by the end of 1945, the League won every Muslim seat in the Central Legislature, and 442 out of 509 Muslim seats in the eleven provinces combined.

The Simla Conference had opened the doors for Jinnah to move towards Pakistan, while the general elections had put a stamp on his total support of the Muslims on an all-India basis. Six months later, in May 1946, the Cabinet Mission plan virtually granted Jinnah his Pakistan in Groups B and C: Punjab, the NWFP, and Sind in Group B; Bengal and Assam in Group C. It was under the fictitious concept of keeping India united. Jinnah seemed satisfied, as he was getting Hindu Assam and non-Muslim East Punjab and West Bengal. In the federal structure envisaged, Jinnah would have dominated India with the support of pro-League Muslims in India—the vanguard of Jinnah's fight for Pakistan. As later events proved, Jinnah would have mustered support of some of the Indian princes through horse-trading. Congress rejection of the plan shattered his dream. A deeply frustrated Jinnah called on the Muslims, on 30 July 1946, to launch "Direct Action" in his declaration: "This day we bid goodbye to constitutional methods . . . Today we have also forged a pistol and we are in a position to use it."[17]

The British-owned and edited *Statesman* of Kolkata called Jinnah's "war" the "Great Calcutta Killing". A year later it turned into the "Rape of Rawalpindi", called so by a leading Punjab Youth Congress leader and member of the Punjab Legislative Assembly, Probodh Chandra. Both happenings were gruesome tales of sadistic carnage and butchery.

In Kolkata, the first to answer Jinnah's call was the Bengal premier, H. S. Suhrawardy, with twin objectives: to terrorise the Hindus and force them to leave Kolkata; and to fill their places by arranging migration of Bihari Muslims to Kolkata and thereby turn the city into Muslim majority, and claim it as part of Pakistan.

The "Great Calcutta Killing" was an unimaginable tragedy. "An orgy of killing, loot and arson, incredible in its manifestation of communal savagery and hatred: corpses piled one on top of the other like corn sacks in a railway yard, headless bodies sprawled on the streets, walls bespattered with blood everywhere, shops broken open and rifled, cars burnt without intervention of the police . . . the streets flowed with blood."[18] Much to Suhrawardy's utter disappointment, of around 6,000 killed, more than 4,500 were Muslims.

Further, the *Statesman* considered the happenings

the worst communal rioting in India's history—a political demonstration by the Muslim League . . . This is not a riot. It needs a word found in mediaeval history: a fury . . . there must have been some deliberation and organisation to set this fury on the way. Hordes, who ran about battering and killing with eight-foot lathis . . . bands found it easy to get petrol and vehicles when no others were permitted on the streets. It is not mere supposition that men were imported into Calcutta . . . On all sides are death, injury and destruction. Houses have been destroyed with men, women and children in them. Men have returned home in the evening to find neither wife nor children. The homeless are lying about unsheltered and starving along the streets, in any open space, wherever they can find room or a little hospitality. Some who gave shelter to the homeless have been dragged out and bludgeoned for doing it . . . Thousands are brutally hurt. Smashed jaws, burst eyes, fractured limbs.[19]

To avenge his failure, Suhrawardy carried the "war" to Noakhali and Tipura in East Bengal. Nehru called this "mass slaughter . . . far worse than the Calcutta killings". East Bengal happenings set a chain reaction. The Muslim League's communal war travelled to Bhagalpur in Bihar, to Gharmukhteshwar in Uttar Pradesh, and, in its final phase, to Punjab and the NWFP.

Jinnah's silence was taken as his approval of such an orgy of violence. But inflammatory speeches by his chief lieutenants worked up the passion and greed of the Muslims. Suhrawardy had threatened: "Let the Congress beware that it is not going to fight just a handful of people fighting for power but a nation which is struggling for its life."

In Punjab, the Nawab of Mamdot declared: "I ask the Mussalmans to be prepared . . . if there were to be a war, we shall accept the challenge." The most provocative was Firoz Khan Noon, a former member of the viceroy's Executive Council, who called upon Muslims to outshine Genghis Khan and Halakku. That let loose genocide in West Punjab: large-scale murder, arson, loot, and, most tragic, rape and abduction of women and young girls. Nehru, who visited some of the affected areas, was appalled by "ghastly sights", and "heard of behaviour of human beings which would degrade brutes". The British deputy inspector-general of police, Rawalpindi Range, J. A. Scott, admitted: "I could never believe that such barbarous acts as were committed on innocent people in rural areas of Rawalpindi district could be possible in Punjab." Home secretary to the Punjab government A. A. MacDonald admitted that it was all pre-planned. Mobs of a few thousand, armed with sten-guns and Bren-guns and led by demobbed military personnel, attacked defenceless Hindus and Sikhs in remote, isolated villages.

What was the genesis of the genocide in Punjab? Penderel Moon (ICS), a senior British bureaucrat from Punjab, thought that since Jinnah could never make his "planned exchange of population a live issue", it was considered that "brute force or overwhelming fear would drive non-Muslims to leave their ancestral homes . . . to make room for incoming Muslims".[20] Jinnah feared that the strong, sturdy, virile Sikh colonists from Central Punjab would be a stumbling block, and could be made to leave through the use of force. Sikander Hyat had told Moon as early as 1937: "Pakistan would mean a massacre."[21] That took place a decade later in 1947.

I personally witnessed Lahore's fate hanging in the balance from May onwards. Many localities were under siege—some under 72-hour curfew. At night, from our terraces, we witnessed, in mute silence, the horizon lit up by red fire; by day it turned into thick black smoke darkening the skyline. In June, in a single night, in a locality, Shahalami, 200 houses were set on fire. Not to let the residents escape, curfew was imposed. Death faced them grimly. A senior government official, who ventured to come out on duty, was shot dead. To their rescue came Dogra troops who happened to be on their routine round. The residents were carried in their trucks to the safety of a newly opened refugee camp.

Thereafter, panic spread fast. Fear gripped our minds with increasing intensity. 13 August proved the worst. Murder, arson, loot reached "a new peak". A desperate people began leaving their houses quickly and unnoticed, escaping detection. Suddenly my locality too looked deserted. Looming large was the rumour of an attack by hooligans. I locked my house and moved to a safer place, a hotel near my office—the *Civil & Military Gazette*—where I worked as a journalist and was required to report at seven o'clock every morning for the newspaper to come out on time under disturbed conditions. I never thought of leaving Lahore. It was unacceptable to me. For Jinnah's surprisingly most secular broadcast on 11 August had assured the non-Muslims of peace and equal status as citizens of Pakistan. Conditions, nevertheless, went on worsening. I left Lahore, hopeful of an early return to unlock my house as soon as conditions settled down. That day never came. I was, like others, thrown into

permanent exile. Lahore became a distant dream for me. I
had lived there for as many as 28 years from my childhood.

General K. S. Thimayya, India's nominee on the Boundary
Force, had a most traumatic experience. One night his sleep
was disturbed by a dreadful dream. He recounts that he saw
"Sheikhupura in flames" and he could "hear the cries of the
dying". In his words: "Nothing like this ever happened to me
before or since". He felt restless, and could not go back to
sleep. By 3 a.m. he and his party headed west. As he
approached Sheikhupura, "the town smelled of smoke . . .
we heard machine-gun fire . . . The street was lined with shops
which had been owned by the Hindus. Every shop had been
smashed open and looted . . . The street itself was strewn
with hundreds of bodies . . . Many seemed to have been
chopped with axes. Women had their breasts cut off; children
murdered as brutally as the adults . . . Police and army men
were firing on helpless civilians. Bullets zipped over my head,
but I ducked and raced on through without being hit."[22]

Thimayya launched a search for those who had survived.
They were found hiding in a school, in a gurdwara, and in a
mosque (where a mullah had hidden about a hundred people
at great personal risk). They were driven to Lahore to join
the long march to India, which Thimayya called "the largest
mass movement in history". Thimayya has written:

Most refugees walked. An average foot convoy
comprised 150,000 people and clogged a road for
20 miles . . . The danger of epidemics terrified us.
The question of water and food kept us awake . . . The
construction of camps . . . was a never-ending problem.
One never knew whether to stretch the insufficient
supplies between a hundred, a thousand or a million
people . . .

Most of all, the refugees needed hope; few knew anything but the horror of the past, and all were nearly insane with fear for the future. The seriously ill had to be given treatment. Orphans had to be cared for. And always there was the problem of disposal of the dead . . . They died of exhaustion, exposure, disease, malnutrition, thirst, and, most of all, they were slaughtered by gangs of opposing religious groups.[23]

A sea of humanity was on the move; that too, on foot, braving many hardships and dangers. Luckier ones—in their thousands too—came by rail in jam-packed compartments, some sitting on open tops in sun, wind or rain, and some even hanging dangerously from the sides of compartments, holding on to whatever their hands could clutch. It was Patel who had realised more than others the need for "timely assistance to escape from sad and almost desperate plight". He lost no time in impressing upon the railway minister, John Mathai: "It must be borne in mind that evacuation must claim prior and sole attention during the present emergency."[24]

Patel's next anxiety was even more daunting: cooling down people's boiling tempers, and stopping retaliatory killings, so as to pull out, at the earliest, those stranded in West Punjab and beyond. He visited Amritsar on 30 September and made "a big speech to what was perhaps the most representative gathering of Sikh leaders since the transfer of power. Nearly all the Jathedars had been present, and had responded favourably to his call for moderation".[25]

It did not take long for the refugees to overcome the past by settling down in their new homes and professions. Credit for that should be shared equally by the government and the refugees: the former for providing opportunities for training and rehabilitation; the latter for grasping them with extraordinary speed to learn and to resettle themselves. As proud people, the Punjabis believed in self-help: to earn through their sweat, toil, and tears. One could not see a Punjabi beggar in the streets of the capital. The best showpiece of their endeavours is the row of refugee shops on Janpath in New Delhi—neat, clean, with a variety of quality products that attract even foreign visitors to New Delhi. Moon, who knew the Punjabis intimately, has written:

> If the massacres of 1947 showed the Punjabis at their worst, the enforced migration brought out some of the best of their qualities. The fortitude with which they bore the sudden uprooting from their homes and the vigour with which they set about establishing themselves in new ones were such as few other peoples could have equalled. They showed all the cheerful vitality of birds which, when robbed of their nest, will start immediately to build a fresh one. The conditions were harsh, but not too harsh to suppress or even check the surge of life in these sturdy, virile people.[26]

It was the enactment of a great human drama, in the success of which the locals played a notable role: laudable for their spirit of tolerance and accommodation. It was no less than a miracle, which can be described best by borrowing an analogy from nature. The refugee-influx into India was like a stone flung into a large tank, creating ripples that started disappearing one after another in quick succession and in no time got dissolved into the whole expanse of water. In the same way ended the refugees' separateness. They became one with the rest—indivisible as Indians, whether in Maharashtra, Tamil Nadu, or Assam.

One painful thought ever troubled their minds: their women and daughters whom they left behind under forced conditions. What fate had the living ones suffered? The women were the worst sufferers. Abduction figures were only estimates: nearly 50,000 from a few districts of West Punjab. Their plight was pitiable, heart-breaking. They were defenceless victims of brute force: abducted, raped and sold in a sex-starved market—in some cases changing hands from person to person. Yet, some saved their honour in a burning fire, some jumped into wells, and some welcomed being hacked to death by the sword of their equally brave menfolk. Their number may not be large but their sacrifices were acts of heroism, unparalleled in the annals of history.

Mridula Sarabhai, daughter of Ahmedabad's leading industrialist, Ambalal Sarabhai, worked in West Punjab, along with other equally brave women, on abducted women rescue work. It was "a heart-rending experience to hear them talk to each other . . . as woman to woman, baffled, humiliated, stunned, and full of doubts for the future".[27] With a heavy heart and lost hope, a forlorn abducted woman lamented: "What is left in me now—religion or chastity?"[28]

Many Indians have continued to express the thought long after independence: if only Patel had lived a little longer! Some, however, pertinently ask: Could Patel have averted India's partition? Possibly so, they believe, if Patel had held the reins of the Congress at the Simla Conference in 1945, been vice-president in the interim government in 1946, and become India's first prime minister in 1947. Patel had told General Roy Bucher, commander-in-chief of the Indian Army, that "if he had sensed what tragedies would result from Partition, he would never have agreed to it".[29]

Jayaprakash Narayan stated: "If Sardar Patel, and not Pandit Nehru, had been the first Prime Minister of India, maybe, Partition of the country could have been averted."[30] Judging by Patel's past, JP's comment was not an underestimate. Patel was confident of derailing Jinnah's bandwagon, and preventing it from reaching its destination—Pakistan. At Karachi, in January 1946, Patel had nearly done that! The 1945 provincial election results were for him "most encouraging". Jinnah had failed to secure an absolute majority in the Sind legislature. In a house of 60, the League had won 27 seats against the Congress' 22. The remaining 11 provided Patel easy manoeuvrability to gain the upper hand to form a non-League ministry. He had nearly succeeded. At such a crucial moment, Azad, as president, threw a spanner in the works by coming to Jinnah's rescue—like Wavell at the Simla Conference—by cancelling Patel's political alignments, unmindful of the consequences, which paved the way for Pakistan's creation.

Allah Bux, a leading politician from Sind, was to ink a deal with Jinnah. From Mumbai, Patel had pulled strings, and "much to the astonishment of everyone, Allah Bux backed out of the agreement". To a "shocked" Jinnah, he was "in the hands of the Congress party". For Jinnah, records Stanley Wolpert, "it was a most bitter pill to swallow. He had laboured long and hard for an independent province of Sind . . . the Sardar . . . had snatched this plum from Jinnah's lips just as he was about to savour its sweetness".[31] For Patel, the situation in Punjab was no different. Premier Khizar Hyat Khan Tiwana, being anti-Jinnah, could have easily turned the situation in his favour. But, because of Azad, Patel decided not to go to Punjab.

The other two Muslim leaders in Sind who mattered were G. M. Syed and Ghulam Hussain Hidayatullah. Both were closer to Patel than to Jinnah. In defiance of Jinnah, Syed had demanded "self-determination to establish a Sindhi Pakistan without interference from the League High Command".[32] Hidayatullah too was out of Jinnah's reach. He had proceeded on tour when Jinnah arrived at his residence to stay with him as his guest. Earlier, in 1936, he had defied Jinnah by forming a Hindu-Muslim coalition. In 1946, he held out a promise to Patel that if made premier, he would not only accept Congress nomination, but would help bury Pakistan in Karachi. This would have killed Jinnah's chances of having an all-exclusive Muslim Pakistan. Hindu-Muslim unity was anathema to him. In his capacity as Congress president, Azad preferred a coalition with the League, following his preliminary talks with the Sind League president, M. H. Gazdar, while travelling by plane to Karachi, without Jinnah's prior consent.

That was Patel's last manoeuvre. His failure was not at the hands of Jinnah, but Azad, his party president. Patel was, as Mountbatten called him, "a stern realist"; one, according to Vinoba Bhave, who "knew no retreat". As a bold pragmatist, he changed his course of action to save India in two ways: first, by not letting Jinnah run away with the whole of Punjab and Bengal, together with Assam; second, by not allowing the British to create too many ulcers in India through independent confederations of princely states. His achievement lay in preventing the total balkanisation of India. He wrote to Frank Moraes, a leading Indian journalist, on 22 May 1947: "We are fighting with our backs to the wall against a mighty power armed to the teeth." And to G. S. Bozman (ICS) he wrote on 11 July 1947: "I fully appreciate your reasons for disliking the decision to divide India. Frankly speaking, we all hate it, but at the same time we see no way out of it. We nurse the hope that one day Pakistan will come back to us."

Sarojini Naidu told Sir Stafford Cripps, "When it came to getting things done, Patel was the really effective leader of the Congress."[33] Wavell could not have formed the interim government without Patel's support, which he had sought on his own. Mountbatten too depended on Patel in the expeditious division of assets and liabilities between India and Pakistan. This was most crucial. Without it, transfer of power could not have taken place on the due date—15 August. Mountbatten thought of Patel as "the one man I had regarded as a real statesman with both feet firmly on the ground, and a man of honour whose word was his bond".[34] Even Wavell admitted: "Patel is the recognised 'tough' of the Congress Working Committee, and by far the most forcible character among them. I have a good deal more respect for him than for most of the Congress leaders."[35] Patel's "toughness" alone could have given the malevolent Jinnah and the scheming British tough times, and thereby, possibly, not let the Congress suffer a humiliating defeat in its failure to avert the partition of India.

In the normal, democractic process, Patel ought to have become India's first prime minister but for Gandhi's uncalled for intervention in proposing Nehru's exclusive name for presidentship of the Congress at the working committee meeting in November 1946. This was in spite of the fact that 12 out of 15 pradesh Congress committees had supported Patel. None had favoured Nehru. Gandhi's intervention tilted the scales in Nehru's favour. Congress general secretary J. B. Kripalani later regretted:

I sent a paper round proposing the name of Jawaharlal . . . It was certain that if Jawaharlal's name had not been proposed, the Sardar would have been elected as the President [by virtue of that India's first prime minister] . . . I have since wondered if, as the General

, Secretary, I should have been instrumental in proposing
Jawaharlal's name in deference to Gandhi's wishes . . .
But who can forecast the future? On such seemingly
_ trivial accidents depends the fate of men and even
of nations.[36]

Whoever became president of the Congress was to be
India's first prime minister. Patel was, naturally, much hurt.
In the final hour of the freedom struggle, ending up in the
transfer of power in 1947, Patel missed scaling the summit.
Yet, as a disciplined Congressman, he accepted Gandhi's
decision stoically, and gave his country his best in the creation
of a strong, united India, and took legitimate pride in saying:
"Had anyone dreamt a year or two ago that a third of India
would be integrated in this fashion? This is the first time in
history after centuries that India can call itself an integrated
whole in the real sense of the term."[37] M. N. Roy's tribute to
Patel was most deserving: "When the future is bleak, one
naturally turns to the past, and Sardar Patel can be proud of
his past."[38]

What was Patel's past? As Gandhi often admitted, he was
a pillar of strength to him in his satyagrahas, and a party leader
who built party solidarity that even Subhash Chandra Bose
could not shake. His creation of a single all-India civil service
ensured the country's unity by binding together 28 states; and
his integration of over 560 princely states created One India.
He was Chanakya and Bismarck at the same time; soft or
stern, whichever the situation demanded and whatever served
the country's interests best. He scored over the latter in his
bloodless revolution. He was far from cunning; ever truthful,
gentle, and accommodating.

, What was Vallabhbhai? That has been answered, briefly,
at the start of the book. Now, at its end, this may be
elaborated in the words of J. R. D. Tata:

Vallabhbhai Patel was the one with whom I felt most in tune, and for whom I developed the greatest personal admiration and respect. While I was awed by his formidable political and administrative talents, the source of which was difficult to understand in a man of his background, one could not but be enormously impressed by the clarity of his mind and the simple good sense and logic with which he addressed and solved seemingly intractable problems.

While I usually came back from meeting Gandhiji elated and inspired but always a bit sceptical, and from talks with Jawaharlal fired with emotional zeal but often confused and unconvinced, meetings with Vallabhbhai were a joy from which I returned with renewed confidence in the future of our country. I have often thought that if fate had decreed that he, instead of Jawaharlal, would be the younger of the two, India would have followed a very different path and would be in better economic shape than it is today.[39]

10

WAS KASHMIR SOLD TO GULAB SINGH?

Exploding the Myth

Sheikh Abdullah never lost an opportunity to repeat a myth that the British had sold Kashmir to Maharaja Gulab Singh, the Dogra ruler from Jammu. His malevolence lay in telling the Kashmiri Muslims that they had suffered from the slavery of the Dogras from Jammu, and that Maharaja Hari Singh was an alien, not a son of the soil, and had no right to rule over them. The Sheikh, therefore, demanded of the Maharaja to leave the state bag and baggage. This was revival of his "Quit Kashmir" demand of 1946. He finally succeeded in the expulsion of the Maharaja from the state, including Jammu, with Nehru's blind support.

The manner and extent of such support has never been explained. It was unconstitutional on at least three grounds: First, the Indian Independence Act of the British parliament, under which Britain had transferred power to India and Pakistan, had also given the Indian princes the right to accede to India or Pakistan, or to choose to remain independent so as to join the "Third Dominion" the British wanted to create.

Second: India's presence in the valley was only after the Maharaja had acceded to India. It would not have been possible in the absence of it. Abdullah refused to admit that. Third: the Maharaja was entitled to be treated on par with other princes.

In 1846, with the signing of the Treaties of Lahore and Amritsar, British conquest of northern India was complete. Consolidation of the gains had yet to be undertaken. This seemed more difficult than the military victory—in Kashmir particularly, being isolated from rest of the country. The territory was far-flung, rugged, and not easily accessible. There were high mountains and deep valleys to traverse, a diverse and alien people, and a hostile climate. The British needed the support of a strong, realiable local chieftain to keep under control such strategic areas as Ladakh, adjoining China in the north-east, and Balistan and Gilgit, bordering Russia, in the north-west. Kashmir presented a problem far more difficult and complex than any other state of the empire in India.

The British choice for a chieftain fell on one of Maharaja Ranjit Singh's ablest generals, Gulab Singh, a Dogra from Jammu, to whom Ranjit Singh had granted a number of estates, including Jammu, for conquering many hostile regions, among them Ladakh and Kashmir. Ranjit Singh had elevated him to the status of a raja. The British found their interests "bound up together" with him.[1] Gulab Singh, on his part, had "nicely calculated the precise moment for abandoning the cause to which he owed all his fortune".[2] By way of a reward, the British "promoted that soldier of fortune to the throne in exchange for 75 lakhs of rupees"[3]—a *nazarana* which Abdullah too paid, as per old practice, to Maharaja Hari Singh, on his release from prison in 1947.

The *Times of India* (1886) referred to the Treaty of Amritsar and wrote: "The British Government transfers and makes over

FROM THE 𝕿𝖎𝖒𝖊𝖘 ARCHIVES

MAY 12, 1886

THE PRINCELY THRONE
OF KASHMERE

The Maharajah of Kashmere died eight months ago and on Monday last his son was formally installed on the *gadi* the season of the year was, as His Highness said, "inconvenient ," for it was impossible at the height of the hot weather to dispense the princely hospitality that marked the installations of the Gaekwar of Baroda and the Nizam of Hyderabad. It is difficult to explain the delay in the ceremonial, for as a matter of fact there had been no interregnum. The son succeeded the father at once, and nothing was needed, but the imperial *khillut*

It had indeed been rumoured that many changes would be insisted upon by the government before the *khillut* of investiture with the territories of Kashmere and Jummu was granted, and this was supposed to account for the delay. Nothing, however, of this sort has been attempted. The family originally paid a good round sum to be put on the throne, and they still hold it for the nominal yearly tribute of 'one horse, twelve perfect shawl goats of approved breed — six male and six female — and three pairs of Kashmere shawls. Still the delay must have a meaning of some sort, and it may be that the government of India is just now too busy to have time for any further schemes about the extension of British supremacy. It has been the fashion to suspect the loyalty of Kashmere, chiefly, we imagine, because the Russian frontier line lies just beyod its boundary over a belt of narrow but inaccessible mountains. As a sober matter of fact, however, the reigning family owe everything to the British who placed them there and maintain them there at the head of an alien population. Our interests are bound up together, and their engagements have been most loyally fulfilled ever since 1846 when we prqmoted that soldier of fortune,

Gulab Singh, to the throne in exchange for 75 lakhs of rupees.

The offer was very simply put. Could he find the money, "the British government transfers and makes over for ever, in independent possession, to Maharajah Gulab Singh and his male heirs all the hilly or mountainous country, situated to the eastward of the river Indus and westward of the river Ravee". The ceremony that was so quietly performed on Monday by the new Resident, Mr T.C. Plowden, is another proof, if further proof were needed, of the good faith with which all our treaties are now carried out.

We have seen this of late in Mysore, Kolhapur and Baroda. If there was any hesitation about Kashmere it was probably due to its delightful and salubrious climate, and to a not unnatural desire to extend the terms of the original treaties by opening the country to Europeans as a health resort. Moses, it is said, went there to die and Solomon to recruit, and many Indian statesmen have dreamt of starting a real English colony among its beautiful hills. However, as no change has been made, it is idle to discuss the probability of any change ever having been contemplated.

The Maharajah on his side seems to have done his duty, and something more in his eight months of probation. He has, as he told us in the speech telegraphed by our correspondent, already marked out the lines of his subjects.

1927

for ever, in independent possession, to Maharaja Gulab Singh and his male heirs all the hilly or mountainous country, situated to the eastward of the river Indus and westward of the river Ravee."[4] What did the words "independent possession" convey? In law, "possession" means "actual holding or occupancy, either with or without rights of ownership".[5] The treaty, thus, meant no more than "handing over of Kashmir to"[6] the Dogra chief of Jammu, Gulab Singh, for ruling on their behalf.

Parting with "rights of ownership" would have undermined the interests of the empire. If no other Indian state enjoyed such rights, how could Kashmir? This would have been contrary to Wellesley's policy of subsidiary alliances. "Independence", on the other hand, meant giving Gulab Singh full freedom to rule in the far-flung regions of the empire which the British themselves could not directly and effectively rule. It was explained: "The Government of India is just now too busy to have time for any further schemes about the extension of British supremacy."[7]

As paramount power, the British had posted a resident in Kashmir, under whose surveillance the Maharaja ruled. The resident's writ prevailed in all matters, even relating to succession to the throne. On the demise of Maharaja Ranbir Singh in 1885, the installation of a new Maharaja was delayed by as many as eight months. It took place in May 1886. The reason offered was unconvincing: it was said to be "inconvenient" because of "the height of the hot weather to dispense the Princely hospitability". Weather was a mere excuse. The *Times of India* (1886) wrote: "It is difficult to explain the delay in the ceremonial, for, as a matter of fact, there had been no interregnum. The son succeeded the father at once, and nothing was needed, but the imperial *khillut*."[8]

In the 1880s, the British were worried about new developments across the state's borders with Russia. The

FROM THE Times ARCHIVES

4 October 1889

RUSSIAN APPREHENSIONS RESPECTING CASHMERE.

THE article in the *Novoe Vremya* on this subject, which was thought sufficiently important for a notice in the European telegrams, is as follows:—

"The rumours regarding the intentions of the Salisbury Ministry to incorporate Cashmere in the Indian dominions of the Queen-Empress Victoria are beginning to be realised in spite of all the former denials of the Government.

"Anyone acquainted with the history of the constitution of the British possessions in India as they now exist can only smile, of course, on reading this announcement. In Cashmere is now being repeated to the letter the very same process which has attended the entire series of English seizures of territory in India. The Cabinet of St. James's does not even put itself to the trouble of varying the methods by the aid of which all these annexations have been accomplished. Everywhere and at all times is repeated one and the same tale, which every Anglo-Indian bureaucrat knows by heart, and which, we are told, is gradually bringing about the intellectual development of the natives. The affair begins with a disagreement between 'the native ruler' and the English 'resident' who receives at particular moment instructions from Calcutta to conduct himself in the most provocative manner towards the vassal or the 'friendly' ruler over whom he has been placed for the purpose of surveillance. As soon as misunderstandings have been thus established and have reached the required degree of tension, a rumour is let out that the native ruler has concocted a plot to 'put an end to' the British Resident by means of poison or some other murderous contrivance. For the most part these rumours are devoid of any foundation in fact. The 'ruler' is almost always found to have councillors who incite him to believe that the course of action of the British Resident springs from purely 'personal' motives and not from the instructions of the British Government: so that if the ruler were to rid himself of a disagreeable supervisor he might confidently expect the deputation of a less hostile Resident to his Court. The native sovereigns of India have long been prone to readily listen to such counsels: so a *corpus delicti* is quickly created, and an informant appears at the precise moment at which he may be required with the necessary revelations. The detected ruler is then threatened with severe measures, and he thereupon 'sends in his resignation' in order to avoid the bitter fate which he has so richly deserved, and then they either put in his place some kind of unknown infant, as happened at Baroda, or they make over the administration of the country to a council of natives. In either case the British Resident appears upon the scene as the ruler of the country *de facto*. Affairs now go on so badly for the native inhabitants that they begin a little to even desire the substitution of English authority for their new rulers. The change is accordingly made one fine day without fuss, almost without the knowledge even of the people themselves and with the full complacency of Europe at large. It may, therefore, be confidently foretold that all this procedure will be repeated in the case of Cashmere, which country is evidently doomed to become a new province of British India.

Times of India reported in a headline: "Russian apprehensions respecting Cashmere." In view of such grave developments, the British, apparently, wanted to change Kashmir's status. The report in the *Times of India* (1889) disclosed: "It may be confidently foretold that . . . Cashmere . . . is evidently doomed to become a new province of British India."[9]

The amount of Rs. 75 lakh that Gulab Singh paid to the British was not for a sell-out, but "a tribute" (*nazarana*) that Indian princes paid to the paramount power under Wellesley's policy of "subsidiary alliances", which guaranteed help in defence in difficult circumstances. It "irrevocably attached" the princes to the paramount power, and "any hope of escape was idle".[10] The British, thus, did not sell Kashmir to Gulab Singh, but perforce allowed the Dogra dynasty to rule over Jammu and Kashmir on their behalf on par with the Nizam of Hyderabad and other Indian princes.

The malicious falsehood of Abdullah's hypocritical utterances is proved untrue by the Treaty of Amritsar in Articles 3, 4, and 9. As per Article 3, the payment of Rs. 75 lakh was "in consideration of the transfer made to him and his heirs" of the Kashmir territories. According to Article 4, "the limits of the territories of Maharaja Gulab Singh shall not be at any time changed without concurrence of the British Government". Article 9 maintains supremacy of paramount power by conceding what it had to other princes under Wellesly's "subsidiary alliances": "The British Government will give its aid to Maharaja Gulab Singh in protecting his territories from external enemies." That is what Wellesley had offered to other princes earlier. Gulab Singh was as much subsidiary to the British as were other members of the princely order.

Paramountcy was always supreme, then or later, in all circumstances. Lord Reading had bluntly told the Nizam in March 1926, "The sovereignty of the British Crown is supreme in India, and, therefore, no Ruler of an Indian State can justifiably claim to negotiate with the British Government on equal footing."[11] Nor could the British administrators in India "sell" sovereignty to any ruler under any circumstance. Gulab Singh could be no exception.

11

PLEBISCITE IN KASHMIR

Mountbatten's Offer to Jinnah

Note of a Discussion with Mr. Jinnah in the presence of Lord Ismay at Government House, Lahore, on 1 November 1947.

In the course of 3½ hours of the most arduous and concentrated conversation, Kashmir took up most of the time; Junagadh took next place and Hyderabad the least. We darted about between these three subjects as well as talking about the overall policy affecting States. I have divided this note into four parts, although this was not necessarily the order in which the subjects were discussed, nor, of course, were all the remarks made consecutively.

Part I: India's Policy towards States Whose Accession Was in Dispute

I pointed out the similarity between the cases of Junagadh and Kashmir and suggested that plebiscites should be held under UNO as soon as conditions permitted. I told Mr. Jinnah that I had drafted out in the aeroplane a formula which I had not yet shown to my Government but to which I thought they might agree. This was the formula:

> The Governments of India and Pakistan agree that, where the ruler of a State does not belong to the community to which the majority of his subjects belong, and where the State has not acceded to that Dominion whose majority community is the same as the State's, the question of whether the State should finally accede to one or the other of the Dominions should in all cases be decided by an impartial reference to the will of the people.

Mr. Jinnah's first observation was that it was redundant and undesirable to have a plebiscite when it was quite clear that States should go according to their majority population, and if we would give him the accession of Kashmir he would offer to urge the accession of Junagadh direct to India.

I told him that my Government would never agree to changing the accession of a State against the wishes of the ruler or the Government that made the accession unless a plebiscite showed that the particular accession was not favoured by the people.

Mr. Jinnah then went on to say that he could not accept a formula if it was so drafted as to include Hyderabad, since he pointed out that Hyderabad did not wish to accede to either Dominion and he could not be a party to coercing them to accession.

I offered to put in some reference to States whose accession was in dispute "to try and get round the Hyderabad difficulty" and he said that he would give that his careful consideration if it was put to him.

I then pointed out that he really could not expect a principle to be applied in the case of Kashmir if it was not applied in the case of Junagadh and Hyderabad, but that we naturally would not expect him to be a party to compulsory accession against the wishes of the Nizam.

Part II: Hyderabad

I told Mr. Jinnah how much I regretted that at this serious moment he should have been compromised by the behaviour of the Itttehad-ul-Mussalmin's delegation to Karachi.

He asked me what I meant. I told him that the two delegates, Yamin Zuberi and his companion, who had been reported by the Press as having seen him in Karachi, had returned to Hyderabad and were alleged to have influenced the Nizam into going back on his word to accept the standstill agreement which his Executive Council had passed by six votes to three. The inference had been drawn that they had carried a message to HEH from Mr. Jinnah, and that this was the cause of the latter's reversal of his decision.

Mr. Jinnah assured me categorically that he had merely seen these two men out of courtesy, for a matter of five or perhaps seven minutes. They had told him that HEH was about to sign an instrument of accession to India, and they begged Mr. Jinnah to intervene. Mr. Jinnah had replied that it was outside his power to intervene and that it was only a question for the Nizam and his own Government to decide.

I then recounted to Mr. Jinnah briefly the events which Sir Sultan Ahmed had related to me on 31 October, and Lord Ismay substantiated this account from a letter he had received from Sir Walter Monckton.

Mr. Jinnah once more affirmed most solemnly that he had nothing whatever to do with the recent reversal of the Nizam's decision. He had sent no verbal message whatsoever to Hyderabad. The advice he had tendered to HEH in writing some time ago was that he was between the devil and the deep blue sea. If he acceded to India, there would be bloodshed in Hyderabad; and if he did not accede, there would equally be bloodshed. Thus an agreement, but not accession, seemed to be the only hope.

I told him that the Nizam had sent me a letter through Sir Sultan Ahmed, dated 30 October, in which he implied that if negotiations now broke down with a new negotiating committee he might have to consider entering into an agreement with Pakistan.

Mr. Jinnah laughed and said, "That looks to me as though he is threatening you. It has nothing to do with me. I have never discussed any form of agreement with the Nizam."

I asked him straight out whether he would be prepared to sign a standstill agreement with Hyderabad if he were asked to by the Nizam. He replied that a standstill agreement implied that there were relations or intervening factors which formed the basis for a standstill [agreement]. He could not think of any such factors between Pakistan and Hyderabad, and whereas he did not envisage wishing to sign such an agreement, he would have to examine the matter carefully, if it were put to him, before refusing.

I drew his attention to the unfortunate effect it would have if in fact he were to start negotiations with the Nizam after they had been broken off with the Dominion to which he was irretrievably linked geographically and by majority of population.

Mr. Jinnah said he would bear this in mind.

Part III: Junagadh
I read out to Mr. Jinnah the following extract from a statement made by Mr. Liaquat Ali Khan, which

had been published in the *Statesman* of Friday, 21 September:

> The correct position is that the Indian Independence Act of 1947 has left all Indian States completely free to join either one Dominion or the other or to enter into treaty relations with either. Legally and constitutionally there can be no question of putting limitations on this right of the States. Muslim League leaders before 15 August and the official spokesmen of the Pakistan Government thereafter have publicly declared their agreement with this view; and have since rigorously stood by it. No objection has been raised by Pakistan to any State acceding to the Dominion of India.

I asked Mr. Jinnah if he still stood rigorously by his Prime Minister's statement. He looked somewhat uneasy but admitted that it represented the legal position. I told him I would revert to this when talking about Kashmir, but in the meanwhile wanted to know what he proposed to do about Junagadh.

He admitted that there was no sense in having Junagadh in the Dominion of Pakistan, and said that he had been most averse from accepting this accession. He had in fact demurred for a long time, but had finally given way to the insistent appeals of the Nawab and his Dewan.

I told him that in the case of Babariawad and Mangrol, it was clearly the wish of the people that they had in fact signed instruments of accession to that effect. How then could he refuse them the right of accession? He said that Mangrol's accession had been forced on him, and withdrawn almost before the ink was dry. In any event, he had persuaded the Nawab of Junagadh to accept legal arbitration.

I told him that the Government of India would not have minded the position so much if Junagadh had played the game and not interfered internally in these small States; but that they were oppressing the people, imposing fines and removing their grain. I pointed out that repeated telegrams had been sent protesting at this. Mr. Jinnah denied this, and stated categorically that neither Pakistan nor Junagadh had sent any soldiers or armed police into these States.

I told him that we had definite information that Junagadh had sent armed police into both of them, and that they were oppressing the people. Pandit Nehru had telegraphed to Mr. Liaquat Ali Khan about this, and the latter had undertaken to ask Junagadh to withdraw their forces.

When they had failed to do so, the Government of India had telegraphed, a few days back, saying that we would have to protect the interests of these States if the Junagadh forces were not withdrawn. Since they had not been withdrawn, India were going to put in forces to protect their interests, subject to a plebiscite being subsequently held in these States about final accession. They would go in under a flag of truce, with loud-hailers and inviting the cooperation of Junagadh authorities.

Mr. Jinnah lamented that the Government of India had not invited the co-operation of Pakistan before hand. I pointed out that they had in fact been unable to enforce their own orders and that so far as I was aware, Indian forces had been sent into these two States that very day.

Part IV: Kashmir

I handed Mr. Jinnah a copy of the statement of events signed by the Indian Chiefs of Staff, which I had shown to Mr. Liaquat Ali Khan. He asked if he could keep it, but I made him return the original and gave him an unsigned copy.

Although he expressed surprise at the remarkable speed at which we had been able to organise sending troops into Srinagar plain, he did not question the document or my statement.

Mr. Jinnah's principal complaint was that the Government of India had failed to give timely information to the Government of Pakistan about the action that they proposed to take in Kashmir.

I pointed out the speed at which events had moved. It was not until the evening of the twenty-fourth that reliable reports had been received of the tribal incursion, and it was not until the twenty-fifth that observers had been sent up to confirm these reports. Thus the decision to send in troops had not been taken until the twenty-sixth, by which date the Maharaja had announced his intention of acceding to India. There had not been a moment to lose. I added that I could not recall the exact time, but that it was my impression that Pandit Nehru had telegraphed to Mr. Liaquat Ali Khan on the twenty-sixth, immediately the decision to send in troops had been taken.

Mr. Jinnah complained that this information should have been sent much earlier—in fact on 24 October. "If," he said, "they had on that date telegraphed saying that a critical situation was reported to be developing in Kashmir and they had sent in observers to confirm these reports and suggested that Pakistan should co-operate in dealing with the situation, all the trouble would have been ended by now."

Lord Ismay agreed that the Government of Pakistan should have had the earliest possible notification. This was the first thing that had occurred to him on his return to Delhi from the United Kingdom, and, indeed, he was under the impression that it had been done. To the best of his recollection, Pandit Nehru had told him on the twenty-eighth that he had kept Mr. Liaquat Ali Khan in touch with what was happening all the time. If this had not been done, the oversight must have been due to the pressure of events, and not because the Government of India had anything to hide.

Mr. Jinnah looked up his files and said that the telegram had arrived after the troops had landed, and that it did not contain any form of an appeal for co-operation between the two Dominions in this matter; it merely informed him of the accession and the landing of troops. Continuing he said that the accession was not a bonafide one since it rested on "fraud and violence" and would never be accepted by Pakistan. I asked him to explain why he used the term "fraud," since the Maharaja was fully entitled, in accordance with Pakistan's own official statement, which I had just read over to him, to make such accession. It was therefore perfectly legal and valid.

Mr. Jinnah said that this accession was the end of a long intrigue and that it had been brought about by violence. I countered this by saying that I entirely agreed that the accession had been brought about by violence; I knew the Maharaja was most anxious to remain independent, and nothing but the terror of violence could have made him accede to either Dominion; since the violence had come from tribes for whom Pakistan was responsible, it was clear that he would have acceded to India to obtain help against the invader. Mr. Jinnah repeatedly made it clear that in his opinion it was India who had committed this violence by sending her troops into Srinagar; I countered as often with the above argument, thereby greatly enraging Mr. Jinnah at my apparent denseness.

From this point, he went on to say that the Government of India authorities had encouraged the Kashmir Government to massacre Muslims in the Poonch and Mirpur areas. I repudiated this as obvious nonsense. He then said, "Very well, it was the Congress party that did it." I pointed out that if there had been any such massacre by Hindus in the Poonch area (which I did not deny) this had been done entirely by Kashmir Hindus and could hardly have been done with the object of inciting the tribes to invade Kashmir and come so close to capturing Srinagar, merely to afford the Maharaja an excuse for acceding to India for the purpose of obtaining help.

I then explained to Mr. Jinnah, at some length, the policy which I had consistently pursued in regard to Kashmir, namely—trying to persuade the Maharaja to institute progressive government, ascertain the will of the people and then accede to the Dominion of the people's choice before 15 August. I recounted how I had tried to persuade HH to do this during my visit to Kashmir in July, and how I had told him my views privately whilst driving in the car with him; but that when I had wished to have a formal meeting with him in the presence of his Prime Minister and my Private Secretary (Sir George Abell) on the last day of my visit, he had pleaded illness and gone to bed to avoid the meeting. On leaving Srinagar, I had instructed the Resident (Colonel Webb) to continue to give the Maharaja this advice officially; and finally Lord Ismay had gone up at the end of August with instructions to advise the Maharaja to hurry up and ascertain the will of the people. But the Maharaja had invariably avoided the issue, and had always turned the conversation to lighter topics.

Mr. Jinnah paid a handsome tribute to the correctness of my policy and admitted that it was I who had put the ex-Premier of Kashmir (Pandit Kak) in touch with him when he came to Delhi.

Mr. Jinnah next referred to the statement which he had issued to the Press that day and enlarged on his difficulties in not being able to have any reasonable conversation, either personally or through representatives, with the Maharaja or even with his Prime Minister; and that, not only had the Maharaja brought his troubles upon himself by this attitude, but had greatly aggravated them by the massacres to which he had incited his Dogras against innocent Muslims. He said that even today at Jammu 90,000 Muslims were in danger of being massacred.

I told Mr. Jinnah that Pandit Nehru had expressed horror at the massacres that had taken place and had issued stringent orders that everything possible was to be done to stop them. Only the night before I had supplemented those instructions myself through an Indian Brigadier who had just returned from Kashmir and who fully agreed with the necessity for stopping any further killing of Muslims.

I informed Mr. Jinnah that we already had a Brigade Group of 2,000 men in Srinagar; that a 4th Battalion would be flown in that day, and a 5th Battalion within the next two days. I said that we should have no difficulty in holding Srinagar and that the prospect of the tribes entering the city in any force was now considered remote.

Lord Ismay suggested that the main thing was to stop the fighting; and he asked Mr. Jinnah how he proposed that this should be done. Mr. Jinnah said that both sides should withdraw at once. He emphasised that the withdrawal must be simultaneous. When I asked him how the tribesmen were to be called off, he said that all he had to do was to give them an order to come out and to warn them that if they did not comply, he would send large forces along their lines of communication. In fact, if I was prepared to fly to Srinagar with him, he would guarantee that the business would be settled within 24 hours.

I expressed mild astonishment at the degree of control that he appeared to exercise over the raiders.

I asked him how he proposed that we should withdraw our forces, observing that India's forces were on the outskirts of Srinagar in a defensive role; all the tribes had to do was to stop attacking. I also pointed out that we could not possibly afford aeroplanes to fly the Indian troops back. Lord Ismay suggested that they should march back via Banihal Pass.

I asked Mr. Jinnah why he objected so strongly to a plebiscite, and he said he did so because with the troops of the Indian Dominion in military occupation of Kashmir and with the National Conference under Sheikh Abdullah in power, such propaganda and pressure could be brought to bear that the average Muslim would never have the courage to vote for Pakistan.

I suggested that we might invite UNO to undertake the plebiscite and send observers and organisers in advance to ensure that the necessary atmosphere was created for a free and impartial plebiscite. I reiterated that the last thing my Government wished was to obtain a false result by a fraudulent plebiscite.

Mr. Jinnah repeated that he and I were the only two who could organise a plebiscite and said that we should do it together. Lord Ismay and I went to great trouble to explain that I was a constitutional Governor-General and a Britisher, and that even if my Government would trust me sufficiently to see this through, I was sure that Mr. Attlee would not give his consent.

Mr. Jinnah complained bitterly that after the extremely generous gesture on the part of the Government of India in accepting his invitation to come to discussions at Lahore, the illness of one man should have prevented some other Minister from coming to conduct the negotiations; why, for example, could Sardar Patel not have come? It was a matter of the greatest urgency to get together on this problem, and he asked me how soon Pandit Nehru could come to Lahore.

I countered by saying that it was now his turn to come to Delhi since I had come to Lahore, and I invited him cordially to stay as my guest, when I would take him to see Pandit Nehru in his bedroom. He said that this was impossible. I pointed out that I had been to see Pandit Nehru personally in his bedroom and that I had now been to see his Prime Minister [of Pakistan] in his bedroom, and that I failed to see what was improper in this suggestion. He assured me that it was not a question of going to anybody's bedroom, but that he was so busy he simply had no time to leave Lahore while his Prime Minister was on the sick list.

I asked him afterwards if there was any single problem more serious or urgent than Kashmir. I pointed out that when one was so busy one had to arrange work in order of priority. If he admitted that Kashmir was top priority, then all other work should stand aside for it and he should come to Delhi at once. He said he regretted that this was impossible, for the whole burden of events was on his shoulders at Lahore. I explained that he need only be gone for the inside of a day and that I was anxious to return his hospitality. He said, "I would gladly come a hundred times to visit you; I just cannot manage it while my Prime Minister is ill." I asked him to come as soon as his Prime Minister was well enough to travel, and he said, "We shall have to see."

Lord Ismay pointed out that the best way to stand well in world opinion was for him now to come and return my visit and discuss Kashmir with Pandit Nehru. Mr. Jinnah said that he had lost interest in what the world thought of him since the British Commonwealth had let him down when he had asked him to come to the rescue of Pakistan.

I ended the meeting, as I had started it, by making it quite clear that I had come unbriefed and unauthorised to discuss Kashmir, since I had not had a chance of seeing Pandit Nehru after he had informed me he would be unable to accompany me. I told him I was speaking not as Governor-General of India but as the ex-Viceroy who had been responsible for partition and was anxious to see that it did not result in any harm coming to the two Dominions. He said he quite saw this but hoped that I would be able to discuss the various proposals which we had been talking about with Pandit Nehru and send him a firm telegram. I undertook to convey this message to Pandit Nehru.

Round about 5.00 p.m. it was obvious that we were going to be too late to go and see Mr. Liaquat Ali Khan again, so Lord Ismay left the room to telephone our apologies to him. I took the opportunity of Lord Ismay's absence to "tell off" Mr. Jinnah. I told him that I considered it was unstatesmanlike, inept and bad mannered for him to issue a statement which directly accused the Government of India of "fraud and violence" in Kashmir a few hours before he expected the Prime Minister of India to come and discuss this very question in a friendly manner; and that had he been feeling well enough to come, such a studied and ill-timed insult would have been enough to send his temperature up again. I finally pointed out that Pakistan was in my opinion in a much weaker position than India, not only from the obvious military point of view, but I was sure, the world would think they were in the wrong; and that this form of abuse before a discussion commenced could only put Pakistan even deeper in the wrong.

At the end Mr. Jinnah became extremely pessimistic and said it was quite clear that the Dominion of India was out to throttle and choke the Dominion of Pakistan at birth, and that if they continued with their oppression there would be nothing for it but to face the consequences. However depressing the prospect might be, he was not afraid; for the situation was already so bad that there was little that could happen to make it worse.

I pointed out that war, whilst admittedly very harmful for India, would be completely disastrous for Pakistan and himself.

Lord Ismay tried to cheer him up out of his depression but I fear was not very successful. However, we parted on good terms.

12

COMMUNAL REPRESENTATION

Patel's Views in the Constituent Assembly

New Delhi, 27 August 1947

Sardar Patel, Chairman of the Advisory Committee on Minorities, Fundamental Rights etc, today in the Constituent Assembly (while submitting the reports of the committees) congratulated the various minorities who had taken a correct perspective of the problems and helped in arriving at unanimous conclusions on many items.

In considering his report, Sardar Patel appealed to the House to eschew heat and bitterness, to recognise the present state of affairs in the neighbouring areas and avoid the raising of controversies which would have unfortunate reactions elsewhere.

Despite bitter controversy on occasions, the Sardar said he was happy to note that the report he was presenting was the result of a general consensus of opinion among the minorities themselves and between the minorities and the majority. It was not possible to satisfy all, but the House would see that the recommendations were practically agreed ones. The Committee had taken into consideration the points of view, sentiments and feelings of the minorities, big and small, and as far as possible tried to meet their wishes.

There was a complication and there were conflicting interests among the minorities themselves. There was a minority within the minority. The committee did not take advantage of such differences, and saw to it that the minorities, instead of dividing themselves, presented a united front. Such difficulties which arose were sought to be solved without bitterness and controversy. He hoped the House would deal with the reports in a friendly atmosphere and with goodwill.

Referring to joint versus separate electorates and representation in legislatures, the Sardar said those issues had been discussed for over a decade, produced so much of controversy and they had suffered and paid heavily for it. But today fortunately they had been able to deal with them in an amicable manner and there was unanimity on the point that there should be no more separate electorates and they should have joint electorates.

On the question of weightage, they had agreed that there should be no weightage and the various communities should be represented according to the proportion of the population. They had thought it fit to agree to reservation of seats in proportion to the population of minorities. Some of the minorities had gladly surrendered their rights. They desired neither separate electorates, nor reservation, and wanted to merge into the nation and stand on their own legs. He congratulated those who had taken that stand.

Referring to the position of the Anglo-Indians, Sardar Patel said that that community at present enjoyed certain privileges and concessions in certain services as the railways, posts and telegraph etc. To ask them to surrender these concessions at present would put them in a difficult position. They might not be prepared for it now, and sufficient time should be given to them to adjust themselves.

Congratulating the Parsis for the stand they had taken, Sardar Patel said that the Parsis had voluntarily abandoned any claims for concessions. Though small, the Parsis were a very powerful community, and perhaps most wise. They knew that concessions would do more harm than any benefit, because they could make their way anywhere and in such a way that they would get more than they would secure by reservations and other methods.

Dealing with the questions of representation in Services, the Sardar said that the main consideration should be that posts must go by merit. If they were to dilute the principle, the general administration would suffer.

There remained, however, Sardar said, one matter of controversy and that was on behalf of the Muslim League and the Scheduled Castes. A point was raised that members of those communities should poll certain percentage of votes of their community to be declared successful in the elections. The matter was discussed and the Advisory Committee rejected the suggestion by a large majority.

Frank Anthony paid a tribute to the far–sighted statesmanship of Sardar Patel whose realistic approach to the question had made agreement possible in the committee . . . The findings of the report were a happy augury for the future. By being generous, the majority community had assuredly harnessed the loyalty of the minorities to the tasks of nation- building facing the country. Every minority should look forward to the time, sooner or later, when it would take its place not under communal or racial label, but as part and parcel of the whole Indian community.

Chaudhury Kaliquzzaman pleaded for granting of separate electorates for the Muslims. Addressing Sardar Patel, he said, "You have become the final arbiter of the fates of the minorities. If you grant us separate electorates, what is the harm if the Muslim community feels it will help in determining their true representative character? After all they will appeal to you and not to any Third Power—not even to Pakistan—for redress of their grievances. I beg of you to consider the new situation in which this question is now being discussed."

Earlier referring to the new factor that has emerged, namely, the disappearance of the Third Party, he said that in the light of that, if the country really visualised the situation existing today in its true perspective, much of the suspicion that hung around separate electorates would disappear. There was no longer any Third Party to whom the Muslims could go and appeal. There was no doubt that if things untoward happened anywhere, they must now go to Sardar Patel.

Replying to the debate, Sardar Patel said he was surprised that there should have been such a debate on the motion . . . His mind (the Sardar said) went back to this day when the question of separate electorates was first discussed. Many eminent Muslims had recorded their view that communal electorates were a serious flaw in the body politic. Many Englishmen had also admitted that the country had to be partitioned today because of separate electorates.

The Sardar said, "When Pakistan was conceded, at least it was assumed that there will be One Nation in the rest of India and that there will be no attempt to thrust the Two-Nation theory here. It is no use saying, we shall ask for separate electorates, but will abide by your decision. We have heard this for many years . . . Do you still want there should be two nations? Will you show one free nation which has a religious basis? If this unfortunate country is to be again oppressed by this, even after its division, then woe betides it. It is not worth living for."

Chaudhury Khaliquzzaman had said that the British had gone and, therefore, we must forget past suspicion. The British had not expected to go so soon. They had left enough mischief behind: we did not want to perpetuate that mischief. That British had introduced communal electorates for easy administration, but the legacy left behind must be liquidated.

"You say you want to be loyal to the nation. May I ask you, is this loyalty?"

Sardar Patel said he had not intended to speak, but apparently there was something still wrong in the land. "If you want peace in this land—you can do nothing either here or in Pakistan without peace—I appeal to you at least at this stage to show that everything is forgotten. I appeal to you to withdraw your amendment and pass this clause unanimously so that the world outside may understand that we have forgotten."

Times of India, 28 August 1947

New Delhi, 28 August 1947

Speaking in the Constituent Assembly, Sardar Patel said that so far as the amendment moved by the representatives of the Muslim League was concerned, he found he was under a mistaken impression. Otherwise he would have agreed to no reservation at all.

"When I agreed to reservation on population basis, I thought that our friends in the Muslim League will see the reasonableness of our attitude and accommodate themselves in the changed circumstances after the separation of the country. But I now find repetition of the same methods which had been adopted when separate electorates were introduced in the country. In spite of ample sweetness in the language used by the speakers, there is a full dose of poison in the methods adopted."

Quoting the analogy of the younger brother making suggestions to an elder brother used by a speaker, the Sardar said, "The last speaker (Naziruddin Ahmed) has said we will lose the affection of the younger brother if we do not accept the amendment. I am prepared to lose it because otherwise it would prove the death of the elder brother."

The formula suggested by the amendment had a history behind it, the Sardar said. It was known as the Mohammed Ali formula. The formula had been evolved by nationalist Muslims to prevent separation of the communities from each other. But now separation was complete and the country was divided, he did not understand the demand for its introduction.

Sardar Patel said, "If the process that was adopted in the past, which resulted in the separation of the country, is to be repeated, then those who want that kind of thing can have a place in Pakistan, not here. We are laying the foundation of one nation. And those who think of dividing again and sow the seeds of disruption will have no place and no quarter here.

"You must change your attitude and adapt yourself to changed conditions, and do not pretend to say our affection is very great for you. We have seen the affection. Let there be no talk about it. Let us face realities. The point is whether you really want to cooperate with us, or want to adopt disruptive tactics. I appeal to you to have changed hearts, and not merely change your tongues, because it would not pay.

"If you think this is going to pay, you are mistaken. I know how much it costs me to protect Muslim minorities here in the present conditions and in the present atmosphere. I appeal to you to forget the past. You have got what you wanted. And remember, you are the people who are responsible for Pakistan, and not those who live in Pakistan. You led the agitation. What is it you want now? We do not want the country to be divided again.

"I sincerely tell you there will be no injustice done to you. There will be generosity towards you, but there must be reciprocity. If it is absent, then you take it from me that no soft words can conceal what is behind the words. Let us forget the past and let us be one nation."

Times of India, 29 August 1947

13

COULD INDIA HAVE SAVED TIBET?

Patel's Historic Letter to Nehru

New Delhi
7 November 1950

My dear Jawaharlal,

Ever since my return from Ahmedabad and after the
Cabinet meeting the same day which I had to attend at
practically 15 minutes' notice and for which I regret I was
not able to read all the papers, I have been anxiously thinking
over the problem of Tibet and I thought I should share with
you what is passing through my mind.

I have carefully gone through the correspondence between
the External Affairs Ministry and our Ambassador in Peking
and through him the Chinese Government. I have tried to
peruse this correspondence as favourably to our Ambassador
and the Chinese Government as possible, but I regret to say
that neither of them comes out well as a result of this study.

The Chinese Government have tried to delude us by professions of peaceful intentions. My own feeling is that at a crucial period they managed to instil into our Ambassador a false sense of confidence in their so-called desire to settle the Tibetan problem by peaceful means. There can be no doubt that during the period covered by this correspondence the Chinese must have been concentrating for an onslaught on Tibet. The final action of the Chinese, in my judgment, is little short of perfidy. The tragedy of it is that the Tibetans put faith in us; they chose to be guided by us; and we have been unable to get them out of the meshes of Chinese diplomacy or Chinese malevolence. From the latest position, it appears that we shall not be able to rescue the Dalai Lama. Our Ambassador has been at great pains to find an explanation or justification for Chinese policy and actions. As the External Affairs Ministry remarked in one of their telegrams, there was a lack of firmness and unnecessary apology in one or two representations that he made to the Chinese Government on our behalf. It is impossible to imagine any sensible person believing in the so-called threat to China from Anglo-American machinations in Tibet. Therefore, if the Chinese put faith in this, they must have distrusted us so completely as to have taken us as fools or stooges of Anglo-American diplomacy or strategy. This feeling, if genuinely entertained by the Chinese in spite of your direct approaches to them, indicates that even though we regard ourselves as friends of China, the Chinese do not regard us as their friends. With the Communist mentality of "whoever is not with them being against them," this is a significant pointer of which we have to take due note. During the last several months, outside the Russian camp, we have practically been alone in championing the cause of Chinese entry into the UNO and in securing from the Americans assurances on the questions of Formosa.

We have done everything we could to assuage Chinese feelings, to allay its apprehensions and to defend its legitimate claims in our discussions and correspondence with America and Britain and in the UNO. In spite of this, China is not convinced about our disinterestedness; it continues to regard us with suspicion and the whole psychology is one, at least outwardly, of skepticism, perhaps mixed with a little hostility. I doubt if we can go any further than we have done already to convince China of our good intentions, friendliness and goodwill. In Peking, we have an Ambassador who is eminently suitable for putting across the friendly point of view. Even he seems to have failed to convert the Chinese. Their last telegram to us is an act of gross discourtesy not only in the summary way it disposes of our protest against the entry of Chinese forces into Tibet but also in the wild insinuation that our attitude is determined by foreign influences. It looks as though it is not a friend speaking in that language but a potential enemy.

In the background of this, we have to consider what new situation now faces us as a result of the disappearance of Tibet, as we knew it, and the expansion of China almost up to our gates. Throughout history we have seldom been worried about our north-east frontier. The Himalayas have been regarded as an impenetrable barrier against any threat from the north. We had a friendly Tibet which gave us no trouble. The Chinese were divided. They had their own domestic problems and never bothered us about our frontiers. In 1914, we entered into a convention with Tibet which was not endorsed by the Chinese. We seem to have regarded Tibetan autonomy as extending to independent treaty relationship. Presumably, all that we required was Chinese counter-signature. The Chinese interpretation of suzerainty seems to be different. We can, therefore, safely assume that very soon they will disown all the stipulations which Tibet has entered into with us in the past. That throws into the melting pot all frontier and commercial settlements with Tibet on which we have been functioning and acting during the last half a century. China is no longer divided. It is united and strong. All along the Himalayas in the north and north-east, we have on our side of the frontier a population ethnologically and culturally not different from Tibetans or Mongoloids. The undefined state of the frontier and the existence on our side of a population with its affinities to Tibetans or Chinese have all the elements of potential trouble between China and ourselves. Recent and bitter history also tells us that communism is no shield against imperialism and that the Communists are as good or as bad imperialists as any other. Chinese ambitions in this respect not only cover the Himalayan slopes on our side but also include important parts of Assam. They have their ambitions in Burma also. Burma has the added difficulty that it has no McMahon Line round which to build up even the semblance of an agreement. Chinese irredentism and Communist imperialism are different from the expansionism or imperialism of the Western Powers. The former has a cloak of ideology which makes it ten times more dangerous. In the guise of ideological expansion lie concealed racial, national or historical claims. The danger from the north and north-east, therefore, becomes both communist and imperialist. While our western and north-western threat to security is still as prominent as before, a new threat has developed from the north and north-east. Thus, for the first time, after centuries, India's defence has to concentrate itself on two fronts simultaneously. Our defence measures have so far been based on the calculations of a superiority over Pakistan. In our calculations we shall now have to reckon with Communist China in the north and in the north-east, a

Communist China which has definite ambitions and aims and which does not, in any way, seem friendly disposed towards us.

Let us also consider the political conditions on this potentially troublesome frontier. Our northern or north-eastern approaches consist of Nepal, Bhutan, Sikkim, the Darjeeling [area] and tribal areas in Assam. From the point of view of communications, they are weak spots. Continuous defensive lines do not exist. There is almost an unlimited scope for infiltration. Police protection is limited to a very small number of passes. There, too, our outposts do not seem to be fully manned. The contact of these areas with us is by no means close and intimate. The people inhabiting these portions have no established loyalty or devotion to India. Even the Darjeeling and Kalimpong areas are not free from pro-Mongoloid prejudices. During the last three years we have not been able to make any appreciable approaches to the Nagas and other hill tribes in Assam. European missionaries and other visitors had been in touch with them, but their influence was in no way friendly to India or Indians. In Sikkim, there was political ferment some time ago. It is quite possible that discontent is smouldering there. Bhutan is comparatively quiet, but its affinity with Tibetans would be a handicap. Nepal has a weak oligarchic regime based almost entirely on force; it is in conflict with a turbulent element of the population as well as with enlightened ideas of the modern age. In these circumstances, to make people alive to the new danger or to make them defensively strong is a very difficult task indeed and that difficulty can be got over only by enlightened firmness, strength and a clear line of policy. I am sure the Chinese and their source of inspiration, Soviet Russia, would not miss any opportunity of exploiting these weak spots, partly in support of their ideology and partly in support of their ambitions. In my judgment, therefore, the situation is one in which we cannot afford either to be complacent or to be vacillating. We must have a clear idea of what we wish to achieve and also of the methods by which we should achieve it. Any faltering or lack of decisiveness in formulating our objectives or in pursuing our policy to attain those objectives is bound to weaken us and increase the threats which are so evident.

Side by side with these external dangers, we shall now have to face serious internal problems as well. I have already asked [H. V. R.] Iengar to send to the E. A. Ministry a copy of the Intelligence Bureau's appreciation of these matters. Hitherto, the Communist Party of India has found some difficulty in contacting Communists abroad, or in getting supplies of arms, literature, etc. from them. They had to contend with the difficult Burmese and Pakistan frontiers on the east or with the long seaboard. They shall now have a comparatively easy means of access to Chinese Communists and through them to other foreign Communists. Infiltration of spies, fifth columnists and Communists would now be easier. Instead of having to deal with isolated Communist pockets in Telengana and Warangal we may have to deal with Communist threats to our security along our northern and north-eastern frontiers where, for supplies of arms and ammunition, they can safely depend on Communist arsenals in China. The whole situation thus raised a number of problems on which we must come to an early decision so that we can, as I said earlier, formulate the objectives of our policy and decide the methods by which those objectives are to be attained. It is also clear that the action will have to be fairly comprehensive, involving not only our defence strategy and state of preparations but also problems of internal security to deal with which we have not a moment to lose. We shall also have to deal with administrative and political problems in the weak spots along the frontier to which I have already referred.

It is, of course, impossible for me to be exhaustive in setting out all these problems. I am, however, giving below some of the problems which, in my opinion, require early solution and round which we have to build our administrative or military policies and measures to implement them.

a)   A military and intelligence appreciation of the Chinese threat to India both on the frontier and to internal security.

b)   An examination of our military position and such redisposition of our forces as might be necessary, particularly with the idea of guarding important routes or areas which are likely to be the subject of dispute.

c)   An appraisement of the strength of our forces and, if necessary, reconsideration of our retrenchment plans for the Army in the light of these new threats.

d)   Long-term consideration of our defence needs. My own feeling is that, unless we assure our supplies of arms, ammunition and armour, we should be making our defence position perpetually weak and we would not be able to stand up to the double threat of difficulties both from the west and north-west and north and north-east.

e)   The question of Chinese entry into UNO. In view of the rebuff which China has given us and the method which it has followed in dealing with Tibet, I am doubtful whether we can advocate its claims any longer. There would probably be a threat in the UNO virtually to outlaw China in view of its active participation in the Korean war. We must determine our attitude on this question also.

f)   The political and administrative steps which we should take to strengthen our northern and north-eastern frontiers. This would include the whole of the border, i.e. Nepal, Bhutan, Sikkim, Darjeeling and the tribal territory in Assam.

g)   Measures of internal security in the border areas as well as the States flanking those areas, such as UP, Bihar, Bengal and Assam.

h)   Improvement of our communications, road, rail, air and wireless, in these areas and with the frontier outposts.

i)   Policing and intelligence of frontier posts.

j)   The future of our mission at Lhasa and the trade posts at Gyangtse and Yatung and the forces which we have in operation in Tibet to guard the trade routes.

k)   The policy in regard to the McMahon Line.

These are some of the questions which occur to my mind. It is possible that a consideration of these matters may lead us into wider questions of our relationship with China, Russia, America, Britain and Burma. This, however, would be of a general nature, though some might be basically very important, e.g. we might have to consider whether we should not enter into closer association with Burma in order to strengthen the latter in its dealings with China. I do not rule out the possibility that, before applying pressure on us, China might apply pressure on Burma. With Burma, the frontier is entirely undefined and the Chinese territorial claims are more substantial. In its present position, Burma might offer an easier problem for China and, therefore, might claim its first attention.

I suggest that we meet early to have a general discussion on these problems and decide on such steps as we might think to be immediately necessary and direct quick examination of other problems with a view to taking early measures to deal with them.

Yours,
Vallabhbhai Patel

Prime Minister Nehru's Note on China and Tibet dated 18 November 1950

[The note was obviously forwarded to Sardar Patel as it answered indirectly some of the matters raised in Sardar's letter of 7 November 1950.]

1. The Chinese Government having replied to our last note, we have to consider what further steps we should take in this matter. There is no immediate hurry about sending a reply to the Chinese Government. But we have to send immediate instructions to Shri B. N. Rau as to what he should do in the event of Tibet's appeal being brought up before the Security Council or the General Assembly.

2. The content of the Chinese reply is much the same as their previous notes, but there does appear to be a toning down and an attempt at some kind of a friendly approach

3. It is interesting to note that they have not referred specifically to our mission [at] Lhasa or to our trade agents or military escort at Gyangtse etc. We had mentioned these especially in our last note. There is an indirect reference, however, in China's note. At the end, this note says that "As long as our two sides adhere strictly to the principle of mutual respect for territory, sovereignty, equality and mutual benefit, we are convinced that the friendship between China and India should be developed in a normal way and that problems relating to Sino-Indian diplomatic, commercial and cultural relations with respect to Tibet may be solved properly and to our mutual benefit through normal diplomatic channels." This clearly refers to our trade agents and others in Tibet. We had expected a demand from them for the withdrawal of these agents etc. The fact that they have not done so has some significance.

4. Stress is laid in China's note on Chinese sovereignty over Tibet, which we are reminded, we have acknowledged, on Tibet being an integral part of China's territory and therefore a domestic problem. It is however again repeated that outside influences, have been at play obstructing China's mission in Tibet. In fact, it is stated that liberation of Changtu proves that foreign forces and influences were inciting Tibetan troops to resist. It is again repeated that no foreign intervention will be permitted and that the Chinese army will proceed.

5. All this is much the same as has been said before, but it is said in a somewhat different way and there are repeated references in the note to China desiring the friendship of India

6. It is true that in one of our messages to the Chinese Government we used "sovereignty" of China in relation to Tibet. In our last message we used the word "suzerainty". After receipt of the last China's note, we have pointed out to our Ambassador that "suzerainty" was the right word and that "sovereignty" had been used by error.

7. It is easy to draft a reply to the Chinese note, pressing our viewpoint and countering some of the arguments raised in the Chinese note. But before we do so we should be clear in our minds as to what we are aiming at, not only in the immediate future but from a long-term view. It is important that we keep both these viewpoints before us. In all probability China, that is present-day China, is going to be our close neighbour for a long time to come. We are going to have a tremendously long common frontier. It is unlikely, and it would be unwise to expect, that the present Chinese Government will collapse, giving place to another. Therefore, it is important to pursue a policy which will be in keeping with this long-term view.

8. I think it may be taken for granted that China will take possession, in a political sense at least, of the whole of Tibet.

There is no likelihood whatsoever of Tibet being able to resist this or stop it. It is equally unlikely that any foreign power can prevent it. We cannot do so. If so, what can we do to help in the maintenance of Tibetan autonomy and at same time avoiding continuous tension and apprehension on our frontiers?

9. The Chinese note has repeated that they wish the Tibetan people to have what they call "regional autonomy and religious freedom". This autonomy can obviously not be anything like the autonomy verging on independence which Tibet has enjoyed during the last forty years or so. But it is reasonable to assume from the very nature of Tibetan geography, terrain and climate, that a large measure of autonomy is almost inevitable. It may of course be that this autonomous Tibet is controlled by communists alone in Tibet. I imagine however that it is, on the whole, more likely that what will be attempted will be a pro-communist China administration rather than a communist one.

10. If world war comes, then all kinds of difficult and intricate problems arise and each one of these problems will be inter-related with others. Even the question of defence of India assumes a different shape and cannot be isolated from other world factors. I think that it is exceedingly unlikely that we may have to face any real military invasion from the Chinese side, whether in peace or in war, in the foreseeable future. I base this conclusion on a consideration of various world factors. In peace, such an invasion would undoubtedly leas to world war. China, though internally big, is in a way amorphous and easily capable of being attacked on its sea coasts and by air. In such a war, China would have its main front in the South and East and it will be fighting for its very existence against powerful enemies. It is inconceivable that it should divert its forces and its strength across the

inhospitable terrain of Tibet and undertake a wild adventure across the Himalayas. Any such attempt will greatly weaken its capacity to meet its real enemies on other fronts. Thus I rule out any major attack on India by China. I think these considerations should be borne in mind, because there is far too much loose talk about China attacking and overrunning India. If we lose our sense of perspective and world strategy and give way to unreasoning fears, then any policy that we might have is likely to fail.

11. While there is, in my opinion, practically no chance of a major attack on India by China, there are certainly chances of gradual infiltration across our border and possibly of entering and taking possession of disputed territory, if there is obstruction to this happening. We must therefore take all necessary precautions to prevent this. But, again, we must differentiate between these precautions and those that might be necessary to meet a real attack.

12. If we really feared an attack and had to make full provision for it, this would cast an intolerable burden on us, financial and otherwise, and it would weaken our general defence position. There are limits beyond which we cannot go, at least for some years, and a spreading out of our army on distant frontiers would be bad from every military or strategic point of view.

13. In spite of our desire to settle the points at issue between us and Pakistan, and developing peaceful relations with it, the fact remains that our major possible enemy is Pakistan. This has compelled us to think of our defence mainly in terms of Pakistan's aggression. If we begin to think of, and prepare for, China's aggression in the same way, we would weaken considerably on the Pakistan side. We might well be got in a pincer movement. It is interesting to note that Pakistan is taking a great deal of interest, from the point of view, in

developments in Tibet. Indeed it has been discussed in the
Pakistan Press that the new danger from Tibet to India might
help them to settle the Kashmir problem according to their
wishes. Pakistan has absolutely nothing in common with
China or Tibet. But if we fall out completely with China,
Pakistan will undoubtedly try to take advantage of this,
politically or otherwise. The position of India thus will be
bad from a defence point of view. We cannot have all the
time two possible enemies on either side of India. This danger
will not be got over, even if we increase our defence forces
or even if other foreign countries help us in arming. The
measure of safety that one gets by increasing the defence
apparatus is limited by many factors. But whatever that
measure of safety might be, strategically we would be in an
unsound position and the burden of this will be very great on
us. As it is, we are facing enormous difficulties, financial,
economic, etc.

14. The idea that communism inevitably means expansion
and war, or to put it more precisely, that Chinese communism
means inevitably an expansion towards India, is rather naïve.
It may mean that in certain circumstances. Those
circumstances would depend upon many factors, which I need
not go into here. The danger really is not from military invasion
but from infiltration of men and ideas. The ideas are there
already and can only be countered by other ideas. Communism
is an important element in the situation. But, by our attaching
too great importance to it in this context, we are likely to
misjudge the situation from other and more important angles.

15. In a long-term view, India and China are two of the
biggest countries of Asia bordering on each other and both
with certain expansive tendencies, because of their vitality.
If their relations are bad, this will have a serious effect not
only on both of them but on Asia as a whole. It would affect

our future for a long time. If a position arises in which China and India are inveterately hostile to each other, like France and Germany, then there will be repeated wars bringing destruction to both. The advantage will go to other countries. It is interesting to note that both the UK and the USA appear to be anxious to add to the unfriendliness of India and China towards each other. It is also interesting to find that the USSR does not view with favour any friendly relations between India and China. These are long-term reactions which one can fully understand, because India and China at peace with each other would make a vast difference to the whole set-up and balance of the world. Much of course depends upon the development of either country and how far communism in China will mould the Chinese people. Even so, these processes are long-range ones and in the long run it is fairly safe to assume that hundreds of millions of people will not change their essential characteristics.

16. These arguments lead to the conclusion that while we should be prepared, to the best of our ability, for all contingencies, the real protection that we should seek is some kind of understanding of China. If we have not got that, then both our present and our future are imperilled and no distant power can save us. I think on the whole that China desires this too for obvious reasons. If this is so, then we should fashion our present policy accordingly.

17. We cannot save Tibet, as we should have liked to do, and our very attempts to save it might well bring greater trouble to it. It would be unfair to Tibet for us to bring this trouble upon her without having the capacity to help her effectively. It may be possible, however, that we might be able to help Tibet to retain a large measure of her autonomy. That would be good for Tibet and good for India. As far as I can see, this can only be done on the diplomatic level and by

avoidance of making the present tension between India and China worse.

18. What then should be our instructions to B. N. Rau? From the messages he has sent to us, it appears that no member of the Security Council shows any inclination to sponsor Tibet's appeal and that there is little likelihood of the matter being considered by the Council. We have said that [we] are not going to sponsor this appeal, but if it comes up we shall state our viewpoint. This viewpoint cannot be one of full support of the Tibetan appeal, because that goes far and claims full independence. We may say that whatever might have been acknowledged in the past about China's sovereignty or suzerainty, recent events have deprived China of the right to claim that. There may be some moral basis for this argument. But it will not take us or Tibet very far. It will only hasten the downfall of Tibet. No outsider will be able to help her and China, suspicious and apprehensive of these tactics, will make sure of much speedier and fuller possession of Tibet than she might otherwise have done. We shall thus not only fail in our endeavour but at the same time have really a hostile China on our doorstep.

19. I think that in no event should we sponsor Tibet's appeal. I would personally think that it would be a good thing if that appeal is not heard in the Security Council or the General Assembly. If it is considered there, there is bound to be a great deal of bitter speaking and accusation, which will worsen the situation as regards Tibet, as well as the possibility of widespread war, without helping it in the least. It must be remembered that neither the UK nor the USA, nor indeed any other power is particularly interested in Tibet or the future of that country. What they are interested in is embarrassing China. Our interest, on the other hand, is Tibet, and if we cannot serve that interest, we fail.

20. Therefore, it will be better not to discuss Tibet's appeal in the UN. Suppose, however, that it comes up for discussion, in spite of our not wishing this, what then? I would suggest that our representative should state our case as moderately as possible and ask the Security Council or the Assembly to give expression to their desire that the Sino-Tibetan question should be settled peacefully and that Tibet's autonomy should be respected and maintained. Any particular reference to an article of the Charter of the UN might tie us up in difficulties and lead to certain consequences later, which may prove highly embarrassing for us. Or a resolution of the UN might just be a dead letter which also will be bad.

21. If my general argument is approved, then we can frame our reply to China's note accordingly.

J. Nehru

18 November 1950

14

A BUNCH OF UNPUBLISHED LETTERS

i) Sir Hugh Garrett, ICS

16 August 1968

Dear Mr. Krishna,

I have read with great satisfaction your letter printed in the *Daily Telegraph* on 16 August. I, who knew him very well, always called him Vallabhbhai. For many years in Ahmedabad I had constant dealings with him. He was, of course, a pillar of the Congress party but that in no way caused ill-feeling on my side, nor, I hope, did he feel any against me.

As an example of our friendly relations, I may relate an incident. He came to see me and related how a *fakir* had built a tomb in the middle of a road in the city's outskirts. He said the *fakir* had threatened him with a sword. He asked if I would deal with the situation. He did not want a police or magisterial case. I accordingly got my car and went to the place and found it as stated. I spoke to the *fakir* and ordered removal of everything within two hours. I went back and found all done.

Later, of course, I had much to do with him, but I had faith in him. He was honest and frank. I hope he had the same view of me!

Of all the Indians I ever met, I place him as the greatest. His premature death was a shock to me and a terrible loss to India.

Yours sincerely,
Sir Hugh Garrett
(88 years old!)

ii) Field Marshal Sir Claude Auchinleck

4 January 1969

Dear Mr. Krishna,

Thank you for your long letter of 9 December. I apologise for the delay in answering it due to my having been away in Spain and elsewhere since before Christmas.

As to your question about my talk with Mr. Jinnah when I flew up to meet him in Lahore . . . I simply told him that if he persisted in his plan to send the Pakistan army against India, all British officers (and there were many, including General Gracey, the C-in-C, in important posts) would be withdrawn at once as it was inconceivable that British officers, commissioned by the British Sovereign, should lead Pakistani troops against Indian troops similarly commanded. It followed, of course, that, if it came to war between India and Pakistan, all British officers serving with Indian troops would be similarly withdrawn. Confidential orders to this effect had been issued by me to all concerned some time before . . . My concern was as Commander-in-Chief to preserve the safety of the British officers for whom I, and I alone, was finally responsible, irrespective of whatever action the Indian or Pakistan Governments might see fit to take.

Yours sincerely,
Auchinleck

iii) Air Marshal Sir Thomas Elmhirst, C-in-C, Indian Air Force

8 January 1969

Dear Krishna,

I have your letter of the 9 December together with your most helpful questionnaire. Reading the letter makes me realise how little I did know of a man whose intelligence, firmness and strength of character I much admired.

My first contact with Sardar Patel was sitting at a conference table in the Governor-General's House in New Delhi, late August or early September 1947, when on the day in question, Delhi appeared to be in the hands of armed Sikhs. The city was certainly not under control of the police or armed forces.

An emergency meeting had been called to consider and deal with the situation . . . The meeting asked Mountbatten to take the chair and Pandit Nehru sat on one side of him and Sardar Patel on the other.

There was fear in the highly charged atmosphere as views were expressed as to how the Government could regain control. Life in Delhi that day was at a standstill, with rebels in control. Someone expressed a view that was absurd. Sardar Patel laughed heartily and made a remark that caused most of us to laugh. The tension was broken and he followed up with a wise suggestion that brought general agreement. He was the man.

I saw more of Sardar Patel in 1948 and 1949, the period of the first Kashmir war. As you say in your questionnaire, he appealed to me, an Englishman, because he was obviously a man of action, of few words, frank, straightforward and unequivocal. He also had that fierce piercing look in his eye I have seen in the eyes of Winston Churchill and Ataturk [Kemal Ataturk of Turkey].

To me Sardar Patel was no enigma like Mahatma Gandhi. Even Pandit Nehru to me was an enigma if he was discussing Kashmir.

I remember an evening when, in Nehru's absence abroad, he sent for me, as Chairman of the Chiefs of Staff Committee, to discuss a point relating to the Kashmir war. He was not well and the meeting was in the sitting room of his home and we were alone. He said something to this effect: "If all the decisions rested on me, I think that I would be in favour of extending this little affair in Kashmir to a full-scale war with Pakistan now, and let us get it over once and for all and settle down as a united continent."

I liked Sardar Vallabhbhai Patel and admired him.

Yours sincerely,
Thomas Elmhirst

iv) General Sir Roy Bucher, C-in-C, Indian Army

24 July 1969

My dear Mr. Krishna,

Thank you very much for your letter of the 14 July. Obviously the repercussions of what happened in Calcutta in August '46 were very widespread. Inter-communal rioting—slaughtering might be a better word—took place in East Bengal, in Bihar, in Assam, in the Central Provinces, in the United Provinces and finally in the Punjab. I personally never thought that any subsequent Partition of India could be completed without recurrence of inter-communal fighting. What however did become clear from the happenings in Calcutta and elsewhere was that the soldiers of the Indian Army, no matter of what class or creed, could, one and all, be relied upon to carry out their full duty in support of Government. Before these outbreaks, Indian soldiers had not been used in any very large numbers in support of the civil authority.

From my own knowledge, I am quite sure that Maulana Azad's charge that Sardar Patel was responsible for the murder of the Mahatma was absolutely unfounded. At our meeting in Dehra Dun, the Sardar told me that those who persuaded the Mahatma to suggest that monies held back in India should be despatched to Pakistan were responsible for the tragedy, and that after the monies had been sent off, the Mahatma was moved up to the first to be assassinated on the books of a very well-known Hindu revolutionary society. I distinctly remember the Sardar saying: "You know quite well that for Gandhiji to express a wish was almost an order."

I was bidden to his house and there were a number of his Cabinet colleagues present. The Sardar pressed me to order

Indian troops into Hyderabad and at once. When I demurred, he obviously was much put about and his colleagues showed extreme anxiety. When I stuck to my point, the Sardar said words to the effect that there would not be a Government of India for very long and that the fault would be Roy Bucher's. He then said: "Come and sit on my bed and I will tell you a story." He did just that and his story was a very amusing one about goings-on within the United Nations Commission for India and Pakistan.

I think Mr. Jinnah's attitude was indicated when he ordered General Gracey to send a Brigade of Pakistani regular troops into Kashmir to catch up with the raiders. General Gracey reported these orders to Field Marshal Sir Claude Auchinleck with the result that the latter met Mr. Jinnah in Lahore, I think, and more or less forced him to cancel his instructions.

My Commander-in-Chief, General Sir Rob Lockhart, certainly received information from the Governor of the North-West Frontier Province that his Government was encouraging raiders to enter Kashmir and was giving them transport and other facilities. Shortly afterwards came the accession to India.

In regard to the final cease-fire, the only people with whom I had consultations and conversations about this were the Minister of Defence Sardar Baldev Singh and the Prime Minister himself Pandit Jawaharlal Nehru. At that time I had no idea of what Sardar Patel's views were, and I did not meet him then.

Early in 1948 I remember a discussion in the Prime Minister's office when certain marked maps showing a possible partition of Kashmir were produced. A month or two later a cease-fire lasting a few days took place . . . Sardar Patel certainly gave me the impression (at a meeting at Dehra Dun) that he was not resolutely opposed to the partition of

Kashmir, but he did say most emphatically, if there were to be new boundaries, these must be capable of being seen and easily recognised on the ground itself, and that vague lines on maps or down the centres of rivers were of no use at all.

With every good wish,

Yours sincerely,
Roy Bucher

v) General Sir Roy Bucher, C-in-C, Indian Army

30 July 1969

My dear Mr. Krishna,

I now attempt to recall the matters which Sardar Patel and I discussed in Dehra Dun . . . I was in Mussourie at that time, and Mr. Birla suggested I should call in on the Sardar who was convalescing in Dehra Dun. It was arranged for my wife and I to lunch at the Circuit House there with the Sardar and his daughter.

After luncheon, the Sardar invited me into the room he was using as a study. He began by saying he was going to tell me of certain matters of which I, as C-in-C, should be thoroughly cognisant; he also said that if I repeated the conversation about to begin to others he, the Sardar, would merely say that my side of the story was inaccurate.

The Sardar next said that he had been blamed for the Mahatma's death because no special security arrangements had been laid on; that had been quite impossible because Gandhiji had forbidden any special precautions. I was told that I knew perfectly well that the Mahatma's wishes were akin to orders to Congress leaders like himself and Pandit Jawaharlal Nehru.

Certain people had argued with force that monies held back in India on Partition and due to Pakistan should be sent across. When, therefore, the Mahatma expressed a wish that this should be done, arrangements for the despatch of these monies were put in hand. When this became known, coupled with the fact that a visit by Gandhi to Pakistan was being planned, the assassination was decided upon by the well-known revolutionary body to which the murderer belonged. The Sardar was extremely vehement on the guilt of those who had so strongly advocated the despatch of monies to Pakistan; he also said he never had any intention of retaining these monies permanently in India, but that in view of the distressful relations between India and Pakistan he had thought it wise to withhold these monies.

The Sardar next spoke of internal security and said that he did not need the Armed Forces, as he could do all that would ever be necessary with the Police and the Armed Police. Naturally I could not agree with him on this in view of what had happened in the past and because of the troubled state of the country generally. The Sardar went on that everyone thought he was anti-Muslim, but this was quite untrue as he realized he was responsible for the lives and livelihood of all Muslims and that as long as he was in his present position no Muslim would be harmed or put at a disadvantage. To trust Muslims, however, was quite another matter. He found this almost impossible for him in view of the 1946 rioting which had begun in Calcutta and for which the Muslim League Government of Bengal was responsible, and also because of

Partition with all its consequences. It was very easy to be wise in retrospect, but if he had sensed what tragedies would result from Partition he would never have agreed to it.

On Hyderabad the Sardar said the Nizam's Government was not in control and that the Razakars under Razvi were organizing a full-scale Muslim rebellion within the State. He spoke of the Moplah rebellion and the difficulties in suppressing that. He also mentioned gun-running from Pakistan into Hyderabad and how the general danger was increased because of Communist pockets around the State in Madras and elsewhere. He was adamant that the Government of His Exalted Highness must accept, without equivocation, the Government of India's minimum demands, otherwise India must enter the State in the interest of law and order all over India. An alien Government in the "tummy" of India was an absolute impossibility.

He then said: "If you can do anything to persuade the Nizam's Government to accept our demands, I give you a free hand, and you can even go to Hyderabad if you wish." He considered that Lord Mountbatten was in error in thinking that he could get a solution to the Hyderabad problem; the only one was the acceptance of the Government of India's conditions . . . I was very much in agreement with the Sardar and our only difference really was a question of timing. I did make touch with Zain El Edroos the C-in-C in Hyderabad, Brigadier Nepean and John Graham both in Hyderabad. I also recommended that the Government of India should appoint a senior soldier as its representative in the State in place of Mr. Munshi. Nothing came of these efforts of mine. When Indian troops did enter the State, the climate of world opinion was favourable to India and the manner in which the operations were carried out practically eliminated all criticism.

The Sardar gave me the impression that he was quite in favour of partition, but that he was dead against a Plebiscite anywhere. To him, possible partition seemed to be for those parts of the State north of the Jhelum River and west of the Poonch River to go to Pakistan, the rest to India. The Sardar said that it was absolutely essential for any new frontiers to be easily seen and recognized both on maps and on the ground, and that vague lines across country or down the centres of rivers could not be countenanced.

Before General Messervy, C-in-C Pakistan, went home he was asked to come to New Delhi by the Governor-General. This happened in late February and I believe the arguments in favour of Kashmir being ceded to Pakistan were advanced, and that India's Prime Minister was present at these discussions. Be all that as it may, I remember being called along to Pandit Jawaharlal in the Secretariat and being shown certain marked maps portraying a possible division of Kashmir as between India and Pakistan . . . nothing came of these discussions because Ghulam Bakshi Mohd., the Deputy Prime Minister of Kashmir, was opposed to any part of Titwahl going to Pakistan.

Some time later, in March I think, General Gracey, now C-in-C in Pakistan, said to me that he thought a cease-fire in Kashmir might be arranged. I informed my Prime Minister of this, and he replied "I will try anything once". A cease-fire did occur, but it could not be sustained as the Prime Minister of Pakistan wished Pandit Nehru to treat with the head of the Azad Government. This was an impossibility because India did not recognize any such Government. So fighting began again and an opportunity presented by India was lost. In verification of this last I wrote in my D.O. No. 18/C. in C. of 30 March 1948 to General Gracey: "It is sad that your Prime Minister could not find an approach to the Government here."

It has remained clearly in my memory, as it was after my interview, that I realised, far more than formerly, what a very wise and determined man the Sardar was.

Kind regards,

Yours very sincerely,
Roy Bucher

vi) General Sir Roy Bucher, C-in-C, Indian Army

(Note dated 6 March 1969)

I cannot quite remember whether it was late in 1946 or early in '47 when I went to New Delhi for an Army Commanders' Selection Board Meeting. I was invited to go and have tea with Mahatma Gandhi, but it was not deemed advisable for me to accept. I subsequently went to have tea with Sardar Patel. This was the first time I had met him in person. In his drawing-room he greeted me with: "You are a very good hotel-keeper, quite one of the best." I said: "Surely you cannot be referring to the time when you and your colleagues were detained in Ahmednagar Fort?" The Sardar replied: "Indeed I am and we were never more comfortable as the King's guests."

All the detailed arrangements for the funeral of Gandhi were made in the sitting-room of our bungalow in York Place. The members of the Government of India were present. It is interesting that neither the Prime Minister nor the Home Minister interfered in any way with proposals for the conduct of the funeral, or made any criticism afterwards of the arrangements which had been carried through.

At the time I recorded that rioting had broken out in and around Belgaum and that we became very busy rounding up certain private armies in an effort to stamp out communalism throughout the country once and for all. The Maharajah of Alwar was removed from his State about this time and I have a note that certain other rulers were similarly to be dealt with.

The load on Sardar Patel must have been very heavy indeed in his dual capacity as Home Minister and Minister for States. There were twenty-nine Battalions in Kashmir where heavy fighting was taking place; aggression into Jaisalmer State and also from West Bengal into Assam occurred. It would have been small wonder had the Sardar become worried or perturbed, but I personally never saw him other than absolutely composed and determined to uphold law and order throughout India. Later I was to see him in a rage and realised how his colleagues were dominated.

Roy Bucher

vii) General Sir Roy Bucher, C-in-C, Indian Army

(From a letter of 10 August 1948 to his daughter, Elizabeth Bucher)

Elements of the Pakistan Regular Army are now taking part in the fighting (in Kashmir). I do not know exactly how many units or sub-units are involved, but there appears to be quite a number. What is more, they are supported by Artillery. As you can imagine, this has altered the whole situation. To me it all seems utter madness, and especially as no warning was given by Pakistan of their intentions.

The Government of the North-West Frontier pushed Mahsuds and Wazirs into the Jhelum Valley which forced Kashmir to accede to India. There was no other alternative— the fates of Kashmiri Muslims, non-Muslims and Christians in Muzaffrabad, Uri and Baramulla, etc. are ample grounds for saying that but for the advent of Indian Army troops, no one in the Valley would have been spared and that Srinagar would have been looted and burnt to the ground.

Roy Bucher

viii) Sir G. S. Bozman, ICS

20 August 1968

Dear Mr. Krishna,

I have seen you letter in the London *Daily Telegraph* of 16 August and was glad to read of the forthcoming biography of Sardar Vallabhbhai Patel. I was Secretary of the Information & Broadcasting Department in Delhi when he took over the portfolio.

I can contribute nothing to the political aspect of Sardar Patel . . . His was, nevertheless, an example, if one were needed, of his straightforward and clear-headed approach to all matters of administration. In this field, there could be no doubt that he far outshone all his colleagues and most of his officials. I often wondered if he knew how greatly these officials, including myself, admired his outstanding ability.

Yours sincerely,
Sir G. S. Bozman

ix) Sir G. S. Bozman, ICS

10 October 1968

Dear Mr. Krishna,

I must apologise for the long delay in answering your long letter of 30 August. Unfortunately, just after I received it, I fell seriously ill...

Sardar Patel excelled in planning and getting things done, while Nehru's role was more idealistic and less practical. The two together, of course, made a team—so long as they agreed together—of great force and character.

Yours sincerely,
G. S. Bozman

x) Andrew Mellor, Correspondent in India of the London *Daily Herald*

18 November 1968

Dear Sri Krishna,

I am sorry not to have replied earlier to your letter of 2 October. During my stay in India, I was representing the *Daily Herald*. The period was 1947-49 and Sardar Patel was, in my opinion, the strongest of the group of strong men who were engaged in the tremendous task of ending the Raj and seeing through the transfer of power—with the involvement of nothing less than the division of the sub-continent.

I saw him first very soon after my arrival in New Delhi and was deeply impressed by his imposing presence. He had the appearance, I thought, of some great Roman consul. It was, I suppose, the immediate impression of strength and power which created that idea in my mind.

The broad and heavy features, the great head and the generally unmoving, almost unblinking gaze from eyes which were extremely penetrating could not fail to have a considerable effect.

With Nehru, the charm immediately reached out and one felt his humanity and friendliness. Patel was altogether different. He gave a feeling of aloofness, almost grimness, and certainly inspired awe. Nevertheless, I know that he was personally kind and patient.

Returning from Kashmir, I saw him one evening and was describing the difficulties of terrain for Indian troops moving through the passes from Jammu towards Nowshera and the Pathan-invaded border towns.

I had seen several guns which had rolled over at road curves and fallen hundreds of feet. It seemed to me that these difficulties were appalling, if not insurmountable. "The roads are so bad that a lot of vehicles cannot, in my opinion, be got up," I said. "They must be got up," he replied, "and they will be." They were.

Yours sincerely,
Andrew Mellor

xi) C. W. E. U'ren, British Indian Police Officer

18 March 1969

Dear Krishna,

Your letter to me of 14 January. I was ASP Ahmedabad during the Gujarat floods of 1927. You may recall that they were very serious indeed and at one time practically the whole of Ahmedabad was a few feet deep in water. This was due to the fact that the Ahmedabad rain-water drains, which were all directed into the river Sabarmati, could not function as the river was in high flood. I well remember Sardar's calling a meeting (he was then President of the Ahmedabad Municipality), which was attended by the Collector, DSP, myself and several other municipal officers . . . He kept discussions strictly to the point, having heard the various opinions expressed, made up his mind on the spot.

He impressed us all by his extreme calmness and dignity at this critical juncture. Just before we left, he said he hoped, one day, Ahmedabad would be modelled on the lines of a western city—particularly insofar as its municipal services were concerned. In other words, even in a crisis he was able to look forward to better days for the city he was administering.

When the All-India Congress Committee passed its "Quit India" Resolution on the evening of 8 August 1942, the Government of India issued orders that all the members of the committee, plus Gandhiji, were to be detained. It fell to my lot to serve orders on the Sardar, his daughter Maniben and Acharya Kripalani (then AICC General Secretary) and to take them to Victoria Terminus (GIPRy) where a special train waited to take the party to Poona and Ahmednagar. I well remember Maniben's asking her father whether the detention documents were in order. Mainly, I think, to pacify her, the Sardar asked to see the order relating to his own case and having scanned it rapidly, nodded his head. He was most dignified throughout and his example to the other two made my task a comparatively simple one.

The Sardar was a "big" man in every way—a great administrator, of few words with the gift of getting to the root of a complicated problem very quickly indeed.

Yours sincerely,
C. W. E. U'ren

xii) K. B. Lall, ICS

24 June 1970

My dear Shri B. Krishna,

Your letters of 12 June and 15 June were transmitted to me while I was enjoying a 10-day break in the Simla hills.

Around 20 August 1947, Delhi was in the grip of a most serious disorder since 1857, resulting in a virtual breakdown of civil order and governmental authority. On that date, V. P. Menon, H. M. Patel and myself had gathered at Sardar Patel's residence to discuss with him the issue of payment to Pakistan of Rs. 55 crores which she had been demanding. It was during the course of this meeting that a man rushed into Sardar Patel's room, bitterly complaining about the murders which were being committed, and asking him to do something effective to stop them.

The Sardar's face suddenly darkened with pain. In a voice filled with agony, he asked me, who belonged to Delhi and resided in my ancestral home in old Delhi, as to why I could not do something effective about the matter. Since the Sardar was not in the habit of saying much, these words of his could have been taken for an order from the Home Minister.

A day later, we three met again at Sardar Patel's residence. During the course of this meeting, a man ran into Sardar Patel's house shouting that a couple of Muslims had been stabbed to death near Sardar's residence. This shocked Sardar beyond measure. His face showed tremendous grief. The agony of helplessness was writ large on it. With some annoyance he asked me as to what I had done to tackle the communal situation.

He could not bring himself to say that no specific responsibility had been entrusted to him. He did say, however, that as far as he knew there were no armed forces nearabout and the majority of police armed force consisted of Muslims who were themselves seething with revolt. The local Muslims had been collecting arms for many months and the refugees, Sikhs and Hindus, having suffered atrocities in the Punjab, were bent on wreaking vengeance and on forcibly evicting Muslim residents in order to gain shelter for themselves. The Sardar was both impatient and angry. He only muttered in great anguish to me: "Why can't you get on with the job?"

Acting on the Sardar's *firman*, I set up headquarters of an Emergency Committee at the Town Hall and organised a "Control Room". In a couple of days, the situation was brought under control. The Muslim pockets around Jama Masjid and Bali Maran were fully protected against attacks by infuriated refugees. The Muslims living in these areas were also provided with food and fuel in their houses. A number of camps were set up for the Muslim refugees, the chief among which was in Purana Qila. A total of 150,000 were fed, clothed and provided with blankets and medical attendance.

*

Being Administrator of the United State of Matsya, I was travelling by car from Alwar to Jaipur to attend the inauguration of Greater Rajasthan. A man standing on the roadside stopped my car and showed me a note from the Private Secretary to the Deputy Prime Minister, V. Shankar, saying that the Dove carrying him and his party had force-landed.

I took over an hour to travel a distance of four miles and found Sardar Patel and his daughter, Maniben, settled comfortably in two chairs which had been detached from the aircraft. Some other members of the party were seated on the *charpoys* which the neighbouring villagers had provided.

On seeing me, the Sardar gave a broad smile and enquired as to how I managed to reach the spot. I briefly replied: "A note from your Private Secretary called me to my duty." The Sardar's humour had not deserted him and he quipped: "Somehow you manage to turn up from nowhere in critical situations.!"

The Sardar's face showed no sign of anxiety or agitation. He appeared well composed. He was at peace with himself and content with the situation in which he found himself. There was no trace of worry or annoyance or agitation. There was no excitement either. He seemed willing to let others do what was necessary to be done to take him from the site of landing to his destination in Jaipur.

I requested Sardar Patel and his party to get into my car. He, however, insisted that he must wait for the Maharaja of Jodhpur, who had gone to the main road to organise rescue from there. On being assured that the Maharaja would be looked after, he moved into the car with great reluctance. He desired that adequate arrangements should be made for the crew's comfort.

Yours sincerely,
K. B. Lall

xiii) K. B. Lall, ICS

17 May 1974

Dear Balraj Krishna,

Your letter of 3 May. The Sardar led the Indian team to the Partition Council. The breaking up of a single entity into two independent units was a complex operation. So much was to be done. So little time to do.

The Sardar kept all the ropes in his own hands. At the same time he believed in decentralisation and had confidence in the competence and patriotism of Civil Servants and military officers. He welded them into a united team.

The Sardar had an eye for the essential and yet no detail escaped his attention. He defended with determination every Indian interest. He had no difficulty in reconciling it with generosity and goodwill for Pakistan. On all but three issues agreed decisions were reached. At the last meeting of the Partition Council, Abdur Rab Nishtar, while taking leave of him, admired his statesmanship, applauded his constructive approach and affirmed that the Pak Ministers would continue to look upon him as their elder brother.

Opposition wilted before his firmness; flexibility converted opponents into friendly followers. He listened to everyone, without exception; but at the end he expected to be listened to. He was both respected and feared at the same time. He handled men, both admirers and critics, as human beings. Pettiness and prejudice had no place in his versatile repertoire. He was harsh if the occasion so demanded. He was kind and considerate, even to those who worked against him.

India's State structure and administrative system bear testimony to his patriotic vision and wise statesmanship. The monument to the Sardar as leader of men is enshrined in the hearts and deeds of those whose minds he transformed, whose actions he inspired, and whose determination he helped to steel!

Yours sincerely,
K. B. Lall

xiv) N. Senapati, ICS

24 April 1969

Dear Mr. Krishna,

I thank you for your letter of 21 April 1969. When Sardar Patel came to Cuttack on 13 December 1947, I was present at the various conferences he had with the Ruling Chiefs of Orissa. In the meeting at Governor's residence, a 21-year old Prince started talking about: "My people want . . ." Sardar Patel remarked: "They are not your people, Your Highness. They are my people. Leave them to me." A saffron-robed Prince started talking about Princely duty. Sardar Patel remarked: "Your Holiness is not fit for Princely duties." When Maharaja of Mayurbhanj said that he had transferred power to his Ministers, Sardar Patel left him out of the discussion with the remark: "I will deal with Your Highness later".

At the public meeting held at Cuttack, on 14 December 1947, large numbers of people from the Princely States had come. They demanded that power in the feudatory States should be transferred to the Ministers in each State and not given to the Government of Orissa. Sardar Patel remarked: "Shall I take from a thief and give to a dacoit?"

After signing an agreement on 15 December 1947, at one of the meetings with Sardar Patel at Delhi, the Ruling Chiefs produced legal arguments to justify their demand to be left as separate entities and not be merged with Orissa. Sardar Patel heard the Princes for about half an hour and remarked: "Your Highnesses may consult lawyers, but I make the law." To the demand of the Princes to form a Union, Sardar Patel remarked: "I am prepared to leave each of your Highnesses as a separate unit, but will not allow Your Highnesses to form a Union. Remember, if any of Your Highnesses wants my help to deal with your people, I will not come to your help."

Yours sincerely,
N. Senapati

xv) K. P. S. Menon, ICS, Foreign Secretary

22 October 1968

Dear Sri Krishna,

Many thanks for your letter of 9 October. Here's the story about the Jam Saheb of Nawanagar. In 1949, when I was Foreign Secretary, we were selecting our delegation to the General Assembly of the United Nations. At that time, we followed the British practice of invariably including a representative of the Princes. A reference was made to the State Department, which was included in the Home Department under Sardar Patel; and the name suggested by them was the Jam Saheb of Nawanagar. I mentioned this to Jawaharlal Nehru. He did not like this nomination and exclaimed: "I am damned if I send him on our delegation. He and his diamond buttons!" I then went to Sardar Patel and said that the Prime Minister would like to have another name for inclusion in the delegation. Sardar Patel kept quiet for a few seconds and said: "I have given my nomination and I stick to it." Panditji accepted the nomination without further ado.

Yours sincerely,
K. P. S. Menon

xvi) K. P. S. Menon, ICS, Foreign Secretary

24 February 1970

My dear Krishna,

Many thanks for your letter of the 18 February. I can well understand why your biography of Sardar Patel is taking so much time. I am sure it will be a valuable contribution to the history of our times.

As regards your query about Sir C. P. Ramaswamy Iyer, all I can say is that he declared Travancore independent in a moment of megalomania. Not only did he declare Travancore independent but he expressed his intention to establish diplomatic relations between Travancore and Pakistan, and even selected a retired Police Officer for the post of Ambassador of Travancore in Karachi. Sir CP was a man of great ability and resourcefulness, but he was also a superb egoist.

With kind regards,

Yours sincerely,
K. P. S. Menon

xvii) Shavax A. Lal, ICS

6 January 1970

Dear Shri Krishna,

I am really very sorry for not having replied to your letter
of 5 October 1969 and the previous one of 2 August.

Your letter kindled a host of memories of my association
with Sardar Patel and it was not easy to pick one which was
free from political overtones. I have always scrupulously
avoided politics of any kind and that was perhaps one reason
why the Sardar had implicit faith in the objectivity of my
opinions. I have, however, no hesitation in recalling the
following incident:

My first contact with Sardar Patel was soon after the joint
Congress and Muslim League Government was formed (in
1946). I was then Law Secretary and one day the Sardar sent
for me. He asked my opinion on a question which was raised
by the then Governor-General. Having just had a somewhat
unpleasant experience of a straightforward but rather
unpalatable opinion given by me to one of his Cabinet
colleagues, I asked the Sardar whether he wanted my honest
opinion. The Sardar flared up and said tartly: "Does
Government pay you Rs. 4000/- a month for your dishonest
opinions? It is your duty to give an honest opinion and it is
for me to accept it or not."

The incident so impressed me that I remember his exact
words. After this introduction I knew where I stood and never
hesitated to speak my mind whenever the Sardar consulted
me, which was quite often, and the questions were not
confined to legal matters only. It was indeed a pleasure to

work with Sardar because those who worked with him instinctively felt that he would never let them down.

Yours sincerely,
Shavax A. Lal

xviii) K. M. Munshi

17 December 1968

Dear Shri Balraj,

Please refer to your letter of 12 December. The substance of Article 370 of the Constitution was settled before Nehru left for USA. The drafting was left to Sri Gopalaswamy Ayyangar, Sheikh Abdullah and myself. Sheikh Abdullah was unhappy with the Article as we drafted and though he was scheduled to support the Article before the Constituent Assembly, he absented himself.

Yours sincerely,
K. M. Munshi

(Note: *Abdullah didn't do that. In Nehru's absence, Patel was the Prime Minister. He, therefore, preferred to attend the debate on Article 370 in the Constituent Assembly, but could not bear the discussion. He lodged a loud protest by saying: "I am going back to Kashmir." That evening he had settled down in his railway compartment when Mahavir Tyagi entered to deliver Patel's stern message: "You could leave the House; but you cannot leave New Delhi." A tamed Abdullah quietly got down and didn't go back to Kashmir*)

xix) Frank Anthony, MP, leader of Anglo-Indians

31 October 1968

Dear Mr. Krishna,

I am sorry for the delay in my replying to your letter of 18 ultimo. I met Sardar Patel. This was my first meeting. In the popular mind he had been invested with an awesome aura, as the "Iron Man" of India. That *nom de guerre* suggested not only a hard but even ruthless approach to administrative and political problems. As a lawyer I had got into the habit of trying to study those whom I met and of forming an estimate of their qualities.

As I sat down, I scrutinised the Sardar. His heavy-lidded, half-closed eyes and sphinx-like manner did not help in my assessment. I stated the case of the community before him rather fully, setting out the historical and political position and also the special economic needs of the community. Beyond a few non-committal monosyllabic grunts he did not interrupt me. I wondered how much he had taken in. To my surprise he then put me a series of staccato questions which no other leader had asked. I realised then, what further contacts and subsequently increasing close association only helped to confirm.

Here was a man with a crystal-clear mind who could see to the core of a problem within the shortest possible time. He asked me how many seats I wanted. I said three. He asked me how many votes in my opinion would be required to return three candidates to the Constituent Assembly. I said that my estimate was that, on an average, it would require about four votes in each Provincial Assembly to return one representative to the Constituent Assembly. I made it clear, however, that except for Bengal where we had 4 seats, we could not, on our own, return an Anglo-Indian representative to the Constituent Assembly. He asked me how many seats we had in all the Provincial Assemblies. I said 12. How many of these representatives, he asked, would vote according to my direction. I said all 12. He was a little incredulous that I could command the vote of every Anglo-Indian in every Legislature, but I assured him that this was a fact.

He then said that since we had 12 seats in the Provincial Legislatures, he would be prepared, on my assurance of their voting solidly at my direction, to recommend three seats for the community in the Constituent Assembly. He said that the Anglo-Indians would have to vote in support of non Anglo-Indian Congress candidates in States where no Anglo-Indian representative could be returned, but that from three Provincial Assemblies he would ensure, by giving us the necessary number of Congress votes, that three Anglo-Indians are returned to the Constituent Assembly.

Yours sincerely,
Frank Anthony

xx) Lieutenant General L. P. Sen

26 August 1970

Dear Mr. Krishna,

Thank your for your letter of 14 August. In 1955, when I was commanding 4 Division in Ambala, Messervey, as Colonel of the JAT Regiment, came to India to visit the unit. At Army HQ's request he was my guest. One evening I asked him a straight question as to whether he was aware of the preparations being made to invade Kashmir. His answer to me was "Yes." Akbar Khan's office was very close to his, and he had been told to give Akbar Khan all the help he required.

Sardar Patel's attitude towards J&K left no doubts in any one's mind. It had acceded to India and was Indian territory, and as such any invasion of the State must be firmly dealt with. I do know that Sardar Patel had a high opinion of Bakshi Ghulam Mohd whom he regarded as an individual who would get on with the job and not bellyache.

Yours sincerely,
Lieut-Gen. L.P. Sen

xxi) Humayun Kabir, union minister; earlier long-time secretary to Maulana Azad

22 July 1969

Dear Mr. Krishna,

Your letter of 6 March regarding your biography of Sardar Patel. As far as I am aware, there was no sharp difference between Sardar Patel and Maulana Azad till 1945. They had of course occasional differences, but these were not strong. I do not know if the period spent together in Ahmednagar Jail had anything to do with their growing estrangement. After 1945, I think, personal and political factors combined to draw them apart. You may remember that when Maulana Azad's term was over, Mahatma Gandhi had thought of Sardar Patel as the new President of the Congress. This was virtually

choosing Sardar Patel to be the first Prime Minister of India.
Maulana Azad intervened by proposing Pandit Nehru's name.

I think this was the last and perhaps the most powerful
cause of antipathy between Sardar Patel and Maulana Azad.
Maulana Azad at that time thought that Sardar Patel's views
were somewhat narrow, but I think towards the end of his
life, he changed his views.

Yours sincerely,
Humayun Kabir

(The *Statesman* of 25 August 1969: Humayun Kabir stated
that "Maulana Azad in his last days had come to believe that
Sardar Patel would have made a better Prime Minister than
Mr. Nehru".)

xxii) C. D. Deshmukh (ICS)

2 October 1962

Dear Shri Krishna,

Thank you for sending me a copy of your article – I can
only say that I read it with interest. It seems to me that two
propositions are incontestable:

1.   No nation has the good fortune to have an unbroken
succession of supermen, and

2.   Amongst the others who also come to the top,
selection and stability can only come through full operation
of democratic processes. Nominations may work only through

silent acknowledgement. Shri Nehru's leadership began with nomination, but has continued because he is what he is.

Yours sincerely,
C. D. Deshmukh

xxiii) Lord Mountbatten

31 July 1968

Dear Shri Krishna,

Thank you for your letter of the 27 July from which I am glad to note that you have undertaken to write the biography of my friend, Sardar Vallabhbhai Patel.

It would have been easy to help you if you had been in England or I had been in India but more difficult to do so by correspondence.

Yours sincerely,
Lord Mountbatten

xxiv) Lord Mountbatten

3 November 1969

Dear Shri Krishna,

Thank you for your letters of the 20 August and 14 October.

I am afraid your letter of the 20 August arrived while I was abroad, and my archivist started acting immediately on it, and had great difficulty in tracing any of the Patel papers as they are not, unfortunately, all filed under Patel but in several different places.

First of all let me thank you very warmly for having sent me a copy of Sardar Patel's letter to me of the 20 August 1948 which I am delighted to have. I remember it well and I am very sorry to say my archivist has been unable to find the original so far. We are, therefore, particularly glad to have a copy. On the other hand, she has been able to trace the original of the remarks about oil contained in my Farewell Memorandum and your copy is correct, and I have no objection to it being used in your proposed book on the Indian Oil Industry.

Turning to the three letters from Sardar Patel dated the 16 August 1947, 31 October 1947 and 11 July 1948, of which photostat copies have been sent to you. My archivist has not been able to find a copy of my letter to Sardar Patel of the 14 August 1947, but has found those of the 31 October 1947 and 19 June 1948. She had made typewritten copies for you which I enclose.

I am afraid I am under such heavy pressure (last month I made twenty-four speeches) I have not been able to read your articles.

My archivist has also searched for my "excellent note on some of the current problems" to which Sardar Patel referred in his letter of the 11 July 1948, but has not yet been able to find it.

When she does she will send it to you in due course.

Yours sincerely,
Lord Mountbatten

xxv)   Lord Mountbatten's archivist

30 July 1970

Dear Mr. Krishna,

The Secretary of the British Cabinet has now replied on behalf of the Government with reference to the papers which relate to the period when Lord Mountbatten was Viceroy of undivided India. He has given authority for you to have photostat copies of the papers you ask for, and I am prepared to send them on to you, subject to your being prepared to give in return an undertaking which the British Government require you to sign. The reason is that under the 30 year rule these documents would not be available until 1978.

I am, therefore, sending you three copies of the undertaking. Will you kindly sign two copies, one for the Secretary of the Cabinet and one for the Broadlands Archives, and retain the third copy yourself. I will then send on the papers you want, and there will thus be the agreed charge of 1/- per page and an additional charge for the postage under registered cover, as you ask. There is no need, of course, to pay the charges until you receive the copies.

If you wish to have access to the documents relating to the period when Lord Mountbatten was Governor-General of Independent India, after 15 August 1947, then Lord Mountbatten will apply to the Queen's Private Secretary for Her Majesty's concurrence for copies of the documents being given to you, and I know from previous experience that he would require an assurance from your Prime Minister's Private Secretary, which I suggest you should send through me, that the Government of India would have no objection to your having access to these documents.

Since writing the foregoing I realise that these papers are very delicate, and in view of this I will make arrangements to have them forwarded to you, possibly through the British High Commission in New Delhi.

Yours sincerely,
Mollie Travis

15

THE MAN WHO DARED CHURCHILL

But Won His Admiration

None could dare Churchill. He was indomitable. He towered over all around him. His fierce bulldog looks commanded immediate obedience. He was a super egoist too, whose voice drowned out others. It was Patel whose "ironness" quietened the British "bulldog"; even won his appreciation for his unexpected, bold retort. Their spat was over Churchill's unbecoming running down of India in June 1948 while "bemoaning the disappearance of the title of Emperor of India from the Royal titles". In his arrogance Churchill had poured out simply venom: "Power will go into the hands of rascals, rogues and free-booters . . . These are men of straw of whom no trace will be found after a few years."

Patel's unification of India totally falsified Churchill. The evil he and other British diehards like Curzon had sown in India is the evil currently plaguing Britain with dreadful consequences. India has emerged far more stable, making all-round progress, whereas in Britain, society is being torn apart, with British Muslims being considered "an enemy within". Not only did they lend support to local terrorism, but openly showed loyalty to distant Iraqis and Lebanese—unmindful of the welcome the British government and people had shown them on their migration to Britain.

Patel could not stomach the insult to India, as well as to his colleagues in the government of which he was the deputy prime minister. From his sick-bed at Dehra Dun, Patel gave Churchill a blistering reply, calling him, what no one else could have dared: "an unashamed imperialist at a time when imperialism is on its last legs". He even called him "the proverbial last ditcher for whom obstinacy and stupid consistency count more than reason, imagination or wisdom".

Patel did not stop at that. He gave Britain a stern warning none had delivered so far: "I should like to tell His Majesty's government that if they wish India to maintain friendly relations with Great Britain, they must see that India is in no way subjected to malicious and venomous attacks of this kind, and that British statesmen and others learn to speak of this country in terms of friendship and goodwill."[1]

Churchill took Patel's counter-attack in good spirit—as between two great men—by conveying a message to him, through Anthony Eden, earlier his foreign secretary, who was visiting India, that he had "thoroughly enjoyed the retort" and that he had "nothing but admiration for the way the new Dominion had settled down to the tasks and responsibilities, particularly those involving relations with the Indian States". Churchill had specially said that the Sardar should "not confine himself within the limits of India, but the world was entitled to see and hear more of him".[2]

NOTES

Introduction

1. Wavell, *The Viceroy's Journal*, p. 260.
2. Alan Campbell-Johnson, *Mission With Mountbatten*, p. 52.
3. *Sardar Patel's Speeches* (Hindi translation from Gujarati by Narhari D. Parikh), p. 445.
4. The *Hindu*, 16 November 1997.
5. M. N. Roy, *Men I Met*, pp. 15-16.

1: What was Vallabhbhai?

1. *This was Sardar*, Commemorative Volume, vol. I, pp. 447-49.
2. Ibid.
3. Ibid.
4. *Harijan*, 26 January 1951, p. 419.
5. The London *Times*, 16 December 1950.
6. The *Manchester Guardian* (now the *Guardian*), 16 December 1950.

7. Thakur Jaswant Singh, recorded interview with author, 5-7 March 1970.

8. Lieut-Gen. S. P. P. Thorat, *From Reveille to Retreat*, p.119.

9. Khushwant Singh (former Editor, the *Illustrated Weekly of India*), recorded interview with author; also, his autobiography *Truth, Love and a Little Malice*, pp. 116-17.

10. *This was Sardar*, Commemorative Volume, vol. I, p. 168.

11. Ibid, p. 207.

12. A. R. Tiwari, *Making of a Leader—Sardar Vallabhbhai Patel*, p. 6.

13. Narhari D. Parikh, *Sardar Vallabhbhai Patel*, vol. I, p. 27.

14. Tiwari, *Making of a Leader—Sardar Vallabhbhai Patel*, pp. 13-14

15. Ibid, p. 184.

16. *Sardar Patel's Speeches* (in Hindi), 1918-48, p. 467.

17. Parikh, p. 36

PART I: DIRECT ROLE

2: Freedom Fighter

Kheda Satyagraha

1. Pattabhi Sitaramayya, *The History of the Indian National Congress*, part I, p. 239.

2. *Sardar Patel*, by Junius, article in the *Bharat*, 31 October 1951.

3. The *Bombay Chronicle*, 13 January 1915.

4. G. V. Mavalankar, *Sardar Patel*, an article on Patel's 70th birthday in the *Tribune*, Lahore, 3 November 1945.

5. Ibid

6. Narhari D. Parikh, *Sardar Vallabhbhai Patel*, vol. I, p. 67.

7. Ibid, p. 78.

8. Ibid, pp. 49-50.

9. Ibid, p. 58.

10. Ibid.

11. Ibid, p. 60.

12. Ibid, p. 55.

13. Ibid, p. 72.
14. Ibid.
15. *Sardar Patel's Speeches* (in Hindi), pp. 3-4.
16. Parikh, *Sardar Vallabhbhai Patel*, vol. I, p. 74.
17. The *Bombay Chronicle*, 13 April 1918.
18. Ibid.
19. Parikh, *Sardar Vallabhbhai Patel*, vol. I, p. 80.
20. *Sardar Patel's Speeches* (in Hindi), pp. 4-5.
21. Parikh, *Sardar Vallabhbhai Patel*, vol. I, p. 85.
22. The *Bombay Chronicle*, 3 June 1918.
23. Ibid.

Nagpur Satyagraha

1. Narhari D. Parikh, *Sardar Vallabhbhai Patel*, vol. I, p. 204.
2. Ibid, p. 206.

Borsad Satyagraha

1. Narhari D. Parikh, *Sardar Vallabhbhai Patel*, vol. I, pp. 220-22.
2. Ibid, p. 223.
3. Ibid, p. 228 (quote from pamphlet issued by Patel).
4. Ibid, p. 242.
5. Ibid, pp. 242-43.
6. *Young India*, 6 April 1924.

Bardoli Satyagraha

1. Mahadev Desai, *The Story of Bardoli*, p. 107.
2. The *Times of India*, 4 July 1928.
3. Desai, *The Story of Bardoli*, pp. 12-13.
4. Ibid, p. 12.
5. Ibid, p. 14.
6. Ibid, p. 49.
7. Narhari D. Parikh, *Sardar Vallabhbhai Patel*, vol. I, pp. 305-06.
8. Ibid, p. 306.
9. Ibid, p. 321.
10. Desai, *The Story of Bardoli*, p. 58.
11. Parikh, *Sardar Vallabhbhai Patel*, vol. I, pp. 343-44.

12. Desai, *The Story of Bardoli*, p. 97.
13. Ibid, p. 73.
14. Parikh, *Sardar Vallabhbhai Patel*, vol. I, p. 318.
15. Desai, *The Story of Bardoli*, p. 97.
16. The *Times of India*, 4 July 1928.
17. Parikh, *Sardar Vallabhbhai Patel*, vol. I, p. 324.
18. Ibid, pp. 325-26.
19. Desai, *The Story of Bardoli*, pp. 155-56.
20. Ibid, p. 160.
21. Parikh, *Sardar Vallabhbhai Patel*, vol. I, p. 334.
22. Ibid, pp. 336-37.
23. Ibid, p. 338.
24. Desai, *The Story of Bardoli*, p. 197.
25. Parikh, *Sardar Vallabhbhai Patel*, vol. I, p. 347.
26. Ibid, p. 349.
27. Desai, *The Story of Bardoli*, p. 228.
28. Ibid, p. 257.
29. Ibid, p. 260.
30. Ibid, pp. 262-63.
31. Subhas Chandra Bose, *The Indian Struggle*, p. 152.
32. Judith M. Brown, *Modern India*, p. 259.

Dandi March

1. Prof. N. R. Phatak, *Government of Maharashtra Source Material for a History of the Freedom Movement in India*, vol. III, part III, 1929-31, p. 19.
2. Pattabhi Sitaramayya, *The History of the Indian National Congress*, vol. I (1885-1935), p. 638.
3. Phatak, ibid, p. 14.
4. Sitaramayya, ibid, p. 639.
5. Narhari D. Parikh, *Sardar Vallabhbhai Patel*, vol. II, p. 13.
6. Phatak, ibid, p. 12.
7. Ibid, p. 16.
8. William L. Shirer, *Gandhi: A Memoir*, p. 95.
9. Parikh, *Sardar Vallabhbhai Patel*, vol. II, pp. 6-7.
10. *Sardar Patel's Speeches* (Hindi), edited by Narhari Parikh, p. 221.

11. Ibid, pp. 222-23.
12. Parikh, *Sardar Vallabhbhai Patel*, vol. II, p. 9.
13. Ibid, p. 12.
14. Ibid, pp. 10-12.
15. H. N. Brailsford, *Subject India*, pp. 232-34.
16. Ashabhai Patel, recorded interview, 16 March 1969.
17. Shirer, *Gandhi: A Memoir*, p. 98.
18. Ibid, p. 71.
19. Ibid, p. 96.

3: Party Boss

1. Jawaharlal Nehru, *Autobiography*, pp. 328 and 338.
2. M. N. Roy, *Men I Met*, p. 16.
3. Jawaharlal Nehru, *A Bunch of Old Letters*, p. 120.
4. Ibid, pp. 156-57.
5. Ibid, p. 166.
6. Pattabhi Sitaramayya, *The History of the Indian National Congress*, vol. II, p. 8.
7. Ibid, p. 13.
8. Nehru, ibid, p. 175.
9. Ibid, p. 178.
10. Ibid, pp. 197-98.
11. Ibid, pp. 182 and 185.
12. M. R. Masani, recorded interview with author, 25 July 1969.
13. Parikh, *Sardar Vallabhbhai Patel*, vol. II, p. 220.
14. Ibid, pp. 237-38
15. Ibid, p. 283.
16. Ibid, p. 288.
17. Ibid, p. 289.
18. Ibid, p. 287.
19. Ibid, p. 270.
20. Ibid, p. 389.
21. Ibid, p. 390.
22. Ibid, p. 391.

23. Ibid, pp. 393-94.

24. Ibid, p. 396.

25. Sitaramayya, *The History of the Indian National Congress*, vol. II, p. 113.

26. Ibid, p. 115.

27. Roy, *Men I Met*, p. 16.

28. Sarat Chandra Bose, letter to Gandhi dated 21 March 1938, published in *Dr. Rajendra Prasad Correspondence and Select Documents*, vol. 3, p. 214.

29. Subhas Chandra Bose, *Indian Struggle*, p. 333.

4: Administrative Unifier

1. H. V. R. Iengar (ICS), *Vallabhbai Patel: A Birthday Memorial Lecture* at Surat Municipal Corporation, 31 October 1973 (unpublished paper with author).

2. The London *Times*, 23 October 1946.

3. B. K. Nehru (ICS), *Thoughts on Our Present Discontents*, pp. 97-98.

4. Ibid.

5. The *Bombay Chronicle*, 21 April 1947.

6. *Harijan*, A tribute to Patel by a Civil Servant, 26 January 1951, p. 439.

7. H.V. R. Iengar (ICS), *The Image of the Police*, article in the *Indian Express*, 8 September 1966.

8. Kewal L. Punjabi (ICS), *The Civil Servant in India* by ex. ICS, p. v.

9. Judith M. Brown, *Modern India*, p. 347.

10. Iengar: *Administration in India*, p. 40.

11. *Sardar Patel, in tune with the millions—II,* vol. III, p. 129.

12. *Constituent Assembly of India (Legislative) Debates*, vol. II, part II, 4 February to 18 March 1949, p. 1451.

13. H. V. R. Iengar, *Making of Decisions by Government*, the *Indian Express*, 4 February 1964.

14. The *Statesman*, 16 December 1950.

5: Partition

1. H. V. Hodson, *The Great Divide: Britain-India-Pakistan*, p. 200.
2. K. P. S. Menon (ICS), *Many Worlds Revisted: an Autobiography*, p. 262.
3. Pyarelal, *Mahatma Gandhi—The Last Phase*, vol. II, p. 11.
4. Ibid, p. 3.
5. Ibid, p. 35.
6. Alan Campbell-Johnson, *Mission with Mountbatten*, p. 52.
7. Penderel Moon, *Divide and Quit*, p. 64.
8. A. K. Mazumdar, *Advent of Indian Independence* (quotes K. M. Munshi's letter dated 4 December 1962), p. 410.
9. R. J. Moore, *Escape from Empire: the Attlee Government and the Indian Problem*, p. 85.
10. Maulana Azad, *India Wins Freedom*, p. 226.
11. Wavell, *The Viceroy's Journal*, p. 291.
12. Ayesha Jalal, *The Sole Spokesman: Jinnah, the Muslim League and the Demand for Pakistan*, p. 200.
13. Wavell, *The Viceroy's Journal*, p. 260.
14. "The Transfer of Power", 1942-47, Vol. VIII, p. 190; also Wavell, p. 329
15. *Sardar's Letters: Mostly Unknown—I*, vol. IV, p. 238.
16. Wavell, *The Viceroy's Journal*, p. 291.
17. *Sardar Patel's Correspondence*, vol. III, p. 303.
18. Hodson, *The Great Divide: Britain-India-Pakistan*, p. 235.
19. Ibid, p. 179
20. R. J. Moore, *Escape from Empire: The Attlee Government and the Indian Problem*, p. 115.
21. V. P. Menon, *The Transfer of Power in India*, p. 363.
22. Alan Campbell-Johnson, *Mission with Mountbatten*, p. 89.
23. Moore, *Escape from Empire: the Attlee Government and the Indian Problem*, p. 251.
24. Hodson, *The Great Divide: Britain-India-Pakistan*, p. 309.

25. Pyarelal, ibid *Mahatma Gandhi—The Last Phase*, vol. II, (quotes from Patel's speech in the Constituent Assembly in November 1949), p. 184.
26. H. M. Patel (ICS), recorded interview, 25 July 1970.
27. H. M. Patel: *Rites of Passage: a Civil Servant Remembers*, p. 184.
28. K. B. Lall (ICS), letter to author, 17 May 1974.
29. Alan Campbell-Johnson, *Mission with Mountbatten*, p. 214.

6: Creator of One India

1. *The Evolution of India and Pakistan (1858 to 1947): Select Documents* (HMG), p. 425.
2. H. V. Hodson, *The Great Divide: Britain-India-Pakistan*, p. 364.
3. *For a United India*, (Speeches of Sardar Patel), pp. 3-5.
4. *Sardar Patel's Correspondence*, vol. V, p. 392.
5. K. M. Munshi, *Indian Constitutional Documents*, vol. II, pp. 415-16.

Eastern States

1. V. P. Menon, *The Story of the Integration of the Indian States*, p. 163.
2. N. Senapati (ICS), letter to author, 24 April 1969.
3. *Sardar Patel, in tune with the millions—I*, vol. II, pp. 68-69
4. Senapati, letter to author, 24 April 1969.
5. Dr. K. N. Katju, *This was Sardar*, Commemorative Volume, vol. I, p. 22.
6. *Sardar's Letters: Mostly Unknown II*, vol. V, p. 39.
7. *Sardar Patel, in tune with the millions—I*, vol. II, p. 106.
8. *Sardar Patel, in tune with the millions—II*, vol. III, p. 92.

Greater Rajasthan

1. *Sardar Patel, in tune with the millions—II*, vol. III, p. 69.
2. K. M. Panikkar, *An Autobiography*, pp. 190-91.

Travancore

1. The *Bombay Chronicle*, 10 May 1947.

2. K. M. Munshi, *Pilgrimage to Freedom*, vol. I, p. 165.
3. *Hyderabad in Retrospect,* a *Times of India* publication (February 1949), comprising articles by ex-officials of Hyderabad, p. 18. K. M. Munshi, in *Pilgrimage to Freedom* credits this to Ali Yavar Jung, p. 165.
4. The *Indian Express*, 27 April 1947.
5. Patel Papers (unpublished letters).
6. H. V. Hodson, *The Great Divide: Britian-India-Pakistan*, p. 362.
7. The *Bombay Chronicle*, 11 June 1947.
8. M. J. Koshy, *Last Days of Monarchy in Kerala*, pp. 271-72.
9. The *Bombay Chronicle*, 18 June 1947.
10. Ibid, 23 June 1947.
11. Ibid, 25 June 1947.
12. Ibid, 16 June 1947.
13. K. P. S. Menon (ICS), letter to author, 24 February 1970.
14. *Sardar Patel's Correspondence*, vol. V, pp. 446-47.
15. K. M. Panikkar, *An Autobiography*, p. 162.
16. Munshi, *Pilgrimage to Freedom*, vol. I, p. 165.
17. *Sardar Patel's Correspondence*, vol. VI, p. 375.
18. *Sardar Patel, in tune with the millions—II*, vol. III, pp. 74-75.
19. Hodson, *The Great Divide: Britian-India-Pakistan*, vide *Viceroy's Personal Report*, No. 15, 1 August 1947, p. 378.

Jodhpur

1. H. V. Hodson, *The Great Divide: Britian-India-Pakistan*, p. 379.
2. H. V. R. Iengar (ICS), *Sardar's Ways: Focus on Main Tasks*, the *Indian Express*, 31 May 1965.
3. C. S. Venkatachar (ICS), interview with author, 17 May 1969.
4. K. M. Munshi, *Pilgrimage to Freedom*, p. 163.
5. V. P. Menon, *The Story of the Integration of the Indian States*, p. 116.
6. Venkatachar, ibid.

7. *Sardar Patel's Correspondence*, vol. V, Appendices, pp. 515-16.
8. Menon, *The Story of the Integration of the Indian States*, p. 117.
9. Ibid.
10. Mountbatten, *Memorandum of 17 March 1976,* addressed to author.
11. Iengar, recorded interview with author, 25 April 1975.
12. Iengar, *Sardar's Ways . . .*, the *Indian Express*, 31 May 1965.
13. Iengar, interview with author, 25 April 1975.

Kathiawar

1. *Sardar Patel's Correspondence*, vol. V, p. 475.
2. *Sardar's Letters: Mostly Unknown I*, vol. IV, p. 256.
3. Ibid, II (Vol. V), p. 17.
4. Ibid, p. 20.
5. Ibid, p. 19.
6. Ibid, p. 18.
7. V. P. Menon, *The Story of the Integration of the Indian States*, p. 126.
8. *For a United India: Speeches of Sardar Patel (1947-50)*, p.31.
9. Menon, *The Story of the Integration of the Indian States*, p. 197.
10. Jawaharlal Nehru, *Letters to Chief Ministers*, vol. I, p. 67.
11. *Sardar's Letters: Mostly Unknown II* vol. V, p. 22.

Bhopal

1. Pyarelal, *Mahatma Gandhi: the Last Phase*, vol. II, p. 332.
2. Alan Campbell-Johnson, *Mission With Mountbatten*, p. 147.
3. K. M. Panikkar, *An Autobiography*, p. 138.
4. Ibid, p. 148.
5. Ibid.
6. Ibid, p. 151.
7. H. V. Hodson, *The Great Divide: Britian-India-Pakistan*, p. 365.
8. Ibid, p. 375.
9. Wavell, *The Viceroy's Journal*, p. 383.

10. Hodson, *The Great Divide: Britian-India-Pakistan*, p. 427.
11. *Sardar Patel's Correspondence*, vol. V, pp. 361-63.
12. Hodson, *The Great Divide: Britian-India-Pakistan*, p. 376.
13. V. P. Menon, *The Story of the Integration of the Indian States*, p. 119.
14. Hodson, *The Great Divide: Britian-India-Pakistan*, p. 376.

Junagadh
1. *Sardar Patel, in tune with the millions—II*, vol. III, pp. 4-5.
2. H. V. Hodson, *The Great Divide: Britain-India-Pakistan*, p. 430.
3. *Sardar Patel's Correspondence*, vol. I, p. 220.
4. Hodson, *The Great Divide: Britain-India-Pakistan*, p. 430.
5. *Sardar's Letters: Mostly Unknown II*, vol. V, p. 74.
6. Alan Campbell-Johnson, *Mission With Mountbatten*, p. 192.
7. Hodson, *The Great Divide: Britain-India-Pakistan*, p. 428.
8. V. P. Menon, *The Story of the Integration of the Indian States*, p. 125.
9. Hodson, *The Great Divide: Britain-India-Pakistan*, p. 429.
10. Menon, *The Story of the Integration of the Indian States*, pp. 128-29.
11. Ibid, p. 127.
12. Alan Campbell-Johnson, *Mission With Mountbatten*, p. 191.
13. *Sardar Patel's Correspondence*, vol. VII, p. 335.
14. Menon, *The Story of the Integration of the Indian States*, p. 129.
15. Ibid, p. 130.
16. Alan Campbell-Johnson, *Mission With Mountbatten*, p. 194.
17. Menon, *The Story of the Integration of the Indian States*, p. 138.
18. Ibid, p. 141.
19. Hodson, *The Great Divide: Britain-India-Pakistan*, p. 438.
20. Menon, *The Story of the Integration of the Indian States*, p. 143.
21. Hodson, *The Great Divide: Britain-India-Pakistan*, p. 438.
22. Alan Campbell-Johnson, *Mission With Mountbatten*, p. 237.

23. Menon, *The Story of the Integration of the Indian States*, p. 147.
24. *Sardar Patel, in tune with the millions—I*, vol. II, p. 62.
25. Menon, *The Story of the Integration of the Indian States*, (quoted), p. 149.
26. *Sardar Patel's Correspondence*, vol. VII, pp. 392-93.

Hyderabad
1. *For a United India: Speeches of Sardar Patel (1947-50)*, p. 11.
2. Alan Campbell-Johnson, *Mission With Mountbatten*, p. 360.
3. H. V. Hodson, *The Great Divide: Britain-India-Pakistan*, p. 382.
4. Alan Campbell-Johnson, *Mission With Mountbatten*, p. 198.
5. Ibid, p. 295.
6. Ibid, p. 199.
7. H. V. Hodson, *The Great Divide: Britain-India-Pakistan*, p. 478.
8. R. J. More, *Escape from Empire: The Attlee Government and the Indian Problem*, pp. 305-08.
9. *Sardar Patel's Correspondence*, vol. VII, pp. 29, 30, 38.
10. K. M. Munshi, *Pilgrimage to Freedom*, vol. I, p. 166.
11. The *Indian Express*, 7 June, 1947.
12. V. P. Menon, *The Story of the Integration of the Indian States*, p. 317.
13. *Sardar Patel's Correspondence*, vol. VII, letter dated 31August 1947 from Arvamudh Aiyangar, member, Nizam's Executive Council, to Gopalaswami Ayyangar, p. 56.
14. Ibid, p. 109.
15. *Sardar Patel's Correspondence*, vol. VII, pp. 59-60.
16. Menon, *The Story of the Integration of the Indian States*, pp. 323, 327, 329, 330.
17. *Sardar Patel's Correspondence*, vol. VII, pp. 53, 54, 87.
18. Ibid, p. 111.
19. Ibid, pp. 80-81.
20. *Sardar Patel's Correspondence*, vol. VII, pp. 125-26.
21. Ibid, p. 134.

22. Ibid, p. 118.
23. Ibid, K. M. Munshi's letter of 17 May 1948 to the Nizam, p. 158.
24. Ibid, p. 110.
25. Ibid, pp. 105, 95.
26. Menon, *The Story of the Integration of the Indian States*, pp. 354-55, 348, 350-52.
27. *This Was Sardar—Commemorative Volume*, vol. I, pp. 244-45.
28. Jawaharlal Nehru, *Letters to Chief Ministers (1947-64)*, vol. I, p. 147.
29. *For a United India, Speeches of Sardar Patel (1947-50)*, p. 40.
30. K. M. Munshi, *The End of an Era: Hyderabad Memories*, p. 177.
31. *For a United India, Speeches of Sardar Patel (1947-50)*, p. 41.
32. V. P. Menon, *The Story of the Integration of the Indian States*, p. 368.
33. *Sardar Patel's Correspondence*, vol. VII, p. 217.
34. Munshi, *The End of an Era: Hyderabad Memories*, pp. 190, 180.
35. *Sardar Patel's Correspondence*, vol. VII, p. 194.
36. General Roy Bucher, C-in-C, Indian Army, letter to author, 19 December 1968.
37. Ibid.
38. Munshi, *The End of an Era: Hyderabad Memories*, p. 202.
39. General J. N. Chaudhuri, *An Autobiography*, p. 146.
40. The *Times of India*, 6 August 1958.
41. H. V. R. Iengar (ICS), *On Working Together*, the *Indian Express*, 18 September 1969.
42. Munshi, *The End of an Era: Hyderabad Memories*, pp. 239, 237.
43. Iengar, *On Working Together*, the *Indian Express*, 18 September 1969.
44. *Sardar Patel's Correspondence*, vol. VII, p. 242.
45. Bucher, letter to author, 19 December 1968.
46. Ibid, letter to sister, 4 April 1948.
47. *Sardar Patel's Correspondence*, vol. VII, pp. 266, 241, 246, 250, 255.

48. Jawaharlal Nehru, *Letters to Chief Ministers*, vol. I, pp. 206-07.
49. *Sardar Patel's Correspondence*, vol. VII, pp. 309-10, 315.
50. Bucher, letter to author, 19 December 1968.
51. W. Gordon Graham, the *Christian Science Monitor*, 1 February 1951.

7: Demolisher of Princely India

1. Vincent A. Smith, *The Oxford History of India*, p. 552.
2. C. S. Venkatachar (ICS), the *Hindu*, 11 July 1999.
3. *Sardar's Letters: Mostly Unknown II*, vol. V, p. 152.
4. K. P. S. Menon (ICS), the *Sunday Standard*, 12 September 1976.
5. Smith, *The Oxford History of India*, p. 664.
6. *Sardar Patel*, by Junius, article in the *Bharat*, 31 October 1951.

PART II: SUPPORTIVE ROLE

8: Kashmir, Tibet and Nepal

Mature and Far-sighted Advice
1. Subimal Dutt (ICS), *With Nehru in Foreign Office*, pp. 52-53.
2. *Sardar Patel's Correspondence*, vol. X, pp. 104-107.
3. Ibid, p. 90.
4. Ibid, pp. 9-10.

Kashmir
1. Alan Campbell-Johnson, *Mission with Mountbatten*, p. 225.
2. Ian Stephens, *Horned Moon*, p. 211.
3. Lieut. Gen. L. P. Sen, *Slender was the Thread*, p. 54.
4. Ibid, pp. 76-77.
5. *This was Sardar—Commemorative Volume"*, vol I, pp. 252, 253, 255
6. Soli Sorabjee, *Ninety Cheers for Sam Bahadur* in the *Indian Express*, 2 April 2003.
7. Air Marshal Thomas Elmhirst, letter to author, 8 January 1969.

8. *Sardar Patel's Correspondence*, vol. I, pp. 80-81.
9. Ibid, p. 73, Mountbatten's Note: A Discussion with Jinnah in Lahore on 1 November 1947
10. John Connell, *Auchinleck: A Biography of Field-Marshal Sir Claude Auchinleck*, p. 932.
11. Ajit Prasad Jain, *What Really Happened*, p. 14.
12. *Sardar Patel's Correspondence*, vol. I, p. 51.
13. *Sardar Patel's Correspondence*, vol. VI, p. 387.
14. Jawaharlal Nehru, *Letters to Chief Ministers*, vol. I, p. 43.
15. Ibid, p. 61.
16. Ibid, p. 119.
17. *Sardar Patel's Correspondence*, vol. I, p. 249.
18. Lieut.-Gen. S. P. P. Thorat, *From Reveille to Retreat*, p. 101.
19. Sarvepalli Gopal, *Jawaharlal Nehru*, vol. III, p. 263.
20. Stanley Wolpert, *Nehru: A Tryst With Destiny*, p. 424.
21. Prem Nath Bazaz, *The History of Struggle for Freedom in Kashmir*, p. 248.
22. Ibid, p. 272.
23. *Sardar Patel's Correspondence*, vol. I, p. 130.
24. Ibid, pp. 119-22.
25. K. M. Munshi, letter to author, 17 December 1968.
26. Mahavir Tyagi, interview with author; also narrated by Prakash Vir Shastri, MP, in *Swatantra Jyoti* (Sardar Patel Number), 1973, p. 27.
27. H. V. Kamath, MP, *Sardar Vallabhbhai Patel: Some Memories*, in *Bhavan's Journal*, 26 January 1982, p. 63.
28. M. P. Masani, letter to author, 25 July 1969.
29. Shahid Hamid, Major-General, *Disastrous Twilight*, p. 293.
30. Jayaprakash Narayan, *Sardar's Immortal Legacy* in the *Swatantra Jyoti*, Special Patel Number 1973, p. 13.
31. M. N. Roy, *Men I Met*, p. 17.

Tibet

1. Sarvepalli Gopal, *Jawaharlal Nehru*, vol. III, pp. 223-237.
2. Ibid, p. 33 (quoted from A. Pant's *Mandala*).

3. *Sardar Patel's Correspondence*, vol. VIII, p. 136.
4. K. M. Munshi, *Pilgrimage to Freedom*, p. 175.
5. *Sardar Patel's Correspondence*, vol. X, pp. 336-41.
6. Brown, Judith M., *Modern India: The Origins of an Asian Democracy*, p. 128

Nepal
1. K. P .S. Menon (ICS), *Memories and Musings*, p. 46.
2. Sarvepalli Gopal, *Jawaharlal Nehru*, vol. III.
3. The London *Economist*, 22 April 2006.

PART III: APPENDICES

9: A Churchillian Plan

1. Wavell, *The Viceroy's Journal*, p. 120.
2. Cited in *The Untold Story of India's Partition* by Narendra Singh Sarila, Oriental & Indian Collection, British Library, London, (hereafter OIC) p. 25.
3. Ibid, p. 26.
4. *The Transfer of Power 1942-4*, vol. I, the Cripps Mission, January-April 1942, Document 208, pp. 282-84.
5. Ibid, Document 375, p. 468.
6. Sarila, ibid (OIC cited), p. 24.
7. Ibid, p. 22.
8. Ibid, p. 23.
9. Lieut-Gen. L. P. Sen, *Slender was the Thread: Kashmir Confrontation 1947-48*, p. 22.
10. The *Times of India*, 14 June 1987.
11. Durga Das, *India from Curzon to Nehru and After*, p. 216.
12. *The Transfer of Power*, vol. VI, pp. 71-72.
13. Ayesha Jalal, *The Sole Spokesman: Jinnah, the Muslim League and the Demand for Pakistan*, p. 83.
14. John Glendevon, *The Viceroy at Bay*, p. 198.
15. H. V. Hodson, *The Great Divide: Britain-India-Pakistan*, pp. 124-25.
16. Ibid.
17. Ibid, p. 166.

18. *Sardar Patel's Correspondence*, vol. III, p. 179 (G.L. Mehta's letter to Patel).
19. The *Statesman*, 21 August 1946.
20. Penderel Moon, *Divide and Quit*, p. 69.
21. Ibid, p. 20.
22. Humphrey Evans, *Thimayya of India: A Soldier's Life*, p. 253.
23. Ibid, pp. 255.
24. *Sardar Patel's Correspondence*, vol. IV, pp. 320-21, letter dated 1 September 1947.
25. Alan Campbell-Johnson, *Mission with Mountbatten*, p. 214.
26. Moon, *Divide and Quit*, p. 247.
27. Mridula Sarabhai, the *Tribune*, 16 April 1948, cited in *South Asia*, journal of South Asian Studies, vol. XVIII, 1995, p. 70.
28. *South Asia*, p. 67.
29. Roy Bucher, letter to author, 30 July 1969 (reproduced on p. 201).
30. The *Times of India*, 14 December 1981.
31. Stanley Wolpert, *Jinnah of Pakistan*, p. 164.
32. Ayesha Jalal, *The Sole Spokesman: Jinnah, the Muslim League and the Demand for Pakistan*, p. 165.
33. Hodson, ibid, p. 137.
34. Ibid, p. 350.
35. Wavell, ibid, p. 495.
36. J. B. Kripalani, *Gandhi: His Life and Thoughts*, pp. 248-49.
37. *Sardar Patel, in tune with the millions—I*, vol. II, p. 106.
38. M. N. Roy, *Men I Met*, pp. 15-16.
39. J. R. D. Tata, *Keynote*, p. xiii.

10: Was Kashmir sold to Gulab Singh?

1. The *Times of India*, 12 May 1886.
2. Vincent A. Smith, *The Oxford History of India*, pp. 617-18.
3. The *Times of India*, 12 May 1886.
4. Ibid.
5. *The Random House Dictionary (College Edition)*, p. 1035.
6. Smith, *The Oxford History of India*, p. 617.

7. The *Times of India*, 12 May 1886.

8. Ibid.

9. The *Times of India*, 4 October, 1889.

10. Smith, *The Oxford History of India*, p. 552.

11. Report of Indian States Committee, 1928-29, Appendix II, Lord Reading's letter of 27 March 1926 to the Nizam: cited in R. C. Mazumdar's *Struggle for Freedom*, p.805; also quoted in *The Evolution of India and Pakistan 1858-1947: Select Documents* (HMG), p. 419.

(Reproduced on pp. 196 & 198 are the two references from the *Times of India* of 12 May 1886 and 4 October 1889.)

15: The Man who dared Churchill

1. *Sardar Patel, in tune with the millions—I*, vol. II, pp. 305, 307.

2. ·V. Shankar, *My Reminiscences of Sardar Patel*, vol. I, p. 126.

BIBLIOGRAPHY

Books

A. K. Majumdar, *Advent of Indian Independence.*

Ajit Prasad Jain, *What Really Mattered.*

Alan Campbell-Johnson, *Mission with Mountbatten.*

A. P. J. Taylor, *Bismarck – The Man and the Statesman.*

A. P. J. Taylor, *Europe – Grandeur and Decline.*

Ayesha Jalal, *The Sole Spokesman: Jinnah, the Muslim League and the Demand for Pakistan.*

Bridwood, Lord, *A Continent Divides.*

B. K. Nehru (ICS), *Thoughts on Present Discontent.*

Bombay Gazetteer, Vol. III.

B. N. Mullik, *Kashmir.*

B. R. Nanda, *Mahatma Gandhi.*

C. D. Deshmukh, *The Course of My Life.*

C. F. Andrews, *His Life and Times.*

Conrad Corfield, *The Princely India I Knew.*

Constituent Assembly of India (Legislative),Vol. II, Part II (1949).

Constituent Assembly of India (Legislative), Debates Vol. II, Part II, 18 March 1949.

Durga Das, *India from Curzon to Nehru and After.*

D. V. Thamankar, *Sardar Patel.*

Evolution of India and Pakistan. 1858 to 1947: Select Documents (H.M.G.).

For a United India (speeches of Sardar Patel).

G. Ramanujam, *Story of Indian Labour.*

H. M. Patel (ICS), *Rites & Passage – a Civil Servant Remembers.*

H. N. Brailford, *Subject India.*

Harekrushna Mehtab, Chief Minister of Orissa, *Beginning of an Era*: Preface by Sardar Patel.

Humphrey Evans, *Thimayya of India.*

H. V. Hodson, *Great Divide: Britain-India- Pakistan.*

H. V. R. Iengar (ICS), *Administration in India.*

H. V. R. Iengar (ICS), *Vallabhbhai Patel: Birthday Memorial Lecture (Surat).*

Ian Stephens, *Horned Moon.*

Jagmohan, *My Frozen Turbulence in Kashmir.*

General J. N. Chaudhri, *An Autobiography.*

Ismay, Lord, *The Memories of Lord Ismay.*

Jawaharlal Nehru, *A Bunch of Letters.*

Jawaharlal Nehru, *Autobiography.*

Jawaharlal Nehru, *Letters to Chief Ministers.*

Jamnadas Dawarkadas, *Political Memoirs.*

J. B. Kripalani: *Gandhi, His Time and Thoughts.*

John Connel, *A Biography of Field Marshal Sir Claude Auchinleck.*

John Glendevon, *The Viceroy at Bay (Lord Linlithgow).*

J. P. Dalvi, Brigadier, *Himalayan Blunder.*

Judith M. Brown, *Modern India: The Origins of an Asian Democracy.*

Kanji Dawarkadas, *India's Fight for Freedom 1913 to 1937.*

Kanji Dawarkadas, *Ten years to Freedom 1938 to 1947.*

Kewal L. Punjabi (ICS), *The Civil Servant in India.*

K. M. Munshi, *Pilgrimage to Freedom.*

K. M. Munshi, *End of an Era – Hyderabad Memories.*

K. M. Munshi, *Indian Constitutional Documents.*

K. M. Panikkar, *An Autobiography.*

K. P. S. Menon (ICS), *Many Worlds Revisited – an Autobiography.*

K. P. S. Menon (ICS), *Memories and Musings.*

Leonard Mosley, *The Last Days of the British Raj.*

M. A. Karandikar, *Islam in India's Transition to Modernity.*

Mahadev Desai, *The Story of Bardoli.*

Mahadev Desai, *The Righteous Struggle.*

Mahavir Tayagi, *Meri Kaun Sunega* (Hindi).

Manmath Das, *Partition and Independence of India.*

Maulauna Azad, *India Wins Freedom.*

Mehr Chand Mahajan, *Looking Back (autobiography).*

Memories of Aga Khan.

Minoo Masani, *Bliss Was It In That Dawn.*

Michael Brecher, *Nehru – A Political Biography.*

M. J. Koshy, *Last Days of Monarchy in Kerala.*

Motilal Nehru, *Selected Works.*

Mountbattten, Lord, *Memorandum of 17ᵗʰ March1976.*

M. N. Roy: *Men I Met.*

M. S. Venkataramani & B. K. Srivastava, *Quit India.*

Narhari D. Parikh, *Sardar Vallabhbhai Patel Vols. I & II.*

N. R. Pathak (Prof.), *Government of Maharashtra Source Material for History of Freedom Struggle in India, Part III.*

Narendra Singh Sarila, *Untold Story of India's Partition.*

N. V. Gadgil: *Government from Inside.*

Pattabhi Sitaramayya, *The History of the Indian Congress Vols. I & II.*

Penderel Moon, *Divide and Quit.*

Penderel Moon, *Strangers in India.*

Prem Nath Bajaj, *History of Struggle for Freedom in Kashmir.*

Pyarelal, *Mahatma Gandhi – the Last Phase, Vols. I & II.*

P. A .Gaitonde, *The Liberation of Goa.*

Rajendra Prasad, *Correspondence & Select Documents.*

R. C. Majumdar, *Struggle for Freedom.*

R. C .Majumdar, *Advanced History of India.*

R. J. Moore, *Escape from Empire – Attlee Government and the Indian Problem.*

Report of Indian States Committee 1928-29.

Robert Dayne, *The Life and Death of Mahatma Gandhi.*

Sardar Patel, *Correspondence Vols. I to X.*

Sardar Patel, *In Tune with Millions, Vols. II & III.*

Sardars Patel's Letters, Mostly Unknown, Vols. I & III.

Sardar Patel, *Speeches in Hindi (from Gujarati).*

Said the Sardar (speeches published by Hyderabad State Congress).

Sarvepalli Gopal, *Jawaharlal Nehru, Vol. III.*

Sen, Lieut-Gen L. P., *Slender was the Thread.*

Shahid Hamid (Major General from Pakistan), *Dangerous Twilight.*

Stanley Wolpert, *Nehru: A Tryst with Destiny.*

Subhas Chandra Bose, *The Indian Struggle.*

Subimal Dutt (ICS), *With Nehru in Foreign Office.*

Sudhir Ghosh, *Gandhi's Emissary.*

This was Sardar, Commemorative Volume I.

Tata, J. R. D., *Keynote.*

Thorat, Lieut-Gen. S. P. P., *From Reville to Retreat.*

Tiwari, A. R., *Making of a Leader: Sardar Vallabhbhai Patel.*

Transfer of Power 1942-1947 (H.H.G.).

V. Rangaswami, *The Story of Integration: A New Interpretation.*

Vincent Smith, *Oxford History of India.*

V. P. Menon, *Transfer of Power in India.*

V. P. Menon, *Integration of Indian States.*

Wavell, Lord, *The Viceroy's Journal.*

William Shirer, *Gandhi: a Memoir.*

Yusuf Meharally, *Leaders of India.*

Newspapers:

Bombay Chronicle:
1915: January 13/15
       April 2
1918: April 13 / 17 / 20 / 23 / 24 / 28 / 30
       June 3 / 5 / 8
       July 3
1920   August 31
       September 9 / 10 / 11 / 16
1921: December 28
1934: October 26
1945: October 1 / 15 / 31
1946: January 9 / 15 / 17 / 26 / 29 / 30 / 31
       February 1 / 2 / 5 / 7 / 9
       April 1
1947: April 10 / 11 / 15 / 16 / 21
       May 5 / 10 / 20 / 26
       June 10 / 11 / 13 / 14 / 16 / 18/ 23 / 24 / 25
       July 2 / 3 / 5 / 7 / 10 / 11 / 12 / 13 / 18 / 19 /
       23/ 24 / 25 / 26 / 28 / 30
       August 12 / 20 / 28 / 29
       September 13 / 26

Calcutta Review (Calcutta University)
1949: December

Eastern World (London)
1951: February
1961: December
1962: November

Free Press Journal
1951: December 18

Harijan:
1951: January 26

Hindu:
1958: March 21
1991: July 1

Hindustan Times
1949: November 15
1980: October 31

Illustrated Weekly of India:
1950: October 29
1979: October 25

Indian Express:
1947: February 28
       March 18
       June 7
1951: December 16
1964 February 4
       June 8
1965: May 31
1966: September 8
1969: September 18
1972: June 9

Economic Times:
1974: October 27
1975: July 6

1978: October 31
1979   May 13

Manchester Guardian:
1950: October 16

Mangal Prabhat:
1951: January

Modern   Review:
1920: February / June
1922: February

Searchlight:
1967: September 13

Statesman:
1950: October 31
       December 16
1955: May 20
1968   November 1
1969   July 25

Sunday Standard:
1976: September 12

Swantantra Jyoti:
1973: Sardar Patel Number

Times of India, Mumbai:
1886: May 12
1889: October 4
1928   July 4
1929: May 8

1945: October 23
1947: August 28/29
      October 3 / 5
1948: June 30
1949: October 4
      March 2 / 5
1958: August 6
1968: November 1
1981: December 4
1987: August 14

Times, London:
1946: October 23
1948: October 2
1950: December 16

Young India:
1924: April 6
1950: October 16

INDEX

OTHER BOOKS BY INDUS SOURCE

Spiritual Masters: The Buddha
Supriya Rai
ISBN 81-88569-05-4

The Buddha, Siddhartha Gautama, lived and taught over 2500 years ago. His teachings comprised some of the highest moral philosophy then known to man and appealed to the rational and the poetic mind alike. He led a remarkable life, travelling and teaching ceaselessly for 45 years after attaining Enlightenment. Today, Buddhism is one of the world's most widely practised religions, drawing followers from lands far away from that of his birth. In this book, three men narrate the story of the Buddha's life. One is his son and disciple, Rahula. Another is King Bimbisara's charioteer, Triguna, who is a creature of fiction. The third narrator is Ananda, a cousin and disciple of the Master and later, his attendant. Their understanding of the Master's Teaching deepens as they proceed with the narration, enabling each one to achieve his own transformation and self-realisation.

Spiritual Masters: Guru Nanak
Harish Dhillon
ISBN 81-88569-02-X

Guru Nanak, the founder of Sikhism, was born in the 15th century during a period of political and religious turmoil in India. Nanak founded a new religion, a synthesis of Hinduism and Islam, with the belief that God was one. He advocated a casteless society based on truth, brotherhood, and equality.

He spent twenty-three years traveling not only in India but also to Tibet, Ceylon and Central Asian countries of Arabia, Iran and Iraq, preaching the truth as he had perceived it and showing mankind the path to salvation. This book tells the fascinating story of a unique messiah who showed a gentle, peaceful path to realisation of God.

Spiritual Masters: Sai Baba
Sonavi Desai
ISBN 81-87967-64-1

Sai Baba of Shirdi is one of the most well known spiritual Masters of India. He belongs to that brotherhood of saints who crossed the barriers of caste and creed and spoke the universal language of love. He taught the most profound philosophy and the greatest truths in a simple and forthright way.

This book is a collection of stories, portrayed through the eyes of Laxmi, one of his closest devotees. While material facts have been kept intact, an element of fiction has been introduced to weave events from his life into a narrative. This book hopes to encourage the reader to reflect on Baba's teachings and inspire a desire to understand the timeless wisdom passed on through our yesterdays.

GANDHI: A Spiritual Journey
M V Kamath
ISBN 10: 81-88569-11-9 ISBN 13: 978-81-88569-11-3

Beginning with his childhood and early years in South Africa, Gandhi: A Spiritual Journey, explores the search for truth and the spiritual transformation of Mohandas Karamchand Gandhi. Influenced by western thought in his youth, Gandhi underwent a deep inner conflict that drew him to the study of comparative religion. His experiments with spiritual ideas, derived from a living faith in God, led him to propagate the principles of ahimsa and satyagraha. Gandhi was as much in politics as he was in search of God and the desire for God-realisation was the mainspring of all his actions, both political and social. Could Gandhi have internalised his quest for God and still remained a leader of the masses? What is Gandhi's spiritual legacy that continues to inspire so many leaders across cultures? Can Gandhi's philosophy of non-violence address the ills of today's strife-torn world? This book examines Gandhi's spiritual ideology and traces his life-long journey in quest of truth that led him to conclude that Truth is God.

Little Lhasa: Reflections on Exiled Tibet
Tsering Namgyal
ISBN 81-88569-10-0

In the nearly five decades since they anchored on foreign shores, exiled Tibetans have tried to preserve their glorious cultural and religious heritage in exile. As this legacy and responsibility is being passed on to the new generation, it has given birth to a new and distinct Tibetan culture. In these ten essays Tsering Namgyal reflects, with curiosity and compassion on this "in-between world" in which he grew up and which is transforming at a rapid pace. He combines his own experience of growing up among the Tibetan communities of India, his extensive travels, and many interviews to explain to himself and to others why his "virtual home" is so unique and intriguing. And why, despite the poignancy of dislocation, it has a strange ability to touch and inspire.

Shiva to Shankara: Decoding the Phallic Symbol
Dr. Devdutt Pattanaik
ISBN 81-88569-04-6

Disdain for the material world is a dominant theme in philosophical schools that consider Shiva as their patron deity. This disdain manifests in two ways: asceticism and alchemy. In the former, sexual activity is shunned; in the latter sexual activity is merely an occult ritual. And yet, Shiva is represented by a very sexual symbol: the male reproductive organ placed within the female reproductive organ. Why? The easy route is to accept the most common and simplistic explanation: it is a fertility symbol. But to make sense of a mythological image one has to align the language heard (stories) with the language performed (rituals) and the language seen (symbol). All dissonances have to be removed so that the real meaning can be deciphered. The quest for this meaning inspired Dr. Pattanaik to write this book.

Waking Up: A Week Inside a Zen Monastery
Jack Maguire
ISBN 81-88569-01-1

This book is an essential guide to what it is like to spend a week inside a Zen Buddhist monastery. The notion of spending days at a time in silence and meditation amid the serene beauty of a Zen monastery may be appealing-but how do you do it and what can you really expect from the experience? Waking Up provides the answers for anyone who is just curious, as well as for all those who have dreamed of actually giving it a try and now want to know where to begin. A detailed "Guide to Zen and Buddhist Places" and a glossary of terms make Waking Up not only a handbook for the curious seeker, but an excellent resource for anyone wanting to know more about the Buddhist way.

Confucius: A Biography
Jonathan Clements
ISBN: 81-88569-03-8

Although famous worldwide, Confucius is often misunderstood outside China. His sayings are frequently repeated out of context, with little attention paid to the conditions that shaped his view of the universe. Using new translations, Confucius reveals many unexpected sides of the venerable philosopher- his younger years, his feuds with his enemies and even his biting wit. It also shows the way that his life and thoughts were influenced by events in the China of his day-a time when a patchwork of rival kingdoms squabbled over the remains of a lost Golden Age, when corrupt noblemen seized power for themselves, and when the people believed that Heaven had deserted them. This intriguing book explores the teachings of Confucius, the man himself and the world in which he lived. It will appeal to anyone interested in philosophy, Chinese life and China's history.

Chronicles of a Quality Detective
Dr. Shrinivas Gondhalekar & Payal Sheth
ISBN 81-88569-00-3

The journey towards zero-defect manufacturing is a long and checkered one. Checkered because some quality defects are tenacious and they persist even after the most sophisticated quality management techniques have been deployed. This book describes the evolution of a technique, called Differential Diagnosis, which charts a dramatic, new path towards diagnosing root causes. It involves deep observation of the problem, emphasizing the absence of phenomena rather than the presence, thus permitting the elimination of a whole range of possible causes. In the process, the area of search is dramatically reduced and the root cause becomes easily identifiable.

Hinduism: Triumphs and Tribulations

S. K. Kulkarni

ISBN 10: 81-88569-15-1 ISBN 13: 978-81-88569-15-1

Sanatana Dharma, which later came to be known as Hinduism, goes back at least five thousand years. In the course of its long journey through the centuries, it evolved, transformed, flourished, and sometimes floundered. In this honest and introspective study of the history of Hinduism, the author analyses its strengths and weaknesses and addresses its contradictions through contemporary eyes. This book is essential reading for all Indians who cherish the dream of a progressive, prosperous, and united India.

Awakening into Oneness

Arjuna Ardagh

ISBN 10: 81-88569-16-X ISBN 13: 978-81-88569-16-8

A fascinating discovery in southern India has caught the attention of spiritual teachers from every tradition, leaders from around the world, and millions more. It is the phenomenon called the Oneness Blessing (also known as "deeksha" in the East), a powerful transfer of energy believed to elicit the realization of unitive consciousness. *Awakening into Oneness: The Power of Blessing in the Evolution of Consciousness* tells the remarkable story of this radical new gateway to personal and global transformation.

What is it about the Oneness Blessing that has ignited the hearts of so many? You'll find the answer here, in *Awakening into Oneness*.

* * *

Indus Source Books
PO Box 6194
Malabar Hill PO
Mumbai 400006
info@indussource.com
www.indussource.com